For the visitor with three days or with three months to explore the magical world around the Inca capital of Cusco, from the conventional traveler to the intrepid explorer,

Peter Frost's Exploring Cusco

is the ideal companion, like having a private guide at your side.

Since the first edition was published in 1979, *Exploring Cusco* has been recognized as the essential guide to the Cusco region, recommended by leading travel guides such as *The Peru Handbook*, *The Lonely Planet Peru Travel Survival Kit*, *The South American Handbook* and *The Rough Guide to Peru*. Frost is praised for his concise descriptions, lively recounting of Cusco's history, and his careful separation of theory from known fact.

In this expanded and completely revised fifth edition, Peter Frost leads the reader through the history of pre-Inca, Inca and colonial-era Cusco. Renowned Inca sites such as Sacsaywaman, Ollantaytambo, Pisac and the legendary Machu Picchu are described in detail, as well as the Inca Trail and many lesser-known (but equally fascinating) sites dotting the Andean landscape, including Moray, Tipón, Choquequirau and Huchuy Cusco. Also included in this edition is the newly-opened network of trails leading to Machu Picchu along the Urubamba river.

> *A Walking Tour of the City of Cusco*
> *The Lost City of Machu Picchu*
> *Sacsaywaman, Tambomachay, Qenqo*
> *Chinchero, Moray and the Pampa de Anta*
> *The Sacred Valley of the Incas*
> *Step-by-Step Guide to the Inca Trail*
> *Exploring the Remote Vilcabamba Region*

Includes practical information on hotels, restaurants, transportation, shopping, as well as directions on walks ranging from a few hours to a few days. Plus additional information ranging from new theories on Inca technology and cosmology to a recipe for making *quinoa* pancakes while camping along the Inca Trail. *Exploring Cusco* is indispensable.

EXPLORING
CUSCO

by
Peter Frost

5ᵗʰ Edition

Nuevas Imágenes S.A.

Av. S. Antunez de Mayolo 879, Lima 33

First published by Lima 2000, Peru 1979
2nd edition 1980; 3rd edition 1984; 4th edition 1989.

This edition published in 1999 by

Nuevas Imágenes S.A.
Av. S. Antunez de Mayolo 879
Lima 33, Peru
Tel/Fax: 511-448-8513
E-mail: jbar@amauta.rcp.net.pe

Readers are encouraged to send comments to the author at:
pfrost@mail.cosapidata.com.pe

Front cover: composite from two photos of Pisac ruins by the author.

Layout by Rocío Avila, MURA S.A.
Printed at Quebecor Peru S.A., Av. Los Frutales 344 , Ate, Lima

Also by Peter Frost:

Machu Picchu Historical Sanctuary by Peter Frost & Jim Bartle

ISBN # 9972-9015-6-4

Printed in Peru

TABLE OF CONTENTS

Communications - Transportation - Hotels - Bars,
Restaurants, etc. - Arts & Shopping - Adventure -
Provincial Towns - Museums - Peruvian Amazon -
Museums - Calendar - Miscellaneous

History of Cusco and the Spanish Conquest; *Pachacuteq*;
*Cusco before the Empire;*The Lay of the Land; Places of
Interest in the City; *A Quiet Walk through Cusco; Spanish
Walls by Inca Masons; A Song of Cusco*

Walks and Tours Close to Cusco; Sacsaywaman;
The Stones of Cusco; Scribing and Coping: Answer to
an Ancient Riddle?; Qenqo; Puca Pucara; Tambomachay;
Two Half-Day Walks near Cusco; *The Ceque Lines of
Cusco; The Celestial Andes*

Pisac; *A Soft Adventure*; Calca; Yucay; *Huchuy Cusco*;
Urubamba; Ollantaytambo; *Levers and Leapfrogging
Ladders*; Pumamarca

*The Early Days; Machu Picchu Historical Sanctuary;
Conserving the Inca Trail*; Preparing to Walk the Trail;
*Quinoa: The Little Grain That Could...; Nature on the
Inca Trail;* Route Description; *Patallaqta; Runkuracay;
Sayacmarca; Phuyupatamarca; Intipata; Wiñay Wayna;
New Trails Around Machu Picchu*

MAPS & RUINS PLANS

This edition is for
Rosi

ACKNOWLEDGEMENTS TO
THE FIFTH EDITION

In a book like this, with so many details, hundreds of people have helped me. But I should acknowledge first and foremost, the Quechua people of the Cusco region, whose cultural riches, so often generously shared, have been the essential material of this book from the very beginning.

I would like to thank Carlos Milla for being an endlessly patient informant and sometime translator over the years. Dr. Brian Bauer and Dr. Jorge Flores Ochoa deserve special thanks for adding new information to this edition; nor should I forget my earlier contributors, Dr. Gary Urton, Alberto Miori and Carol Stewart. Vincent R. Lee and Nancy Lee have been a fountain of valuable material and assistance concerning the Vilcabamba region, and I am grateful for Vince's permission to publish my version of his ingenious theories concerning Inca construction techniques. Jim Bartle, my editor and publisher, has helped to condense and clarify the text, while overseeing and generating many new ideas for the design of the book. Gary Ziegler has also been immensely helpful concerning Vilcabamba, and has hospitably invited me along on his expeditions. Dr. Jean-Jacques Decoster has frequently been incisive and decisive in clarifying abstruse anthropological and historical data. Juan Nuñez del Prado has initiated me into some of the mysteries of the Andean spiritual path, and in this my thanks also go to Lucas Checa and Amalia Escobar - and to Laura Russell, for numerous introductions and many moments of mutual madness. Timoteo Ccarita generously shared his knowledge of the Andean weaving and festival traditions. Román Vizcarra's help with the musical section was indispensable. Barry Walker of Manu Expeditions, was supportive in many ways, and supplied most of the information on the Manu Biosphere reserve; Mariana van Vlaardingen of Pantiacolla Tours supplied the rest, and generously allowed me to use her office as a support system. Dr. Alfredo

Valencia and Fernando Astete have assisted me with investigations of Machu Picchu; Ruth and Kenneth Wright generously provided information from their studies of the Machu Picchu water and agriculture systems. Dr. Carolyn Dean cast some light into the darkness of my ignorance of Cusco's colonial art and architecture, while Dr. Gordon McEwan did the same for the pre-Inca sites of Pikillaqta and Choquepuquio. María del Carmen Vargas has supplied countless details of Cusco tourism services, while ensuring that I never miss a plane, even if it is already taxiing to the runway. Fredi Vera, Andrew Sullivan, and especially Paul Cripps deserve thanks for the information about mountain biking, as does Claudia Valerín for some new information about the colonial churches of the Vilcanota valley. In the Sacred Valley, Nicholas Asheshov and Wendy Weeks have my gratitude for their open-door policy towards me.

Have I forgotten someone? I'm sure I have, and I apologize. So many people, so many years... I thank you all.

About the Author

Peter Frost lives in Cusco and has been studying and writing about the region for almost 30 years. He is the author of *Machu Picchu Historical Sanctuary*, and numerous magazine articles about the Cusco area. He works as an adventure travel guide, freelance writer and photographer. This is his fifth edition of *Exploring Cusco*, which was first published in 1979.

About the Contributors

Dr. Brian Bauer is an archaeologist at U. Illinois at Chicago who has completed a field study of the Inca *ceque* system, and is conducting an archaeological survey of the Cusco valley.

Dr. Gary Urton is an anthropologist at Colgate University, New York, whose seminal work on Quechua astronomy influenced a generation of Andean scholars.

Dr. Jorge Flores Ochoa is an anthropologist on the faculty of the University of San Antonio de Abad in Cusco. He is noted for his work on the culture of Andean herders, and is currently director of the Inka Museum.

Carol Stewart is an itinerant gourmet, psychologist and tarot reader who lived in Cusco for a time during the 1980s, and discovered that the way to Cusco's heart was through its stomach.

Alberto Miori is a Cusco-based trekking guide and operator, and a noted expert on Andean textiles.

INTRODUCTION
TO THE FIFTH EDITION

This is the "Read Me" section of the book—like those files attached to software applications that everyone ignores. Ignore it, by all means—but it if you read it, it will help you navigate your way around the book, and get my drift more easily.

Exploring Cusco celebrates its 20th birthday this year; its 21st in the year 2000. Coming of age? Coming of youth, too, I hope. The idea of producing new incarnations like this one every so often, is to keep the book fresh and relevant.

Numerous and clamorous have been readers' plaints concerning obsolescence in the 1989 edition, (in which the round trip Cusco-Lima air fare was quoted at US$45, and a double room at the Hotel Libertador was US$34). But plaint no more, faithful readers—here it is, *Exploring Cusco* for the 21st century (the first few years of it, anyway).

Those prices were from the good-old/bad-old days, when the national currency was almost worthless, and dollar-bearing foreigners came here on the cheap...but often lost everything to thieves. It is a pleasure to report that Peru has stabilized considerably, both economically and politically, since then. The Peruvian sol is in slight decline at this writing, but mostly I do not quote prices at all in this edition, because they can change so radically. Where I do quote prices I quote them in U.S. dollars, this being the principal international currency in Peru.

The last edition was full of *caveats*—about political violence, and crime. This time around, I can drop the first altogether and soft-pedal the second. The terrorist movements have generally been cornered and marginalized, and the rampant crime of ten years ago has been reduced to tolerable levels today (knock on wood!—these are, as they say, interesting times...). And remember, this is not an invitation to be careless—tourists are always juicy targets for street criminals.

To Peruvians, Cusco is both a city and a department, the latter a political sub-division of 76,225 square kilometers, with the city of Cusco as its capital. According to the 1993 census figures, the department has about 1.1 million inhabitants, of whom 257,750 live in its capital city. The "Cusco" of this guide lies partway between these two geographical entities—larger than the city, but smaller than the whole department.

Few visitors have the time or interest to "do" the department of Cusco from end to end, and this book is not intended for that purpose But it is an attempt to go beyond the limited Cusco offered to the short-term visitor—a series of standard attractions, established mainly by convention and the convenience of tour operators, consisting of locations within the city itself, Pisac or Chinchero on market day, Ollantaytambo, Sacsaywaman and other ruins along the road to Pisac. And of course, Machu Picchu. What tour agency takes you to Tipón?...to Moray?...to Raqchi?

The magnificent traditional sights should not be ignored, of course, and the essential information on these is here. But even the best-known among Cusco's attractions are often haphazardly and inaccurately documented—and don't expect to find signposts or trustworthy information at the sites themselves. So the visitor has nowhere else to turn for information on the many other fascinating locations within reach of the city.

"Within reach of the city" might serve best, in fact, to define the area covered by this book. Most of the destinations referred to lie within a few hours journey of Cusco, and can be reached without excruciating sacrifice. Hotel accommodations are some places are rustic, but tolerable. Readers who prefer to travel in style will find references to resorts where they can enjoy comforts equal to anything in Cusco itself. And backpackers wanting to leave the main highways will find footpath and camping information here as well. These are some of the criteria I have used in selecting areas for inclusion.

The final chapter on Vilcabamba stands apart. Vilcabamba is the opposite of accessible; Manco Inca retreated there for that very reason after the defeat of his rebellion against the Spanish. It takes about three days on foot or horseback to reach the major ruins of Espiritu Pampa from the nearest roadhead; two days to reach Choquequirau. (But even here matters have improved, with a modest but pleasant hotel now open at Huancacalle—the gateway to Vitcos and Espiritu Pampa—and a sturdy footbridge replacing the fearsome *oroya* across the Apurimac that was previously the only way to reach Choquequirau). But Vilcabamba appears in this book because it was the last stronghold of the Incas during the dying years of the empire, a place of mystery where abandoned ruins lean above idyllic jungle valleys. It is also real, no-holds-barred explorers' territory—easy to get lost in, partly unmapped.

It would be absurd to claim that this publication constitutes an exhaustive survey. On the contrary, there is far more than one could squeeze between these covers. So whenever I have noted or heard talk of an area that looks promising—for ruin-hunting, scenery, local color, history, or whatever—I have passed these leads on to the reader.

So here, a plea: if you follow paths to unknown places, if you come across unexpected delights, or something just plain interesting, if there is anything you feel should be in this book but isn't, I would be grateful to hear from you. My e-mail is pfrost@mail.cosapidata.com.pe.

Hiking. A general point about the hikes suggested in this book, is that the Andes are rugged and rocky, and a good pair of hiking boots or shoes is a distinct asset. Sneakers will do in a pinch, but avoid high heels, sandals, and such. Carry something waterproof, especially during the rainy season (November through March.)

Dogs can sometimes be a problem. Most *campesinos* (peasant-farmers) keep dogs and they sometimes rush upon you in savage-looking packs. The barking is mostly for show, and the mere act of picking up a stone will usually keep them at bay; if not, then throwing it almost certainly will. However, do *not* approach the house that they are protecting unless the owner is close by to help you. And if you should get bitten, don't panic. Rabies does not kill quickly, and normally you have at least ten safe days in which to get your shots—generally much longer. However, in the unlikely event you get bitten anywhere near the head, get your shots as fast as you can.

You will often be walking among fields of crops. Campesinos don't have much, and if you trample their *chacra* they will have even less. Take care about this, and watch out also for the irrigation channels, which are easy to damage if you walk along their banks.

Campesinos, especially children, will often ask for money or gifts. It's depressing when one's human contact routinely begins with an outstretched hand. I seldom give money, except in exchange for a photo. Candy is even worse; you feel like a jerk not giving it to kids when you have it in your pocket—but think what you are doing. If you do a hike, you may find that children come running up to you to demand imperiously, "Dame dulce!" ("Give me sweets!")—and it's because people have been giving them candy.

Giving away food is more in keeping with the system of reciprocity that traditionally underlies all material transactions in the Andes. After all, they grew the stuff (and sold it to you cheap, yes?). So to bring some cooked or baked food (e.g. bread) back to the countryside to give away is to practice reciprocity, the way I see it. People will frequently offer you cooked potatoes or corn in exchange; try not to cause offence by refusing it. Other extremely useful, if not exactly reciprocal, gifts are pencils and school notebooks. Campesinos crave a decent education for their children (it is one of the chief reasons for migration to the cities), and can often barely afford these simple items. If you can think up something their kids can do for you in exchange, you are reinforcing their most vital cultural tradition. For example, ask them to guide you along the trail a little way—say, to the next turn-off *(desvío)*. For adults, coca is cheap, light to carry, and easy to share, so carry extra when you hike. Cigarettes are popular gifts among adult males in the countryside (there is an odd folk myth that they cure headaches). For the giver, they have the advantage of being ultra light; for the receiver, all the well-known disadvantages—but you can take comfort in the knowledge that campesinos simply cannot afford to get addicted to them.   Another suggestion is souvenirs from home—a picture of the Golden Gate bridge or the Kremlin always goes down well. And of course, nothing beats a polaroid camera. What better gift than an instant photo, for people who have never seen a picture of themselves?

Quechuas and Incas. Pre-hispanic history in Peru—as any candid authority will admit—is about 60% speculation, 30% probability, and 10% established fact. Without counting that portion which is totally unknown. Thus, most of what has been written about the Incas is open to dispute. For example, two of the leading scholars are in complete disagreement on an issue as fundamental as whether or not the Incas conceived of the city of Cusco as having the physical shape of a puma (J.H. Rowe/for vs. R.T. Zuidema/against).

To avoid cluttering these lines with qualifiers and academic asides I have adopted the following heresy: wherever a historical or archae-ological assertion comes from a respected source, seems reasonable, and is not contradicted by other plausible theories, I cite it as fact. On the other hand, where a popularly held belief is doubtful or demonstrably erroneous, I try to expose it.

My intention in these matters is to chart a course between the timid reductionism of so much academic interpretation of the Inca past, and the voodoo confabulations of extreme New Agers and assorted wackos.

The Inca language was Quechua. In modern times this has also become the name applied to the people who speak this language, known as the Quechua Indians. There was an effort (which the last edition of *Exploring Cusco* supported) to replace the word Quechua with "Ru-nasimi" (the people's tongue), which is what traditional speakers call it themselves. But it didn't catch on, and since I am no champion of lost causes, this edition goes back to Quechua.

Quechua place names are often graphic and colorful; frequently they describe the history or geography of a location. So wherever possible I have included a translation. But what is a writer to do about Quechua spelling? The original language had no alphabet or written scheme, and there are glottal and aspirate Quechua sounds that don't exist in any language using the Roman alphabet—so from the earliest years of the Spanish Conquest, a bewildering variety of spellings has been used for transliterating Quechua. For example, the glottal stop in "Rit'i" (snow), is usually marked by the European apostrophe—but it is also often spelled "Ritti."

Formal spelling systems have been adopted, but if followed consistently they founder in a morass of extraterrestrial locutions that offend the European eye and violate common Peruvian usage. An example: modern academic convention, replaces the Spanish "hua" (Sacsayhuaman), with "wa" (Sacsaywaman). Attempting dutifully to use this system throughout the new *Exploring Cusco*, I set my remorseless attack dog, the computer's search/change function, to expel the heretic "hua" from these pages. What did I get? Spellings like "Wánuco," "Wallaga," and the low comedy of "Wanka"—spellings that no Peruvian ever uses.

For that matter, should you now be reading the introduction of *Exploring Qosqo?* And what about "Inca"? Somehow it has become pee-cee to spell it "Inka" these days. Ink? Sounds like a sinister blot to darken the reputation of the word. (We know what Kakfa did to the letter "K"!) Amerika? Ku Klux Klan? Inka? No way. My Inkas are Incas. I'll still use "k", where it looks right, I'll use the apostrophe for glottal stops (it'i) when needed, but my "wa" will sometimes be "hua", and there will be other heterodoxies—the seat of my pants being the judge. I've decided to have my "k" and "it'i," too.

Finally, concerning Quechua and other arcana, if you come across a strange word or an abbreviation you don't understand, check the glossary or the list of abbreviations at the back of the book.

———————

Authors run into another problem when writing about "the Incas." The vast agglomeration of peoples under rule from Cusco in the years preceding the Spanish invasion had no collective name that has survived. "Inca" was the Quechua term used to describe just one person, the ruling emperor himself—the Sapa Inca. We have a word for the nobles who ruled under him: *orejones*—big ears—a Spanish word alluding to the huge gold earplugs worn by the aristocracy. But one is stuck for a word to describe the culture as a whole, and so most writing about ancient Peru mingles the correct and incorrect use of the word Inca shamelessly. What follows here is no exception.

One thing is certain—it is wrong to call modern Quechua people "Incas." The broadest possible use of that term includes only the ruling elite of Cusco before the Conquest, a group thought to have numbered around 30-40,000. Today, the Quechua speaking Q'eros people from the remote mountains east of Cusco claim descent from refugees of the Inca nobility (and who knows, perhaps the recent spectacular finds of frozen high-status Inca mummies on Andean peaks will eventually supply a DNA-based ruling on their claim). But be that as it may, most modern Quechua people are not, and never were, Incas.

Any mention of the early chronicles in these pages refers, of course, to post-Conquest Spanish accounts—along with a few mestizo and indigenous documents—transcribed from a multitude of sources. The Incas only had an oral history, plus a rather restricted method of record-keeping on colored strings and knots *(quipus),* as far as we know.

New Ruins. As you amble through the book, you may notice a certain amount of griping about the reconstruction of archaeological sites, and what I consider to be the violence done to many of them—particularly on the Inca Trail and around Machu Picchu. This is a big subject, and if my comments can help to ignite a debate, then all to the good. Because there has never been a debate in Peru on this issue. The authorities in charge of the sites simply go ahead and do it, and no one ever questions how it is done, or whether it should be done at all. Visitors seldom get to see a site which has not been treated this way, and so the shock of "Before" and "After" is not so evident to outsiders as it is to this writer. "Before" is when the site is a ruin, some of the buildings have partially fallen in unruly piles of stone, and all is softened with a green coat of moss, lichens, orchids and bromeliads. "After" is when the site looks as though it were built yesterday, and is waiting for the roof to be added. The walls are utterly bare of vegetation, and the intention is that they should remain so. The overall impression is stark and uninviting.

It is said that when the anthropologists arrive, the gods depart. In my opinion, something similar happens with reconstructers of archaeological sites. Imagination is crushed; the mystery, the allure and the enchantment depart. (Many archaeologists would add: and with them goes a lot of irreplaceable information; for these are sites that can no longer be studied in their particulars.)

Local guides are even told that it is not kosher to call the ancient settlements "ruins"—they are "archaeological sites." But to me they *are* ruins, and that is just the point. It's a fraud to make them look brand new. I am all in favor of consolidation and conservation of ruins, to prevent further deterioration, and some clearing to facilitate access. But let ruins be ruins. If you manage to reach Huchuy Cusco or Vitcos/Rosaspata before they get The Treatment, you may see my point.

There is a phrase that appears on the signboards placed on every reconstruction project: *"puesta en valor"*. It has no easy translation in English, but it means, roughly, "making it worth something". It has been the justification for innumerable radical interventions—include much work that is totally indefensible, where entire walls and even buildings have been assembled upon little more than a vestige of the foundations. Visitors are presumed to be insufficiently intelligent to imagine how an unreconstructed site might have looked.

The unstated assumption behind the words "puesta en valor" is that ruins are worthless until they are reconstructed. Having seen Before and After quite a bit over the years, I immoderately beg to disagree.

GENERAL INFORMATION

Altitude (city of Cusco): 11,150 ft./3400m above sea level.

Population: According to the 1992 census the city of Cusco has about 300,000 inhabitants; the total for the department of Cusco is about 830,000.

Annual Rainfall: 25 in./63 cm.

Climate: During the May-September dry season the weather is generally sunny, with spells of overcast or showers. From October to April the weather is far more variable, with a tendency to sunshine in the morning with rain later. January and February are the wettest months. The Andean seasonal variation seems to have become less reliable in recent years, and the weather less predictable. In recent times the problem of grass and forest fires in the Andes and Amazon has become acute, often leading to very smoky skies in August and September.

Altitude Note: At high elevation air pressure is lower. Each lungful of air captures fewer oxygen molecules. It is definitely worth restraining one's enthusiasm for the first couple of hours when arriving by plane from Lima. Relax, lie down, adjust. Avoid respiratory depressants, such as alcohol, sedatives and sleeping pills. (For better sleep, take Acetazolamide [*see below*] instead). Eat lightly for a day or so. Dehydration occurs very rapidly at high altitude, thus it is vital to drink plenty of fluids. All this will speed acclimatization. In a day you will feel better, and in two days you should be fine.

Hypoxia or AMS (Acute Mountain Sickness), know locally as *soroche*, can be hard to shake off once it starts. Symptoms: shortness of breath, headache, nausea, dizziness, insomnia, loss of appetite, vomiting in bad cases. Descent is the infallible cure for altitude problems. The Sacred Valley, only 45 minutes from Cusco by the most direct route, is about 500m. lower, and this is enough to cure or greatly improve most cases of AMS. However, various remedies and preventatives can help. The local remedy is tea made from coca leaves *(mate de coca)*. This is helpful, but by no means a cure. Peripheral edema (fluid retention, puffiness) is common at high altitude. Any diuretic, such as coca tea, will help alleviate this.

Acetazolamide (Diamox). This drug has shown good results as prophylaxis and treatment of AMS. It is a prescription drug used in the treatment of glaucoma, and as a diuretic. It acts as a respiratory stimulant, and also counteracts the blood alkalosis associated with AMS. Taking the drug at night before sleep is particularly helpful. Most people experience a slight tingling in their extremities as a side effect, some feel drowsy, and a few have more serious adverse reactions. (One common and extremely serious side effect is that it ruins the taste of beer). It is a sulfa drug, and the usual precautions apply. Dexamethasone is an alternative for the sulfa-intolerant. Consult a physician.

Acetazolamide is now usually taken for two or three days to prevent AMS, beginning the day before your journey to high altitude (125-250mg twice a day, or one 500mg sustained release capsule per 24 hrs.) It is available over the counter at Peruvian pharmacies.

Most *controlled* medical conditions show little or no extra risk at high altitude. Young and old, fit and unfit, normal pregnancies, those with diabetes, heart disease, even mild lung disease—all are welcomed by the mountain gods. Consult your medic, nonetheless.

Altitude for hikers. If you are hiking the Inca Trail (max. 4200m.) or one of the other circuits in the region you will be ascending far higher than Cusco. This requires extra acclimatization and precautions. Note that the altitude you sleep at is more important than how high you go during the day.

Very high altitude can produce extremely dangerous conditions known as High Altitude Pulmonary Edema (HAPE) and High Altitude Cerebral Edema (HACE), which can even be fatal if not treated. Taking time for acclimatization, and gradual ascent, are the keys to prevention. To set off for the Inca Trail the day you fly into Cusco from sea level is asking for trouble.

Early recognition of symptoms of progression from AMS to HAPE/HACE is vital to treatment. These are: labored breathing while at rest, ataxia (loss of physical co-ordination), mental confusion, extreme lassitude, cyanosis (purple lips and fingernails), persistent dry coughing, audible congestion in the chest. Coma, then death, are the ultimate consequences.

Treatment for HAPE/HACE: Descend! Immediately! There are no sub-stitutes. Descending 500-1000m. is usually sufficient. If this cannot be accomplished immediately, administer oxygen if available, and Dexam-ethasone. Nifedipine or other vasodilator is also helpful. Keep patient warm, and encourage to purse lips on exhalation (improves oxygen absorption).

(Source: *High Altitude Medicine*, P.H. Hackett & R.C. Roach)

Coca: Controversial, but misunderstood. Cocaine is to coca as ivory is to elephants: a derivative, and very different from the whole beast. Cocaine is obtained by chemically extracting the principal alkaloid from the coca leaf, and dumping all the rest. Most cocaine users are abusers, and the effects are then toxic and addictive. Coca leaf, however, contains a complex of fourteen alkaloids, significant amounts of vitamins A & E, plus iron, potassium, calcium (lots of sodium, too, incidentally), and various other minerals in trace amounts (source: *The Incredible Leaf*—Cochabamba, 1992). It helps maintain blood sugar levels when protein intake is low, which is one of the reasons for its popularity among the highland Indians. It is also said to help regulate the heart rate during the drastic changes in altitude that one undergoes during a trek through the Andes. It certainly does act to counter the effects of high altitude, and, being a stimulant (not a narcotic), it gives a lift when the going gets tough. The effect is not powerful enough to overtax a normally healthy body. Coca chewing also dulls the appetite, which can be helpful when your rations are necessarily limited. It shows no signs of being addictive, and does not get you high unless you chew an awful lot.

Coca is a vitally important element in Andean religion and society. It has been used in the Andes for millenia, and is woven into the very fabric of life, featuring in every traditional ritual, every social and economic exchange, besides its many medicinal uses.

As this edition goes to press, the U.S. government has announced amid fanfare that it is close to perfecting a fungus genetically modified to attack coca plants, which it intends to spread in coca-producing nations—calling it a "silver bullet" in the drug war. The issues of Peruvian sovereignty and the effects of this fungus on coca plantations which supply leaves for legitimate indigenous use were not mentioned.

Coca can be purchased, still legally (may it always be so!), by the main market in Cusco, two or three blocks downhill from the railroad station on the righthand side. If you do chew coca, don't forget the *llibta*, a small block of lime-rich substance that activates the various alkaloids in the leaf. Bicarbonate of soda works even better and is not caustic.

Photography: It's best to have a skylight or u-v filter on your camera to soften the intense blue of light at high altitude. Most common types of film are now available in Cusco, including APS. If you buy film locally, be sure to check the expiration date.

Maps: the best large-scale maps of Peru are available from the Instituto Geográfico Nacional, Av. Aramburu 1190, Surquillo, Lima (8:00-12:30 & 13:30-15:30 Mon-Fri; tel. 451939). They are for sale in Cusco only at the South American Explorers Club.

Tourism Season: the busiest season is May through September. A severe crunch occurs in the latter part of June (due to the Inti Raymi festival), and between July 28 and August 10, when Peruvian national vacationing peaks and all services are overloaded. This is a good time to avoid Cusco; if you can't, then double-reconfirm your plane, train, and hotel reservations. Christmas is also a busy time. Also note that, conversely, in the low tourist season, especially February and March, some of the services mentioned below are cut back or closed altogether.

The South American Explorers Club: In Lima: Av. Portugal 146, Breña; tel. 425-0142. (Mail: Casilla 3714, Lima 100); e-m: montague@ Amauta.rcp.net.pe In USA:126 Indian Creek Rd., Ithaca, NY 14850; tel. (607) 277-0488; e-m: explorer@ samexplo.org From its humble and precarious beginnings 20 years ago, this non-profit organization has grown to become an indispensable resource for backpackers, kayakers, climbers, cyclists and all kinds of expeditionaries to South America, particularly Peru. The Lima & Quito clubhouses are friendly places to visit and offer a variety of services: Books and maps for sale; advice and information; used equipment (buy & sell); networking; a library of books and maps; a place to hang out, meet people, and relax. Sales and services are to members only; membership costs $40 per year (couples $60), which includes four issues of the quarterly magazine *The South American Explorer*.
Now open: the **Cusco Clubhouse!** (a long-awaited event), Av. Sol 930; P.O. Box 500; tel/fax. 223102. e-m: saec@wayna.rcp.net.com

COMMUNICATIONS

Telephone

Peru country code: 51. Lima prefix: 01. Cusco prefix: 084 within Peru, 84 from overseas. All calls within the department of Cusco, e.g. to the Sacred Valley, are local and carry no prefix.

Coin-op telephones are common on the streets, and calling card phones are also plentiful. Calling cards are for sale in the Telefónica offices and from some newspaper kiosks.

Long distance and international: **Telefónica**, Calle del Medio 115 (just off Pl. de Armas); hours 7:00am-1:00am daily; Av. Sol 451; hours 7:00am-11:00pm daily. International calls are expensive, so be aware and check rates first.

Mail

The Post Office is at the corner of Av. Sol and Av. Garcilazo. Since privatization, rates are high and delivery is slow.

Courier Service

World Courier, Av. Sol 615; tel. 234051.

E-mail and Internet

For personal mail on a short-term basis, most local tour operators who are using e-mail will let you receive and send messages if you are a client of theirs.

Public services are available at the University center on Av. Sol, first block, lefthand side facing downhill, first door on the left past the long stone wall...*whew!*... (couldn't they just paint a street number on the doorway?). Also at the **Cyber Cafe**, Espaderos 135, 2nd floor. Longer-term visitors can sign up for a personal account at **UNSAAC**, on Av. la Cultura (location known to all taxi drivers), or **Telser**, at the telephone company offices listed above.

TRANSPORTATION

AIR

Remember to reconfirm reservations which were made elsewhere, especially during high season. Departure times and frequency for comestic flights are too variable to publish.

AeroContinente, Portal de Car-

nes 254, Pl. de Armas. Tel. 235666; 263978. Daily flights to Lima and Puerto Maldonado.

AeroPeru, Av. Sol 319, tel. 240013; 233051. Daily flights to Lima, Arequipa & Puerto Maldonado. Juliaca via Arequipa on Mon-Wed-Fri-Sat. (AeroPeru is currently not operating, its future unclear.)

Lloyd Aereo Boliviano, Av. Pardo 675, tel. 224715, fax 222990. Three flights to La Paz each week—Tues-Thurs-Sat at 11.00am.

HeliCusco, Triunfo 379, 2nd floor; tel. 243555. e-m: dfhr@Amauta.rcp.net.pe Daily helicopter flights to Aguas Calientes for visits to **Machu Picchu**. About 25 minutes flying time. Costs about three times as much as the rail autovagon. Saves time, but don't expect great views; visibility from the helicopter is very limited.

ROAD

Buses

Cusco has a new bus terminal (*terminal terrestre*), on Calle Jorge Chávez, near the Pachacutec monument. More local companies will be moving here, simplifying for travelers the complex local transport system. *An **asterisk*** *means that company has a counter at the bus terminal.*

Current schedules are included,

where known. **Morning departures** are marked in **boldface**, to help travelers find daytime schedules:

Cusco-Arequipa is part paved and part good gravel road, and takes about 12 hours. Buses to **Lima** generally go via Arequipa (paved highway from there to Lima), and take about 30 hours.

Note. All buses to Arequipa, and also to Juliaca/Puno, go via Sicuani.

Ormeño* (nationwide service; recommended); tel. 229763. Arequipa-Lima, daily at 5.00pm.

Cruz del Sur (nationwide service), Av. Pachacutec 512; tel. 222909. Arequipa-Lima, daily at **7.00am**, 4.30pm, 5.30pm, 6.00pm. Juliaca-Puno, daily at 6.30pm; Juliaca-Puno-La Paz, Tues-Thurs at **8.00am**.

Romeliza*, tel. 252994. Arequipa-Lima, daily at 4.30pm.

Puma*, tel. 241242. Arequipa-Lima, every other day at 4.30pm.

Corrales*, tel. 241955. Arequipa-Lima, daily at 6.00pm.

Colca*, tel. 227535. Arequipa, daily at 4.00pm.

Civa*, Arequipa-Lima, daily at 5.00pm. Juliaca-Puno, at 7.00pm

Trans-Prado*, Arequipa-Lima, daily at 4.00pm.

Transzela*, tel. 228988. Juliaca-Puno-La Paz. Daily at 7.30pm.

El Chasqui*, tel. 229784. Arequipa, daily at **6.45am**, 2.00pm and 5.30pm.

Alas Doradas*, tel. 229754. Arequipa, daily at 5.30pm. Puno, daily at 7.30pm.

Guadelupe*, tel. 229962. Arequipa, daily at 5.30pm. Puno-Copacabana-La Paz, daily at 8.00pm. Takes 15 hours to Copacabana, and 20 hours to La Paz.

Continental Sur*, tel. 241242, Juliaca-Puno, daily at 7.00pm Also **Carhuamayo*** (*see below*).

Cusco-Juliaca-Puno-La Paz. This highway is now paved all the way, and Cusco to Puno takes about 7-8 hours by bus. Most companies travel at night, but one or two have morning departures. Luxury buses cost about 20% more, and are well worth it. However, nightime buses in either direction between Cusco and Puno tend to dump hapless travelers on the streets at an ungodly pre-dawn hour, and none of the bus companies claiming to have direct service to La Paz actually have it at this writing—there is always a bus transfer, and several hours of cold, uncomfortable, inconvenient and potentially dangerous delay in Puno.

A new service to Puno, operated by **Amaru Overland**, Av. Pardo 545; tel. 224050, offers this journey as a one-day archeological tour, visiting the ruined Inca temple of Viracocha at Raqchi, the early site of Pucará, and the tombs of Sillustani on the way.

Etrasur*, tel. 229962. Juliaca-Puno, daily at **8.00am** and 8.00pm.

Urkupiña*, tel. 247515. Juliaca-Puno. Claims to have daily departure at **8.00 am**, another at 7.00pm.

Power*, tel. 247515. Juliaca-Puno-La Paz, daily at 8.00pm. Juliaca, daily at 7 pm.

Libertad*. Puno daily at **8.00am**, 7.30pm, 8.00pm.

Trans-America*, Puno daily at 7.40pm.

Also **Cruz del Sur, Alas Doradas*, Civa*, Guadelupe*** (*see Arequipa*) and **Carhuamayo*** (*see Quillabamba*).

Cusco-Sicuani. Good highway, about three hours.

Expreso Oriental, Av. La Cultura at Av. Manuel Prado; tel. 252874. Departures every 20 minutes, from 3.30am to 6.30pm.

Cusco-Andawaylillas-Urcos. Same highway, about 1 1/2 hours. Buses leave every 15 minutes or so from Av. Haya de la Torre, beside the Regional Hospital, about 1/2 block from Av. La Cultura.

Cusco-Abancay-Lima. Soon to be paved all the way, but at this writing paved only from Cusco to shortly beyond Curawasi, and from Chalhuanca to the Pan-American highway at Nazca, with a long, rough gap in the middle.

Expreso Wari*, tel. 261703. Abancay-Lima, daily at **6.30am** and 7.30pm.

Ampay*, tel. 227541. Abancay, daily at **6.00am**, 1.00pm and 8.00pm. Quillabamba, daily at **8.00am** and 6.00pm.

Cusco-Andahuaylas-Ayacucho – Lima. Paved from Ayacucho to the Pan-American highway at Pisco, but nasty between Abancay and Ayacucho. Change buses at Ayacucho for Lima.

San Jerónimo*. Andahuaylas-Ayacucho, daily at **6.00am**, 12.30pm and 6.00pm.

Also, **Expreso Wari*** (*see above*).

Cusco-Quillabamba is a long, gruelling, but spectacular journey up, over, down, up and around the Urubamba gorge, paved only as far as Ollantaytambo, and taking about 10 hours.

Carhuamayo*, tel. 237144. Quillabamba, daily at 5.30pm. Arequipa-Lima, daily at **6.30am** and 5.00pm. Juliaca-Puno, daily at 6.00pm.

Also **Ampay*** (*see above*).

Chinchero-Urubamba / Pisac-Calca—bus station at Calle Intiqhawarina, just off Av. Tullumayo. Departures on both lines every 15 minutes, from 5am to 7.30pm.

Pisac-Calca-Urubamba—Huascar 128. Departures every 15 minutes from 5am to 7pm.

Maras & Salineras— take the bus to Urubamba via Chinchero and get off at the Maras turn-off, about 10km. after Chinchero. Here there are normally taxis waiting for passengers from the bus, and they will take you to Maras or Salineras.

Paucartambo—buses leave from Av. Tomasa Tito, between the Social Security Hospital and the Coliseo Cerrado. There is one a.m. and one p.m. departure on Mon-Wed-Fri, and one p.m. departure only on Tues-Thurs-Sat-Sun. Times variable.

Pilcopata, Atalaya etc., via Paucartambo—trucks leave from same stop as Paucartambo, Mon-Wed-Fri mornings around 10am. Get there early for chance of a seat in the cab.

Paruro, Huanoquite—Empresa Qoyllur Rit'i, Belenpampa J-11. Buses daily at 5am to Huanoquite and Paruro, and at 3pm to Paruro only.

TAXIS

Taxis in Cusco are a cheap and convenient way to get around town. Within the center, a flat fare is charged, which at this writing is less than a dollar. Day and half-day rates for travel around Cusco are similarly low, and between three or four people a day out can be surprisingly economical. It is actually cheaper to hire a taxi with driver than to hire a self-drive rental car.

CAR RENTALS

Localiza, Av. Sol 1089, tel. 242285, fax 263448.

RAIL

Cusco-Juliaca-Puno. Mon-Wed-Fri-Sat at 8.00am. Wanchac station, at the end of Av. Sol. There are three classes: Inca, Pullman and Economy. Inca & Pullman offer lunch & bar service, plus greater security. Inca class has better seats than Pullman. The journey to Juliaca is supposed to take 8 1/2 hrs., to Puno 10 hrs. , though it often takes much longer. The train is slow and uncomfortable, but it travels by day and offers an excellent view of the wonderful scenery and Andean towns along the route. It is no longer possible to take the train direct to **Arequipa**, but there are two connecting Pullman departures per week from Puno, on Mon & Fri at 7.45pm, arriving Arequipa at 6.00am.

Machu Picchu. San Pedro station, opposite the central market. The ticket office is open from 8am-

10am/1pm-2pm/5pm-8pm. Buy your ticket the day before your journey. There are three trains and five classes: the *Autovagon*, departing at 6.00am, costs most ($55 at this writing), leaves earliest, and goes fastest (taking about three hours altogether). If you have only one day at Machu Picchu, the extra time you gain there is worth the extra money. *Inca* ($45), *Pullman* ($34) and *Expreso* ($17) are three different classes on the same train, which leaves at 6.30am and takes about three and a half hours. *Económico* is the local train, which is much slower and is not intended for tourism. This train goes to the end of the line, which until early 1998 was Quillabamba. That year an enormous landslide, which wiped out five bridges and many kilometers of railroad, left the lower limit of the railroad at Km. 121, near the western boundary of the Machu Picchu Historical Sanctuary.

It is possible to board any of these trains at Ollantaytambo, and at peak times the railroad company runs a shuttle between there and Machu Picchu, transporting passengers between Cusco and Ollantaytambo by bus.

HOTELS

Cusco now has hundreds of hotels, without even counting guesthouses in private residences. Here is a small selection of them, in approximately descending order of price and quality. Some hotels offer free transport from the airport. Hotels listed under a) and b) all have private bathrooms; c) and d) may have a mixture or be all communal.

a) **Hotel Libertador**, Plaza Santo Domingo; tel. 23-1961; fax 233152. e-m: hotel@libertador.com.pe After many years in operation, the best-known and most professionally run hotel in Cusco. Colonial building. 212 Rooms.

Hotel Monasterio, Plaza Nazarenas. Tel. 241777; fax 237111. e-m: resrlima@peruhotel.com. Cusco's fancy new hotel, a highly atmospheric restored colonial seminary, with an opulent former chapel serving as conference center. 123 Rooms.

b) **Hotel Don Carlos**, Av. Sol 602; tel. 226207; fax 241375. e-m: dcarloscus@tci.net.pe Comfortable new hotel on main avenue.

La Posada del Inca, Portal Espinar 142; tel/fax 233091. Comfortable new hotel, very centrally located.

Hotel Ruinas, Ruinas 472, tel. 236391. New, pleasant, nr. center, roof terrace. 54 rooms.

Royal Inca I & II, Plaza Regocijo 299 & Santa Teresa 335; tels. 231067. Long-established twin hotels in city center.

Hotel Savoy, Av. Sol 954; tel. 224322; e-m: savoy@mail.cosapidata.com.pe Not central, but comfortable and reasonable.

Los Andes de America, Calle Garcilaso 234; tel. 223058; e-m: andeam@telser.com.pe New hotel, in remodelled colonial building. Central, modern.

IncaTambo, Sacsaywaman. tel/fax 233073. Hacienda-type hotel 2 km. from the city center, close by the famous ruins, horseback riding.

Carlos V Hostal, Tecsecocha 490; tel. 223091. Small, pleasant, central.

Los Portales, Matará 322; tel 222391. Comfort and good service, good value.

c) **El Balcón,** Tambo de Montero 222; tel/fax 236738. e-m: balcon@peru.itete.com.pe Remodelled colonial building in very central location, intimate, with a terrific view.

El Patio, Saphi 440; tel/fax 226241. Another very nice remodelled colonial building with an intimate feel, very close to the main square.

Cusco Plaza, Plaza Nazarenas 181; tel. 263842. Friendly place in quiet but centrally-located old square.

Valichawasi, Saphi 766; tel. 242002; tel/fax 235353. e-m: valicha@chaski.unsaac.edu.pe Small, intimate family hotel in central, remodelled colonial house.

Hostal Adomar, Portal Mantas 128; tel. 232249. Comfortably modern in colonial building, very central.

La Casona del Sol, Plazoleta Santo Domingo 263, tel. 232704; tel/fax 234082. Pleasant, atmospheric and well located.

Casa de Campo, Tandapata 296, San Blas; tel. 244404, fax 241422. An imaginative new hotel, fireplaces in rooms, gardens, and fine view over Cusco.

La Posada del Sol, Atoqsaycuchi 296, San Blas; tel. 228060/fax 242506. Small, homey bar, with fine view.

El Arqueólogo, Ladrillos 425; tel. 232569. Quiet, garden setting. French owner.

Andenes de Saphi, Saphi 848; tel. 227561, fax 235588. Small, central, comfortable, new, personable atmosphere.

Hostal Cahuide, Saphi 845, tel. 222771/fax 222361. Good for large groups, convenient location.

T'ika Wasi, Tandapata 491, San Blas. tel/fax 231609. One of new hotels in San Blas. Has vehicle access, unlike many others in this district.

Hostal Loreto, Intik'ijllu (a.k.a. Loreto) 115; tel 226352. Very small, central, friendly, some Inca walls.

Niños Hotel, Calle Meloc 442; tel. 231424. e-m: ninos@correo.dnet.com.pe. A pleasant, modest hotel in a converted colonial mansion, run by a Dutch couple with an unusual agenda: feed and shelter homeless children, using the profits from their business. Recommended.

Hostal Samana, Nueva Baja 472; tel. 239688. Another converted colonial mansion, giving quite good value.

Pensión Alemana, Tandapata 260; tel. 226861. Pleasant, homey feeling, w/garden, in quiet San Blas. 10 rooms.

d) **Hostal Familiar**, Saphi 661; tel. 239353. Old, pleasant, modest; some private bathrooms.

Hostal Suecia, Suecia 332; tel. 233282. Colonial building, very central.

Hostal Imperio, Chaparro 121; tel. 228981; next to San Pedro Church. Good value, private baths.

Qawarina Hostal, Suecia 575; tel. 228130. Small, friendly, views.

Hostal Quipu, Fierro 495, tel. 236179; fax 260721 Clean, cheap, friendly management, slightly away from center, well located for Machu Picchu train station.

Municipal Hostel. Quiscapata 240; tel. 252506. Hostelling International spot near San Cristobal church, in a high part of town. Fine views.

EATING, DRINKING AND BEING MERRY

Restaurants

A brief selection from the many restaurants in Cusco. Places have been included for some special aspect: food, price, atmosphere. Many local restaurants have an inexpensive set lunch menu. Within the categories featured below, places are approximately ordered in descending price range.

LM = Live music.

LM&FD = Live music & Folk Dance.

SL = Set Lunch—indicates a moderately-priced set lunch is served.

VO = Vegetarian Option. Most places can produce some sort of dish for vegetarians, but VO means there is a special menu or special items.

GV = Great View.

By law, prices featured on the menu must include sales tax.

The following listings are arranged very approximately in descending order of price.

La Retama, Portal de Panes 123, (Pl. de Armas); tel. 226372. One of Cusco's best restaurants, with some unusual dishes, trout a specialty (try the cooked trout cebiche), Andes cream soup delicious. (But time for a wine list to match, eh guys?). LM&FD, GV

El Truco (W. side of Pl. Regocijo); tel. 235295. Local and international food, some good dishes, nice atmosphere and lively but overamplified LM&FD (cover charge).

Mesón de Espaderos, Espaderos 105 (crnr Pl. de Armas); tel. 235307; meaty menu; excellent food, tasty garlic bread, salad bar, and side sauces. GV.

La Estancia Imperial, Portal de Panes 137, 2nd floor (Pl. de Armas); tel. 224621. Salad Bar, local and international dishes. GV.

José Antonio, Santa Teresa 356, tel. 241364. Excellent lunch buffet with local and seasonal Andean dishes. LM&FD

El Paititi, Portal de Carrizos 270, Pl. de Armas; tel. 252686. International food, Inca wall. LM.

Roma, Portal de Panes 105, tel. 24-5041. Inca walls, local and international menu. LM&FD

Trattoría Adriano, crnr Av. Sol and Marques; tel. 233965. Good international food, espresso coffee and exquisite German chocolate cake.

El Mesón de los Portales, Portal de Panes 163 (Pl. de Armas); tel. 235604. Good international food; nice atmosphere.

Pucara, Plateros 300, tel. 22-2027—good national and international cuisine served with the fresh vegetables at reasonable prices. Pleasant atmosphere. Chocolate desserts recommended. SL.

Los Tomines, Triunfo 384, tel. 236671. Local cooking. Pleasant. SL, LM.

Ama Lur, Plateros 372, tel. 224203. Pleasant atmosphere, reasonably priced SL.

Kusikuy, Plateros 348. Good Peruvian-style food, nice atmosphere, SL.

Greens, Tandapata 700, top end of Plaza San Blas; tel. 650587. Small, friendly, pleasant ambience, some oriental dishes.

La Yunta, Portal de Carnes 214, tel. 235103. Busy, noisy, lively. Good food, great pizza, shared tables, slow service.

Haylli, Plateros 363. Snacks, sandwiches, vegetarian SL.

La Ensaladera, Procuradores 371. Good food, inexpensive. SL w/VO.

José Suave's Procuradores 398; tel. 243024. Hamburgers. Chicken wings and Chinese style. Home delivery. SL w/VO.

Ethnic

Kin Taro, Heladeros 149; tel. 226181. Japanese food, ambience, and owner; elegant, simple and reasonably priced. SL.

El Cuate, Procuradores 386. Excellent Mexican food at a very reasonable price. Superb tortilla chips.

Pasta

El Patio, Portal de Carnes 236, Pl. de Armas. Superb pasta with wide range of delicious sauces. VO.

Da Giorgio, Suecia 308; tel. 246357. Italian owner-chef; excellent pasta, cakes, pastries.

Tiziano Trattoria, Tecsecocha 418, excellent homemade pasta, good value, try the canelloni, good SL.

Chez Maggy *(see Pizza)*.

Pizza

New York will crash when the international set finds out about Cusco pizza crust. Cooked in adobe, wood-fired ovens (pizzerías are great places to go if you are feeling the Andean cold), and served at:

Chez Maggy, Plateros 339. Small but good.

Marengo, Plaza Regocijo 246. L-shaped den with excellent pizza.

La Yunta, *(see above)* —pizza also gets high rating.

Chifa (Peruvian-style Chinese)

Sipán, Plateros 358 and Q'era 251; tel. 222246. Chifa is mainly a Peruvian coast tradition, but this is a good local effort.

Vegetarian

Frutos, Sunturwasi (a.k.a. Triunfo) 393; tel. 242953, upstairs, in patio—small, clean, pleasant atmosphere, inexpensive. Sells an interesting selection of books, too. SL. GV.

Auliya, Calle Garcilazo 265, 2nd floor. Pleasant group-size space, quality food. Also sells natural foods (dried fruits, gluten, tofu etc.) produced by owners Michael & Aurora

Schilling in Sacred Valley. SL.

Govinda, Espaderos 128; run by Hare Krishnas; fruit and yoghurt drinks; inexpensive.

Killa Wasi, Saphi 705. Veggie with attitude. Inexpensive. SL.

Seafood

El Mariño, Portal Espinar 108, tel. 236308. Seafood; lunch only.

El Trujillo, Matará 261; tel. 233465. Good food, inexpensive; noisy, funky atmosphere.

Quintas

These are open-air restaurants, serving local highland cooking, weighted towards meat and spice. Lunchtimes only.

Quinta Pacha Papa, Plazoleta San Blas 120; tel. 241318. A new quinta in the traditional-style, in the heart of San Blas.

Quinta Eulalia, Choquechaca 384; delightful open-air eating on a sunny day; cheap regional food.

Quinta Zarate, Totora Paqcha 763, tel. 224145. At the south end of Tandapata in San Blas. Huge portions. GV.

Tradiciones Cusqueñas, Belen 835, Santiago. Indoor quinta, funky local flavor.

Quinta Don Luis, Av. Regional 904; tel. 222073. Longstanding indoor/outdoor quinta in lower part of town.

Breakfast spot

La Tertulia, Procuradores 50, 2nd floor. Excellent breakfast buffet with yogurt, muesli, plus all the usual. Nice atmosphere. Book exchange.

Cafés

El Ayllu, Portal de Carnes 208, Pl. de Armas (to the left as you face the cathedral); good pastries, homemade fruit yogurt, classical music, snacks; fast service; opens early; very busy, not a place to sit down and write postcards.

El Varayoc, Espaderos 142. Good coffee, pastries. Calm atmosphere.

Manu Café, Av. Pardo 1046, tel. 252721. Step out of Cusco's center and into another world—L.A., perhaps. Pricey, w/quality. Exotic coffees. Foreign magazines.

Le Croissant, Pl. San Francisco 134. French-style patisserie, delicious pastries, tea/coffee, breakfast; run by French couple Emmanuelle and Gerard Bance.

Café/Restaurant

Al Grano, Sta. Catalina Ancha 398 (crnr. of San Agustín); tel. 228032. Range of tasty oriental dishes, lunch & dinner. Friendly, comfortable atmosphere. Muffins, brownies, top-rated coffee. Something different.

Bar/Café

Ethnic Café bar, Tecsecocha 458. A calm and tasteful locale, conceived by Cusco's Japanese expat designer, Miki Suzuki, and run by partners Michael Bloom & Carmen Salas. Light dishes and snacks, coffee, drinks etc.

Trotamundos, Portal de Comercio 177, 2nd floor, Pl. de Armas. Pleasant atmosphere, snacks, drinks & lunches. GV.

Los Perros, Tecsecocha 436. Couch bar. Magazines, books, drinks, chat, snacks; comfortable, friendly. Fried wan-tan to die for.

El Plus Café, Portal de Panes 151, 2nd floor, Pl. de Armas. Coffee, chocolate cake, apple pie etc. GV.

Bars

Most Cusco Bars have a Happy Hour when drinks are half price. Check for times.

The Cross Keys, Portal de Confiturías 233, 2nd floor, Pl. de Armas. Open from 11am till 1am daily. The original, founding Cusco pub. Pizza & bar snacks. Pool games free until 6pm. Cable TV, news/ sports. Owner is Brit. hon-consul Barry Walker. Happy hour 6-7pm, and 9-9.30pm. GV.

Paddy Flaherty's Irish Pub, Sunturwasi (a.k.a. Triunfo) 124, 2nd floor. A pleasant and friendly watering hole. Cable TV. GV. Happy hour 6-7pm, and 10-10.30pm.

Norton Rat's Tavern, Intik'ikijllu

(a.k.a. Loreto) 115, 2nd floor. Great location, nice feel and decor by owner, US expat-biker Jeff Powers. Hamburgers, grill. GV.

Kerara, Espaderos 135, 3rd floor. Pool, billiards, backgammon, darts. Calm atmosphere. Live show on weekends. GV.

Rosie O'Grady's, Santa Catalina Ancha 360; tel. 247935. New Irish pub two blocks from Pl. de Armas. Spacious, serves food.

Dance-Bars

Kamikaze, crnr of Plaza Regocijo, above Cafe Varayoc; bar, electro-Andean music, and dancing, sometimes live bands. GV.

Ukukus, Plateros 316, 2nd floor. Funky, good-sized dance space, often live bands.

Uptown Pub, Suecia 302, Pl.

de Armas. Disco dance-floor, good atmosphere, currently techno-pop music.

Mama Africa, Espaderos 135, 2nd floor. Rock, reggae, small and usually packed w/teen to twenties crowd. With attached **Cyber Café**. Serves pizza and pasta till the small hours.

Xtreme Pub, Portal Espinar 108. Adventure sports themed dance hall with adjacent games rooms for pool, darts, pinball etc.

Traditional Dance and Music

Taki Andean Music Museum, Hatunrumiyoq 487, #5. A tiny outpost of authentic Andean music tradition. Thurs. & Sat. events of music & dance.

Centro Qosqo, Av. Sol 604. Nightly music and dance shows in large theatre space.

ARTS, HANDCRAFTS, SHOPPING

Conservation note. Some stores sell such items as jaguar and ocelot skins, macaw-feather arrows and headdresses, collections of butterflies and insects etc. *Please don't buy these!* If you do you are sponsoring the destruction of the region's wildlife. Many of these products violate wildlife protection statutes, and cannot be legally exported, anyway.

Cusco Artists

Cusco has some superb artists and craftspeople. Not all those listed below are from Cusco, and some are not even Peruvian, but all of them live and work in the Cusco region, and have become part of the local scene.

Carlos Chaquiras, has been a major influence on contemporary Cusco jewelry styles. He designs and makes fine-crafted jewelry of silver, gold, and semi-precious stones with pre-Columbian motifs, and sells them at the eponymous store on Sunturwasi (a.k.a. Triunfo) 375, tel. 227470.

Japanese expat **Miki Suzuki** designs fashion clothing, sweaters, cotton prints and many other items, and sells them, along with other interesting local handcrafts, at **Pedazo**, Plateros 334-B, tel. 242967, and

Pablo Seminario, the region's most original ceramic Artist, now gaining an international reputation, sells his work, along with other quality local handcrafts, at **La Mamita**, Portal de Carnes 244, Pl. de Armas; tel. 246093, and also at his pottery in Urubamba (*see Provincial Towns, p. 38*).

Carlos Olivera, Cusco sculptor and artist, noted for his creative, sometimes darkly humorous manipulations of found objects and organic materials. Has no store or gallery, but pieces hang in the Retama restaurant, Uptown Pub, Cross Keys and other locales. Messages: 236695.

Tiburcio Suna, from a remote village in the province of Paucartambo, has created his own style of wooden masks, loosely derived from the festival mask tradition. Funny or scary, but always lively and original, they are a unique contribution to the Cusco handcraft scene. Imitations of his work abound in Cusco stores, but for the authentic originals, contact Numitor Hidalgo at the Pensión Alemana,

Tandapata 260; tel. 226861.

In Urubamba, **Christa Quiróz** makes highly original felt slippers and other items, which are sold in some Cusco stores. Tel. 201390.

Longstanding local artists and artesans of renown in the San Blas district include:

Olave, Calle Plazoleta 651. Quality ceramics.

Mendívil, the Cusco family famous for its giraffe-necked models of saints. Three stores (Plazoleta San Blas 634 & 619, and Hatunrumiyoc 486; tel. 233247/fax 233234),

Mérida, Carmen Alto 133. Clay figurines in a much-imitated, somewhat painful and grotesque style.

Other stores:

Anticuario Artesanal Viracocha, Sunturwasi (a.k.a. Triunfo) 352-B; tel. 236981. Rich collection of antiques, fine handcrafts and traditional weavings, assembled by owners Mauro and Mercedes Alvites. Many items for exhibition only, and worth seeing.

Galería Latina, San Agustín 427; tel. 246588. Upscale collection of very fine, high-priced handcrafts.

Tiendas Museo, Plateros 334; tel. 233484 (and Santa Clara 501; tel 225601—mornings only). Quality traditional weavings.

Pisonay. Q'aphchik'ijllu (a.k.a.

Pasaje Arequipa) 242, tel. 228327. Nice collection of Peruvian handcrafts.

The colonial patio at Sunturwasi (a.k.a. Triunfo) 393 has several good handcraft stores, including **Cariluis** for colorful woven vests (a.k.a. waistcoats), and **Artesanias Maxi**, for high quality dolls.

El Suri, Portal de Carnes 236, Pl. de Armas. Small, diverse collection of handcrafts and jewelry.

Bazaars

Two private markets with a typical range of local handcrafts for one-stop shopping are **Yachay Wasi**, Calle Triunfo 376 (about half a block from Pl. de Armas) and **Bazaar Inca**, crnr of San Andres and Q'era.

On Saturdays there is an open-air handcraft market in the **Plazoleta San Blas.**

If you have limited time and want to hit just one area for browsing and shopping, try starting at the Plaza de Armas and walking up Triunfo, along Hatunrumiyoc, and up the Cuesta San Blas to Plazoleta San Blas; many of the shops mentioned are on this route. Plateros and Plaza Regocijo are also good.

Fine alpaca wool fashions

Alpaca 111, Heladeros 202; tel. 243233

Royal Alpaca, Santa Teresa 387; tel. 252346.

Juana Maria Zamora, Portal de Comercio 141, Pl. de Armas

Alpaca Golden, Plaza Santo Domingo 285; tel. 26-2914.

Galería Latina *(see above)*

Alpaca wool for knitting:

Alpaca Michell, San Juan de Dios 264; tel. 221157

ADVENTURE TOURS AND EXPEDITIONS

(Note that hard-core hiking and rafting trips shut down during the November-March rainy season. However, the Inca Trail is now hiked—and the softer sections of the Urubamba river are rafted—year round.)

Trekking/Hiking

The Cusco region is fabulous country for everything from day hikes to treks and backpacking. This is wide open country; no "Keep Out" signs, or barbed-wire fences. Very intrepid adventurers with compass and map could reach the Peruvian coast on foot from here if they wanted to. The views are astounding and the countryside is endlessly varied.

The Inca Trail is justifiably famous but very heavily used. Meanwhile there are dozens of other hikes and circuits in the area. Some less well known ones are suggested in the appropriate chapters. The 6-day Ausangate circuit is a rigorous gem of a high-altitude hike, while the Mollepata to Santa Teresa route offers a combination of high mountain passes and cloud-forest environments. New routes have opened up in the Machu Picchu area *(see end of Chapter 4),* as less-traveled alternatives to the Inca Trail.

Here are some companies which operate trekking in the area. Note that some of these companies operate river trips, too.

Explorandes, Av. Infancia 440, Huanchac; tel. 238380; fax 233784. e-m: explocus@qenqo.rcp.net.pe. The oldest established and largest in the Peruvian adventure travel scene. Hikes and camping trips into the interior, rafting and kayaking. Not the cheapest services, but experienced and reliable. Group bookings only.

Manu Expeditions, *(see Manu operators, p. 43)*, also operates highland trekking groups.

Mayuc, Portal de Confiturías 211, Pl. de Armas. tel/fax 232666. e-m: mayuc@Amauta.rcp.net.pe; web: www.mayuc.com Backcountry expeditions, strong on rafting and kayaking; takes local bookings, small ad hoc groups. Offers kayaking courses.

Aventours, Cusco: tel/fax 262042. Lima: Av. La Paz 442, Miraflores, tel. 441067. Experienced company in rafting and trekking.

Tambo Treks, Casilla 912, tel. 237718/fax 236229. e-m: tambotrx@ qenqo.rcp.net.pe Strong on long treks focused on local culture. Goes to Bolivia. Group bookings only.

Peruvian Andean Treks, Av. Pardo 705, tel. 225701—e-m: postmaster@patCusco.com.pe (Cusco); US associate: Andean Treks, 32 Russell Av., Watertown, MA. 02172-3456 (USA) e-m: patusa @ziplink.net. Rafting and trekking, local and North America based. Groups only. Associate Nilda Callañaupa arranges interesting weaving demonstrations in Chinchero.

Southern Cross Adventures, Centro Comercial los Ruiseñores, Portal de Panes 123, Of. 301, tel. 237649/fax 239447. Run by veteran trekker Hugo Paullu. Noted for horseback trips in the Cordillera Vilcabamba.

Apu Expeditions—Avda. Sol 395; tel/fax. 228651; e-m: apuexpe@qenqo.rcp.net.pe Owner Alberto Miori strong on local lore, trail knowledge, weavings, antique coins and other arcana.

Trek Peru, Urb. Mateo Pumacahua C-10, Huanchac, P.O Box

1151, Cusco; tel. Trekperu 252899; Fax 238591; e-m: trekperu@correo.dnet.com.pe Wide range of adventure services.

Andean Adventures, Heladeros 157, Of. 201; tel/fax 236201.

Innumerable companies operate the **Inca Trail**. Some of the cheaper ones should be avoided. A basic-services company which has received good reviews is **United Mice**, Plateros 349, tel/fax 221139. **Vilca** *(see Manu operators)*, occupies the middle range, while **Mayuc** *(see above)* has been recommended for the higher-end traveler who wants a little pampering.

A biased recommendation. There are too many adventure travel operators in the U.S., and too many local tour operators in Cusco, for either of those categories to be listed here. However, since I have worked with the following companies personally for many years, I can recommend them. **Adventure travel in the U.S.:** Wilderness Travel, 1102 9th St., Berkeley, CA. 94710. 1-800-368-2794. **Tours in Cusco:** Peru Chasquitur, Calle Maruri 228, Of. 108; tel. 241280—Milla Turismo, Av. Pardo 689; tel. 231710.

Equipment Rental

Quality of equipment available for rent varies enormously. *Check and test everything before you set off on a trip.* **EcoTreks**, Ruinas 435, tel/fax 243129. Has fairly new equipment at this writing. Also, **Soqllaq'asa**, Plateros 359, tel. 252560 and **Vilca**, Amargura 101, crnr. Saphi.

RIVER RUNNING

Cusco is an excellent base for kayaking and rafting on some of the wild Andean rivers. The following are the main rivers run commercially out of Cusco. Class Ratings, with one exception (Checacupe-Quiquijana), apply to the dry season (June-November):

The standard one-day rafting trips out of Cusco are the **Huambutío-Pisac** (Class II) and **Ollantaytambo-Chillca** (Class III) sections of the Urubamba. The first is for almost anybody, the second is scarier but not terrifying, and has the most beautiful scenery. Both sections can become scary monsters for periods during the rainy season.

The **Urubamba** is also run at the short but technical **Huarán** rapids (Class IV+). Further downstream is a beautiful run, the two-day high-jungle **Chaullay to Quillabamba** (Class III+) section of the Urubamba. Rainy season only. Also on the Urubamba, a new one-day run becoming popular in low tourist season is **Checacupe-Quiquijana** (Class IV-V).

The **Apurimac** (Class IV-V), a major river, is rapidly gaining popularity as the new Bio Bio (the famous Chilean river, now lost to a damming project). It's a wild run of two, three or four days, with spectacular scenery, wildlife possibilities, and beautiful camping beaches. Mid-May to mid-November only. *Warning.* Hellish sandflies on the beaches. Take repellent.

The **Tambopata** (Class III-IV, and will turn to V in one rainy night), a 10-12 day (Cusco to Cusco) rafting adventure in wild country along the Bolivian border, in the Department of Puno—a very remote wilderness experience, rich with wildlife. Includes the famous Tambopata macaw lick.

One- or two-day sections of the exciting **Kosñipata** river (Class III+) can be run as part of a journey to Manu, or a visit to the jungle lodges on the Alto Madre de Dios river.

Warning. If you haggle for the cheapest price, you may be cutting corners on safety. Cusco rafting is not regulated, and big rivers like the Apurimac can be dangerous. You may be in a remote area, far from help. There are one or two fatal rafting accidents in the region each year. Guides must be experienced, equipment must be serviceable. There should be a safety kayak or raft for rescues. If you are inexperienced, the trip should ideally include half a day for training at the beginning.

How well is your operator taking care of the environment? There are reports that groups have been trashing the camp sites along the Apurimac. Send back your reports *(see author's e-mail address on copyright page)*.

Some tips from rafter Paul Cripps: If it's an expedition of several days on a big river, try to meet the guide before you sign up. Find out how well he speaks English (incomprehensible instructions can be disastrous), ask what river experience he has. Ask to see equipment. Life jackets should be reasonably new and buoyant. Helmets are a must for big rivers, and should not have been cracked and repaired (I've seen them bandaged with duct tape). Ask to see dry bags, and check for age and leaks. Self-bailing rafts are best for long trips: they are less work, and safer.

Paul Cripps has teamed up with Swiss river guide Stephan Zumsteg to run river trips out of Cusco under the name **Amazonas Explorer**, *Casilla 722, Cusco, tel/fax 236826; (Swiss Office: tel/fax (41) 1-361-4857; e-m: info@amazonas-explorer.com).*

River Operators

Many companies sell rafting trips. Some do not operate them, but merely taking your booking and passing you on to other operators. It is best to go direct to the operator. The following are the main river rafting operators. The first four operate the Apurimac. Mayuc also operates the Tambopata:

Mayuc, *(see Trekking)*

Instinct, Procuradores 50, tel/fax 233451.

Apumayo, Garcilazo 265; #3, in patio; tel/fax 246018.

Eric Adventures, Plateros 324, tel 232244/fax 239772.

Loreto Tours, Calle del Medio 111, tel. 236331.

Kayaking

Some operators offer kayak classes: Eric Arenas (a Peruvian kayak champion), of **Eric Adventures** and **Mayuc** *(see River Operators)*; .

MOUNTAIN BIKING

The Cusco region is terrific for mountain biking, with innumerable bikeable trails close to the city and many more starting a day's drive away. It's easy to put your bike on the roof rack of almost any local bus (make sure they load it properly), and travel to trailheads around the region.

Easy riders (if you're not adjusted to altitude, include yourself in this category no matter *how* fit you are!) can take some of the most spectacular downhill road-runs anywhere in the world. They go on for hours.

Warning: Dog attacks! Homicidal drivers! Suicidal pedestrians! Broken glass! Highway soccer matches (usually on blind curves)!

Be alert.

Here are some options, going from soft to extremely hard. In all cases, take a local bus or taxi and get off at the highest point—unless of course you want to bike the whole way from Cusco *(see **Transport** for buses).* An even better option is to rent a support vehicle to carry your gear and follow you:

One day downhill highway outings:

- **Puente Cunyac.** Start early for this one. Take a local bus heading for Limatambo and ask the driver to let you off at the highest point beyond Izcuchaca, the Abra de Huillque. Ride about three hours downhill all the way to Puente Cunyac, the bridge over the Apurimac river. Take a truck or interprovincial bus back to Cusco. For a longer, harder version of this ride, take a taxi to the "Arco", the high point on the outskirts of Cusco, and bike all the way to Puente Cunyac.

- **Pisac.** Take a bus past Qenqo & Tambomachay, get off at the Abra de Corao. Ride down to Pisac. This is short—about thirty minutes—but fast. (To ride all the way to Pisac from Cusco, including a longish uphill stretch, takes 2-3 hours.) To continue further, take the old road down the left bank of the Urubamba *(see below)*.

- **Urubamba.** Take a bus past Chinchero and get off at Km. 37. Nearly all downhill from here to Urubamba, about one hour. Fabulous views.

Mild off-road experiences:

- Chinchero to Urubamba, via Lake Huaypo, Moray and Salineras. Take bus to Chinchero. A lovely ride, fairly flat, but you've got to know the route. Bike Center *(see below)* has a map.

- Cusco to Pachar, via Izcuchaca and Huarocondo. Take a bus or taxi to El Arco, the high point on the outskirts of Cusco, to avoid a hard urban hillclimb. Then it's an easy ride on excellent paved highway, as far as Huarocondo (take the right fork at Izcuchaca), then moderately rugged, but downhill, following the dirt road which parallels the railroad all the way to Pachar, where you cross the Urubamba river and meet the main highway between Urubamba and Ollantaytambo. If you only want to do the first bit, take public transport back to Cusco from Huarocondo.

- The old road from Pisac to Calca, or further, to Wayllabamba *(see Sacred Valley chapter for full description).* A pleasant, very easy ride down the left bank of the Urubamba, on a road with so little traffic it almost qualifies as a bike path.

More serious outings.

These four downhill road runs take you from the heights of the Andes down into the jungle lowlands. Use public transport to reach the starting point:

- Abra Union to Quincemil, past Ocongate on the road to Puerto Maldonado. This is an entire day of downhill, much of it through spectacular cloud forest, but the road is very rough, and the trip requires panniers, camping gear, planning, and a serious attitude. Expect to rough it. Abra Union can be reached by any truck or bus heading for Quincemil.

- Abra Tres Cruces to Pilcopata, on the road past Paucartambo to Atalaya. Take public transport to Pilcopata (Mon-Wed-Fri only) and get off at the Abra Tres Cruces. Transportation as far as Paucartambo is more readily available, but from there it is 3-4 hours uphill to the Abra. After the Abra it's another incredibly long downhill on a terrible road (currently under improvement) through some of the most spectacular montane forest on the planet, skirting the Manu National Park. Can be included as part of a Manu trip.

- Abra de Málaga to Quillabamba, a vast downhill from the snowy slopes of Mt. Wakay Willka (Verónica) to the coffee and coca belt downstream from Machu Picchu. One option is to ride from Cusco to Ollantaytambo, overnight there, and pick up a bus or truck next day, to spare yourself the brutal climb to the Abra de Málaga.

- Abra de Lares/Abra de Amparaes to Quillabamba, an exciting trip also with spectacular scenery, from the heights north of Calca, down through tropical forest. The road splits before the pass, the lefthand going through Lares, the righthand through Amparaes, joining together again many kilometers down-valley. The Lares road carries less motor traffic.

Terribly serious outings (the previous ones were mostly downhill, on motor roads; these aren't):

- the Ausangate Circuit. It's a trekking route, but hard core locals have done it on bikes. Warning: several high passes, two of them around 5,000m. Steep ascents, pushing bike. Be smart— hire horses to carry your baggage in Tinqui. Four days.

- Mollepata to Km. 88 and Chillca, via the Abra de Incachiriasqa, below Salcantay. A cruel journey, like the previous one. Only one pass, but it's 5200m.—then mostly downhill. Hire horses in Mollepata to take baggage at least as far as the pass. About four days.

Bike Maintenance

Juan Carlos Salazar, tel. 246534. Recommended bike mechanic; has some parts, but no shop at this writing; may be opening soon at new premises in Calle Saphi.

Soqllaq'asa, *(see equipment rental)* and **Loreto Tours** *(see River Operators)* also has a few bikes for rent.

ORGANIZED MOUNTAIN BIKING TRIPS

Amazonas Explorer *(see River Running)*

Ecomontaña. Calle Garcilaso 265, #3 in patio; tel/fax 242030. e-m: ecomontana@hotmail.com. Runs various itineraries out of Cusco from easy to gruelling, from one day to one month, and from Peru to Patagonia. Has bikes, will rent.

Horseback riding

Elías Cosio, 237011/cel. 623070; fax 223271. Inquiries: Saphi 704. Rents horses and guides for local trips in the Cusco area, anything from 1/2 to four days. *(for horseback riding in the Sacred Valley, see Pisac square; Sacred Valley Inn, Urubamba; Perol Chico, Ayllunpampa; Hostal Tambo, Ollantaytambo).*

Paragliding

Mountainous regions high above sea level are not ideal for beginners at this sport. However, **Leo Infanta**, tel. 239476; fax 263115 offers cour-ses. Also inquire at **Mayuc** *(see Trekking).*

Hot Air Ballooning

Globos de los Andes, Hotel la Posada del Libertador, Plaza Manco II, Yucay; tel. 201116; e-m: globossa@aol.com. Flights over the Sacred Valley and the Maras Plateau in small balloon for 3-4 pax. Pricey, but well worth it if you've got the bucks.

PROVINCIAL TOWNS

Note: telephone calls from the city of Cusco to the numbers listed below are now local and require no prefix.

The Sacred Valley

The Valley is an excellent base for exploring the Cusco region, including Machu Picchu and the Inca Trail, and has the advantage of a better climate, lower altitude and calmer environment than the city of Cusco. For independent visitors, traveling the length of the Valley between Ollantaytambo and Pisac on public transport is very easy these days, with cheap and frequent public buses, which can be flagged down anywhere. Some visitors are beginning to use the Valley instead of Cusco as their base, traveling there straight off the plane from Lima. Urubamba is the most central location and has the most services. Pisac is closest to Cusco, while Ollantaytambo is most convenient for Machu Picchu, and both have interesting attractions of their own. Take your pick.

PISAC

Pisac now has a handcraft market on Tues-Thurs-Sun (the original market day). Check out the local bakery on Mariscal Castilla, just off the main square, which bakes excellent bread in a mighty colonial oven.

For transport to the ruins, look out for minibus taxis near the main highway bridge, or in the main square. Horses can be rented in the main square for transport to the ruins on market days.

Hotels

a) **Hotel Royal Inka,** just beyond outskirts of Pisac, on the way to the ruins; tel. 203067. Swimming pool, tennis court.

c) **Hostal Pisaq,** on Pisac main square. Casilla 1179, Cusco tel/fax 203062—sauna, pizza oven, nicely decorated (paintings), pleasant atmosphere, friendly management with owners Román & Fielding Vizcarra, shared bathrooms (one room w/private bath).

Restaurants

Samana, south side of main square. Sunny courtyard, good local food. Transport to ruins.

Intiwasi, 203047. About 1km. outside Pisac on the highway to Calca. Tourist lunches by arrangement. Tasty trout.

CALCA

The **Hostal Pitusiray** is the only decent hotel, located at the edge of town on the main road to Urubamba. Clean with abundant hot water; restaurant. (US$4 per person, sharing double.) The **Quinta El Carmen** on the main road is a pleasant garden spot, serving tasty lunches at reasonable prices. The **Quinta Jacaranda** is an inexpensive restaurant, a bit noisy, serving good local-style food.

There are ruins up the valley that runs northeast from town, and also hot springs, about 8 km. up a narrow road. But the baths are housed in a building so scruffy and rundown that one is not tempted.

HUAYO CCARI—On a bluff on the north side of the river, across from the south-bank village of Urquillos, stands Huayo Ccari, home of the Lambarri family, who are the closest thing to royalty in the Urubamba valley. The family offers exclusive buffet lunches by prior arrangement, and also accommodation in a converted colonial mansion. Inquiries: 241437.

WAYLLABAMBA

Coming someday: Wayllabamba, 8 km. east of Urubamba, is the only major town on the left bank of the river. Just upstream, at Urquillos, lies **Yaravilca**, a working farm and former colonial hacienda which Scottish expatriate Ken Duncan is turning into a very exclusive hotel. The man has excellent taste, so this hotel will probably be the finest in the Sacred Valley, but completion may take a while. Inquiries: tel/fax 232829.

YUCAY

Posada del Inca, Plaza Manco II, tel/fax 201107. Large, spacious hotel, colonial hacienda style, partly original, in pleasant grounds. Small historical museum.

La Posada del Libertador (so named because Simón Bolivar—the Liberator—once stayed there), Plaza Manco II, tel. 201116. Small, pleasant, personal, spacious gardens, colonial house surrounded by cornfields. 20 rooms.

URUBAMBA

The cheap and convenient local transport in Urubamba (also Calca) is the moto-taxi, a kind of motor tricycle with room for three passengers. They can be picked up easily around town, and there is a line of them in the main square.

Hotels

Sacred Valley Inn, edge of Urubamba, on the highway towards Ollantaytambo. Tel. 20-1126/27; Fax 201071. Modern, 65 bungalow rooms, spacious riverside grounds with fine views, large auditorium/conference center, swimming pool, horses for rent. Until recently a hotel, now in transition to a health spa and convention center.

San Agustín, 500m. beyond town, on highway to Pisac; tel. 20143/44; Fax 201025. Pleasant country inn. 42 rooms.

Hostal Willka T'ika, Rumichaca, outside Urubamba on the road to Ollantaytambo, tel./fax 201181. 11 rooms. A small, intimate and comfortable hotel, in an exquisite garden setting, built by *Pachamama's Children* co-author Carol Cumes. Prefers group bookings.

Recoleta, outskirts of Urubamba towards Yucay; partly built in patio of old Franciscan mission. 20 rooms. Tel./fax 201004.

Hostal Hammer, about 1 km. outside Urubamba on road to Ollantaytambo. tel/fax 201194. Small (8 rooms), friendly, comfortable, pleasant location.

Campsites

Follow the road to Pumahuanca, about 1/2 km. past the church of Torrechayoq. First, on the right is **Camping Los Cedros**, shortly beyond it down a lane to the left is **Camping Los Girasoles,** tel. 201390. Both have spacious and pleasant camping areas, with showers and toilets and both rent tents and camping equipment. Partying is in order (Los Cedros specializes in Full Moon parties), and they cater to a young crowd.

Los Girasoles also has hot showers plus indoor accommodations in a pleasant building with bunk beds for up to 20 people, plus two private rooms, and a private bungalow with its own bathroom/toilet. Owner José Luis Quiróz and his wife Christa also organize a beautiful and little-known three-day hike up the nearby Pumahuanca valley and over a high pass (4900m.) to Concani and Lares.

There is another very pleasant campsite with some inexpensive hotel accommodation at **Rumichaca** about 2 kms. from Urubamba, run by Hada Maggiolo. Messages and inquiries to 250266.

Further downstream, to the right of the highway at **Ayllunpampa,** is the **Perol Chico,** where owner Edi rents two small cottages, and offers horse trips with Peruvian pacing horses. (cel. 624475).

Restaurants

El Maizal, on main highway between center of Urubamba and road bridge to Cusco. tel/fax 201054. Buffet lunch on Pisac market days. Local cuisine, relaxing, spacious outdoor/indoor setting with gardens.

Quinta Los Geranios, on main highway, opposite side from El Maizal. Good, inexpensive food in garden setting. Great home-made ice cream.

Hirano on Mariscal Castilla, the main artery of Urubamba, is also good.

Chez Mary, Calle Grau, 6th block, for local food and *ceviche*.

La Terraza, at the intersection opposite the Chinchero-Cusco bridge over the Urubamba. Open air, local food.

Shopping

Ceramic Artist **Pablo Seminario**, whose work is inspired and informed by pre-Columbian designs and techniques, can be visited in his pottery workshop at Av. Berriozabal 405; tel. 201002. e-m: kupa@net. cosapidata.com.pe **Mon Repos** handcrafts store is on the main highway opposite El Maizal restaurant.

River Running

Sacred Valley Adventures, Convención 117; tel. 201217. Whitewater rafting trips, run by veteran guide Carlos Infantas.

OLLANTAYTAMBO (a.k.a. Ollanta)

Hotels

El Albergue, entrance on railroad station platform. tel/fax. 204014; P.O. Box 784, Cusco. Delightful views, location, atmosphere. Sauna. 15 beds. Owner is longtime resident, Artist and U.S. expat Wendy Weeks. (Manager Adela also speaks English). Ask to see the uniquely eccentric store—part shop, part art gallery, part folk-art museum. Try Mama Wendy's *compuesto* (tonic spirits).

Albergue Capuly, entrance by station. Pleasant grounds and accommodations, but at this writing overpriced.

Las Orquídeas, near the center on the way to the railroad station, tel. 204032. Small, simple, with garden, very pleasant atmosphere.

Hostal Tambo, Calle Horno (just

off main square), tel. 204003. Pleasant low-end spot with Bougainvillea-filled patio. Organizes horseback riding excursions.

Villa San Isidro, outside the village on the road leading from Plaza Ruinas. This is a newly-built complex of numerous small, hotels; not central, but very inexpensive. Among them, **Hostal Quishuar** has had good reports.

Coming Someday: a big five-star resort-type hotel with bungalows, tennis courts, and everything you need to make you feel you could be anywhere on the planet. On the Patacancha river, about one km. upstream of village.

Restaurants
Restaurant Ollantay, main square. Good basic food.

River Running
Instinct *(see also Cusco Adventure)* runs rafting trips out of a branch office in the main square.

Horses
Hostal Tambo *(see above)* rents horses, which can be used for trips to the quarries, Pumamarca and elsewhere. Reserve at least 24 hours in advance, more for large groups.

Museum
The new **Museum of Ollantaytambo**, just off the north corner of the main square, is well worth a visit.

MACHU PICCHU

Machu Picchu Ruinas Hotel, tel. 211038/211052 (reservations: Cusco 241777; Lima 221-0826; e-m reserlima@peruhotel.com), located right beside the ruins, is the only place to stay at Machu Picchu itself. The place is comfortable and convenient, but expensive and sometimes hard to get into. It is best to have a reservation if you want to stay here.

The hotel operates the public cafeteria adjacent to the ruins, serving an expensive and time-consuming lunch. If you want to spend less money and have more time in the ruins, buy food in Aguas Calientes (or Cusco, if you are only visiting Machu Picchu for the day), and take it with you. Technically it is forbidden to take lunches into the ruins, but if you don't litter (and you WON'T—WILL you?!), then why not?

Camping in the ruins of Machu Picchu is strictly forbidden. There are campsites by the river, just upstream of Puente Ruinas train station.

AGUAS CALIENTES

A night spent at Aguas Calientes (also known confusingly as Machu Picchu) will allow you more time at the ruins of Machu Picchu. The town is named for the hot springs, which constitute its main visitor attraction besides the famous ruins nearby. The pools were partly wrecked by a landslide in 1995 and again in 1997, and at this writing remain semi-refurbished, and not so very lovely. They are open from 5am to 7pm. No nudes. Swimsuits for rent all over town. Morning is best if you don't like crowds.

Buses to the ruins. A new road connecting Aguas Calientes to the ruins via Puente Ruinas station eliminates the tiresome walk along the railroad tracks, and these days there are plenty of buses to the ruins. First bus leaves at 06.30. (Construction of a controversial cable car to the ruins is imminent.)

Aguas Calientes has two basic axes: one is the railroad track and station, which features a good number of the hotels and restaurants mentioned below; the other is the main walking street leading uphill from the church square. Prices of basic items sold in stores and market stands tend to be cheaper on the main street than at the railroad station.

El Pueblo, (reservations: Lima 422-6574/fax 422-4701; Cusco 232161; e-m: reservas@ inkaterra. com.pe; web: www. inkaterra. com.pe) is the fancy hotel, lovely grounds, bungalow accommodations, but slightly isolated at one end of the village, and a tedious walk along the railroad tracks from the bus stop.

At the railroad station, **El Presidente**, tel. 211065/fax 211034 is a small, comfortable place with private bathrooms. The **Machupicchu** is more basic, shared bath, but clean and pleasant.

Up town a little, the locally renowned **Gringo Bill's,** tel. 211046, is a homey 28-room place for around $10 p/p per night. The restaurant is quite good. For a small fee the hotel performs the valuable, time-saving service of booking and purchasing your return railroad ticket. On the main street to the thermal baths there are several simple hotels. **Hotel Wiracocha** in Calle Wiracocha has been recommended. The **Hostal La Cabaña** (tel. 211048) is pleasant, and the **Hostal Ima Sumac** (tel. 211021) is also okay.

There are plenty of places to eat at the railroad station: **La Choza, El Refugio** and **El Mirador** are quite good. Just across the bridge from the station is the good and slightly pricier **Toto's House.**

Up main street are the upscale **El Indio Felíz** (tel. 211090), tastelessly named, but otherwise tasty; French owner/chef; trés bon—and the **Chez Maggy**, a good pizza and pasta house. Clean, pleasant, live music.

Disco/Bar: Wasicha Pub.

PERUVIAN AMAZON

In south-eastern Peru, the steep gradient of the eastern slope of the Andes has created an extraordinary variety of rainforest habitats within a relatively small area, with unparalleled biodiversity. Two main areas can be visited from Cusco:

MANU

The Manu Biosphere Reserve is one of the major conservation units of South America, encompassing the complete drainage of the Manu river. It is home to much wildlife that has been exterminated or is extremely difficult to see in other parts of the Amazon, including 13 species of primate (the highest count for any one locality in the Americas); the world's largest freshwater carnivore—the giant otter; the world's third largest cat—the jaguar; and a wealth of other animals, birds and reptiles.

The Reserve encompasses an area of almost 1.9 million hectares—the size of Wales. Most of it is unexplored and access is restricted. The **Manu National Park** is the core area, and can only be visited by scientists or anthropologists authorized by the Peruvian Government.

The **Reserved Zone** is essentially the lower portion of the Manu river where the majority of ox-bow lakes occur, and no-one is allowed here without permits, currently costing around US$22.00. The lakes and the trails around them are the main spots for wildlife viewing, and feature prominently in the visitor's itinerary.

Two areas are open to visitors with permits: Cocha Juarez, where the comfortable Manu Lodge is situated; and Cochas Otorongo and Salvador where several eco-tour companies have safari camp concessions. Regulations are strict and all visitors must be accompanied by authorized guides. Independent travellers are not allowed into this area.

Manu is isolated and difficult to get to and consequently is not the most economic rainforest destination; it is, however, one of the best, and although Amazonian wildlife is difficult to observe, Manu provides your best opportunity.

The **Multiple Use Zone** is accessible to anyone who has the time and patience. This area can be reached by road from Cusco via the Kosñipata valley to Atalaya or Shintuya, and then by river.

Downriver from Manu on the Madre de Dios river, the vicinity of the Manu macaw lick (a site where flocks of macaws and parrots gather to eat mineral clays) has a high diversity and concentration of wildlife. Here, 2 hours downriver from Boca Manu and 20 minutes from the macaw lick is the Manu Wildlife Centre, a comfortable lodge set amidst pristine rainforest and ox-bow lakes, with canopy towers and blinds available to guests, and on-site guides. The lodge is jointly owned and operated by Manu Expeditions and Inkanatura Travel, and reservations can be made through either *(see below)*.

How to get there. See Operators *(below)* for visits to the Reserved zone.

Access to the Manu area is possible by light plane from Cusco to Boca Manu and many visitors return to Cusco this way. The outward journey overland down the forested eastern slope of the Andes is utterly spectacular and should not be missed. Tours and expeditions to Manu vary from 4 days (both ways by light aircraft), to 9 days in length.

Buses to the Muliple-Use Zone are non-existent or infrequent. Trucks leave from Cusco's Coliseo Cerrado in Cusco on Mon-Wed- Fri at about 10:00 am and sometimes on Sundays, to Pilcopata, or direct to Shintuya via Atalaya. It's a tough journey of 12 hours to Pilcopata, and about 6 more hours to Shintuya, not counting waiting time in Pilcopata. The ideal situation is to find a truck in Cusco, loaded with cargo and destined for Shintuya. Typically it will be met there by a boat which takes the cargo further downstream, and which can also take passengers. Failing this, it can be a long wait. Downstream, to Boca Manu takes 4 hours, to Colorado 1 1/2 days, and to Puerto Maldonado 2 days. An interesting trip: so-so for wildlife, but the forest and panoramas are impressive, and it is an adventure.

Manu Operators

Some companies are directly involved in rainforest conservation projects, therefore, doing business with them helps to protect this environment. They are:

Manu Nature Tours—Avenida Pardo 1046; tel. 252721/fax 234793 e-m: mnt@Amauta.rcp.net.pe; web www.rcp.net.pe/MANU

Manu Expeditions—Avenida Pardo 895; tel. 226671/fax 236706; e-m: manuexpe+@ Amauta. rcp. net.pe; web: www.gorp.com/adventur.

Pantiacolla Tours—Calle Plateros 360; tel: 238323/fax 252696 e-m: pantiac@mail. cosapidata. com.pe; web: www.pantiacolla.com

Inkanatura Travel—Av. Sol 821, 2nd floor; tel. 243408; fax 226392; e-m: acss@telser.com.pe

Lodges

Within the Reserved Zone, there is a lodge run by Manu Nature Tours (*see above*), and a new one owned and operated by the Machiguenga indigenous tribe at Cocha Salvador. Contact in Cusco: **Apeco**, Saphi 456, Of. J; tel. 223061; fax 221020; e-m; peamanu2@ datos. limaperu.net

In the Multiple Use Zone, **Amazonía Lodge**, Matará 334; tel/fax 231370; e-m amazonia@ correo. dnet.com.pe. Run by the Yabar family, this is a converted tea hacienda and a great place to break the journey to Manu. Further downriver (30 minutes from Shintuya) is another quality operation, **Pantiacolla Lodge**, run by the Moscoso family and managed by Pantiacolla Tours (*see above*).

Cloud Forest Lodges. Both Manu Nature Tours and Inkanatura own and operate lodges in the mountainous forest, on the fringes of Manu, en route to the Manu Biosphere Reserve proper. This is a good way to see this unique habitat and its highly distinct fauna and flora.

Other Manu operators:

Manu Ecological Adventures, Plateros 356; tel. 261640, fax 225562.

Vilca, Plateros 361; tel/fax 251872.

TAMBOPATA

This region lies upstream from Puerto Maldonado, where the Tambopata river joins the Madre de Dios. Biodiversity is tremendous and it is more accessible than Manu (though human impact has been greater here), with daily scheduled jet flights from Cusco to Puerto Maldonado, and a shorter river journey once you are there. Various tourist lodges are located along the river. Generally, the further these are from Pto. Maldonado, the less human presence and the better the wildlife viewing.

All of the following lodges are reached via Pto. Maldonado. They are:

Sandoval Lake Lodge, *(see Inkanatura, above)* located on a great ox-bow of the Madre de Dios river.

Cusco Amazonico, Urb. Santa Monica, Jr. Julio Tello C-13; tel. 245315; fax 244669, Cusco—one of the better lodges located close to Pto. Maldonado, with excellent habitat, though limited wildlife.

Posada Amazonas, a very comfortable lodge co-owned and -operated by Rainforest Expeditions *(see below)* and the Ese'Eja indigenous community, whose special attraction is a harpy eagle nest-site with observation tower.

Explorers Inn, Plateros 365; tel/fax 235342, Cusco—one of the oldest established lodges, with a private rainforest sanctuary, adjacent to the 1.5 million hectare Tambopata-Candamo Reserve. Most of the guides are also involved in biological research.

Tambopata Jungle Lodge, owned and operated by Peruvian Andean Treks *(see p. 30)*—another private-reserve lodge with a network of trails, across the river from the Tambotata-Candamo reserve. Offers visits to the Tambopata macaw lick.

Tapir Inn, tel. 084-571297; e-m: jespinoza@intersoft.com.pe—in Cusco at Mayuc *(see Adventure p. 30)*—a very small lodge in the heart of the Tambopata-Candamo reserved zone, owned and run by veteran guide Orlando James. Offers low prices.

Tambopata Research Center, Rainforest Expeditions (Lima), tel. 421-8347; fax 421-8183. e-m: rainfore@Amauta.rcp.net.pe; web: www.perunature.com—located at the famous macaw lick, about eight hours upriver from Pto. Maldonado, where fabulous gatherings of macaws and parrots may be seen. Visitors break their journey halfway, at the Posada Amazonas *(see above)*.

MUSEUMS

(T.T.) means that entrance is included in the US$10 Tourist ticket which also includes many ruins sites in the Cusco vicinity. *(See p. 47)*

The Inca Museum—located in the Admiral's Palace (#10 on city map, p....) Times: Mon.-Fri. 08.00-17.00; Sat. 09.00-17.00. With a brand new extension, this building now houses a vastly-improved display of mainly Inca material. No information in English, but well worth a visit.

Regional Historical Museum—Casa de Garcilaso (#25 on city map). Mon.-Sat. 08:00-17:30. Collection of archaeological material and colonial paintings. (T.T.)

Museum of Religious Art—crnr of Hatunrumiyoc and Palacio (#15 on City Map). Mon.-Sat. 08.00-11:30 & 15.00-17.30. Contains many colonial paintings. The museum's greatest treasure is a famous and fascinating series of twelve paintings depicting the Corpus Christi processions of 17th-century Cusco—but inexplicably and deplorably, the archbishopric has witheld these paintings from public view for more than four years at this writing. (T.T.)

Santa Catalina Museum— Santa Catalina Angosta (1/2 block from Pl. de Armas). Mon.-Thurs. & Sat. 09.00-15.00. Fri. 09.00-15.00. A collection of colonial-era paintings and artifacts. (T.T.)

Museum of Contemporary Art —Municipal Town Hall, Plaza Regocijo. Daily 09:30-18:00 A permanent collection of work by contemporary Cusco artists, plus special exhibitions from time to time. Entrance free.

Cultural Hall, Banco Wiese, Maruri 315. Weekdays 09:00-19:00, Sat. 09:30-12:30. Has small but interesting exhibitions of different aspects of Cusco culture. Entrance free.

Qoricancha Archaeological Museum, Av. Sol opposite Santo Domingo church. Daily 09.30-18.00. Some artifacts from excavations that were made when the adjacent park was being built. (T.T.)

"Irq'i Yachay" Museum of Andean Children's Art, Choquechaca 491, entrance on Ladrillos; tel. 223390. Something really different. The Mobile Art Workshop's rotating exhibit of astonishing art produced by children in remote Andean villages. Wed.-Sun. 11am-5pm. Entrance free.

CUSCO CALENDAR

Jan. 20—procession of saints in San Sebastián, near Cusco.

Easter Monday—Cusco: parade of the Lord of the Earthquakes, an important religious festival; quite lively. Easter itself is interesting, but this is the day of Cusco's major religious icon.

May 2/3—at all mountaintops with a cross on them: the Vigil of the Cross, a boisterous affair.

Pentecost Sat-Tues— Ollantaytambo: costumed dancers; horseback games; bullfight

Trinity Sun-Tues—, the "Snow Star" festival at the remote Sinakara valley (4,600m elevation) near Mawayani, north of Ausangate.

Thursday after Trinity Sunday (early June, usually)—Cusco: Corpus Cristi; saint effigies from all the churches of Cusco are brought to the cathedral to "sleep" with the other saints, and taken on parade next day; a very colorful and emotional event.

June 17—Raqchi: a lively local festival to the old creator god, Viracocha. Lots of music.

June 24 (and several days before that date)—Cusco: Cusco Week, culminating in Inti Raymi, the pageant re-enactment of the Inca festival of the winter solstice, vigorously celebrated to this day, and by no means staged only for tourists.

July 15-17—Paucartambo (also Pisac, Huarocondo and Quillabamba): festival of the Virgin of Carmen. Costumed dancers enact rituals and folk tales in the streets.

July 28—Peruvian Independence Day. Combapata: Yawar Fiesta ("Blood Festival"), the famous ritual struggle between a condor and a bull, symbolizing the hoped-for triumph of the native people (the condor) over the invader (the bull). Stay away if you love animals.

August 14—Tinta: festival of San Bartolome. Tiobamba: major religious festival and market; well worth a visit. Calca: Virgin of the Assumption; parades and market.

September 14—Huanca: religious pilgrimage to the shrine of El Señor de Huanca. Huge event in awe-inspiring mountain setting.

November 1-2- All Saints and All Souls days, celebrated everywhere with bread dolls, traditional cooking, remembering the dead and visiting cemeteries.

December 24—Cusco: Santorantikuy, "the buying of saints"; massive celebration of Christmas shopping, Cusco-style.

MISCELLANEOUS INFORMATION

US$10 Tourist ticket (T.T.) grants entry to many museums and ruins sites in Cusco and vicinity. Can be purchased at any of the sites included, or at a side door of the Casa de Garcilaso, on Calle Garcilaso (#25 on city map). Mon.-Fri. 08.00-18.00; Sat. 08.30-12.30. Tickets are valid for 10 days.

Money changing. There are numerous Exchange shops and individual money changers on Avenida Sol, giving a better rate than banks. Count your change carefully and watch out for fake bills, which are common in both U.S. and Peruvian currency.

Student cards, will often win a big discount at government-run institutions, such as ruins sites etc.

Horseback riding. Rides starting from near the ruins of Sacsaywaman. Elías Cosio, Saphi 704. Tel. 237011, 623070. Fax 223271.

Doctors—Gladys Oblitas, tel. 227264, combines natural medicine with orthodox therapies. English-speaking doctors: Oscar Liendo, beeper: 242071- #2007; Manrique, tel. 620215; Tejada 233836/621821.

Clinic. Clinica Pardo, Av. La Cultura 710, tel/fax 240387.

Chiropractor. Miguel Chamorro, Av. de los Incas 916; tel. 234473.

Massage. Luz Marina Usca, tel. 225159.

Coin-op laundromat. Lavandería Ñapasña, Saphi 578-A. Can leave clothes to wash , too.

Family laundry, Saphi 675-A. 2 and 4 hour cleaning. **Dry cleaning.** Lavanderia Inka, Ruinas 493.

English books. Librería Jerusalen, Heladeros 143.

English video movie theater. Tumis, Saphi 478.

Natural & Specialty Foods. Auliya *(see Restaurants)* for dried fruits, gluten, tofu; Al Grano *(see Restaurants)* for bread, baked goods; the shop at Ruinas 483 for bread; Granja Heidi, Matará 288, for yogurt, honey, cheese. Saturday morning market at Plaza Tupac Amaru has "Feria de la Miel" stand with several varieties of excellent honey. The bakery at Cuesta San Blas 579 has good bread and pastries.

Gourmet jam fans can try the products of Tierras Altas S.A., particularly the *aguaymanto(Physalis peruviana l.)*, a little-known but delicious native Andean fruit; sold at Plazoleta Nazarenas 211, at the corner of Tucumán.

Camera equipment & repairs. Nishiyama, Sunturwasi (a.k.a. Triunfo) 346 and Mantas 109. Shogun, Garcilaso 290.

Language schools—Excel, Cruz Verde 336; tel. 232272. e-m: esl-exl@qenqo.unsaac.edu.pe;

Amauta, Procuradores 50, 2nd floor; tel/fax 241422. e-m: amautaa@mail.cosapidata.com.pe; web: www.business.com.pe/ Amauta. Centro Cultural Andino, Av. Pardo 689; tel. 231710; fax 231388; e-m: andinos@ wayna. rcp.net.pe Offers language courses combined with Andean cultural education, seminars and visits.

Complaints & grievances. Indecopi, Portal Carrizo 248, Pl. de Armas. Tel. 252974. e-m: sptcuz@ indecopi.gob.pe Toll-free nationwide: 0-800-4-2579. If you've been enticed, sliced and diced, clipped, ripped, and gypped, screwed, blued and tattooed by a travel agency, hotel etc. (many are the ways!), don't hesitate—call the number, or visit the office, of this government agency designed to prevent abuses against tourists. They will try to help. They have an office in the airport, too.

Tourist police. Police station on 1st block of Saphi. File theft reports for insurance purposes, if nothing else. This also helps police know where greatest concentrations of thefts occur.

Robbery. Crime has diminished tremendously since the last edition, but be careful nonetheless, because a tourist is still a thief's favorite free lunch. The common forms are bag-snatching and bag-slashing. Favorite locations are crowded streets and railway stations, on trains and buses, anywhere that confusion reigns. In these situations, have a money belt, hold on to your camera, pay attention. Thieves work in pairs or groups, so be suspicious of attempts to disorient you (soap on your clothes, money on the ground in front of you etc.). It is a good idea to use the safe-deposit if your hotel has one.

Late night choke-hold muggings can also occur, especially in the approaches to Plazoleta Nazarenas, and in the San Blas district. Take a taxi back to your hotel at night. Robberies continue to be reported at Qenqo, Sacsaywaman and environs. Police now patrol these areas, but it is still wise to be clear of them before dusk, unless with a group.

Money Transfers. Western Union, Santa Catalina Ancha 311; tel. 233727.

Immigration and Prefectura. Av. Sol, 1/2 block uphill from the Post Office. Immigration 08:00-13:00/17:00-19:00, weekdays. You can renew your visa once for 30 days, without leaving the country, for a fee of US$20.

Begging. Traditionally Saturday is *"dia de los pobres"* (day of the poor), when it's okay to beg. Here's one way to distribute your alms if you feel sympathy for the innumerable beggars, but overwhelmed by the constant demands: give on Saturdays.

Mountaineering. The region is ripe with potential for ice climbing on beautiful high peaks, but is largely neglected in favor of the Cordillera Blanca in northern Peru. There are three major Cordilleras: the Vilcanota (highest: Ausangate, 20,790 ft./6338m.); the Vilcabamba (highest: Salcantay, 20,575 ft./6271m.); and the Urubamba (highest: Wakay Willka/Verónica, 18,865 ft./5751m.).

Fishing. The Vilcanota/Urubamba river is now too polluted and overfished to be worth considering. For jungle fishing check with the Explorers Inn, or Cusco-Amazonica Lodge, which offer fishing trips on the Madre de Dios and Tambopata Rivers.

Chapter One

THE CITY OF CUSCO

History

According to an Inca myth current at the time of the conquest, the founding Incas, Manco Capac and Mama Ocllo emerged from Lake Titicaca at the islands of the Sun and the Moon, sent to earth by the solar and lunar deities to bring culture to a barbarous world. From there they began a lengthy quest (about 500 km. if they took the shortest route over the La Raya pass) which ended in a valley far to the north, at the spot where Manco probed with his golden staff, and it disappeared into the ground. Here they founded their civilization, and the Inca city of Cusco.

An alternative and contradictory myth of the Inca origins, also current at the time of the conquest, concerns a more complicated family—Manco Capac, the three Ayar brothers, and their wives. They emerged from caves at the mythical origin place of Pacarictambo (Lodging-house of the Dawn), south of Cusco. One of the brothers, Ayar Cachi, was so violent and wild that he destroyed entire mountains with his sling-shots. For safety's sake the rest of the family lured him back into his cave and entombed him there. There he remains to this day, causing occasional earthquakes with his struggles. God forbid he should ever get loose. (Some would argue that he *has* got loose, but that's another story). His wife, Mama Waco, an early feminist, remained free and later more or less single-handedly conquered a town in the Cusco valley, terrifying its inhabitants by ripping the lungs out of one warrior's body and blowing them up like balloons. Of the remaining brothers, one grew wings and flew off into the sun, another turned into a stone on the mountain of Wanacauri, which became one of the most

51

sacred Inca *wacas*, and the last, Manco Capac, inherited all the wives and reached Cusco to found the Inca empire.

Modern archaeology indicates that the Titicaca myth may be closer in spirit to the truth, since the evidence suggests that the Incas established their hegemony in the region by peaceful means *(see Cusco before the Empire, p. 58)*. Cusco began to dominate its neighbors as early as 1100 AD, and these proto-Incas eventually established political influence and a pattern of peaceful regional exchange, sparing this area the centuries of brutal rivalry and constant warfare that characterized the rest of the Andean region after the fall of the Tiwanaku and Wari civilizations.

The previous great periods of "horizon" civilization in ancient Peru—the ones that spread their influence over a wide area of the Andes—were the early Chavín of northern Peru (c. 800-200 BC), and the later Tiwanaku who spread out from Lake Titicaca (c. 600-1000 AD). Both of these civilizations first rose as centers of religious influence, pilgrimage sites which were also favorably located for trade and agriculture. Later on, in the case of Tiwanaku at least, they developed military and imperial characteristics. Cusco's rise to dominance in the Andes may well have followed this same pattern.

The peaceful era of Cusco's dominion came to an abrupt end around 1438, after Cusco was attacked from the north by a tribe called the Chancas. Rallied from near-defeat by the son of the reigning chief, the militarily unprepared inhabitants of Cusco triumphed. The very stones of the mountainsides were said to have sprung to life and fought on the Inca side. The son seized power and took the title Pachacuteq, meaning "Shaker (or Transformer) of the Earth" *(see Pachacuteq, p. 55)* Thereafter, Pachacuteq is credited with an astonishing series of accomplishments: the complete rebuilding of Cusco in the distinct and impressive masonry style whose remains are so admired today; the building of Sacsaywaman, Ollantaytambo, Machu Picchu, Pisac and other sites; the form of worship; the system of government and land tenure.

Pachacuteq may also have been the instigator of the Titicaca origin myth of the Incas; it tended to legitimize Inca authority in the Titicaca region, which was an early target of Inca expansion. But the myth also established an extraordinary relationship between the Inca and his people: he was divinely descended from the Sun; the Coya, his queen (who was also his sister), was in turn the daughter of the Moon. Thus the Inca's power was as absolute and unchallengeable as that of any ruler in history. To rebel was to defy God himself. This was the faith that underpinned the empire, until the rapacious Spaniards arrived and dashed the edifice to the ground.

Pachacuteq's son Topa Inca carried on his father's work, pushing the frontiers of the empire into modern Ecuador, Bolivia, Argentina and Chile. A combination of techniques sustained this expansion. Military conquest played a part, but so did skillful diplomacy—some of the most important territories may have been allied chiefdoms with considerable autonomy, rather than totally subordinate domains. For example, Chincha, a coastal state which virtually monopolized maritime trade, was treated with great caution and respect.

The empire's lifeblood was the practice of reciprocity: ritual generosity and favors to local rulers on a huge scale, in exchange for loyalty, labor and military levies, wives and concubines for the Inca nobility, specialized regional products, and so on. The emperor maintained fabulous stores of sumptuary goods—the "art" for which the Andean region is justly famous—to meet his ritual obligations and create new alliances.

By the time Topa's son Wayna Capac came to power the empire had perhaps already overreached itself, and at Wayna Capac's death it was beginning to fragment. A disastrous civil war broke out between factions of the north and south headed by two of Wayna Capac's sons, Atawallpa and Wascar. After years of strife, the northern faction under Atawallpa prevailed. Perhaps Atawallpa, a strong if rather ferocious leader, would have succeeded in re-unifying the empire in time, but as he was celebrating his victory a mysterious group of bearded men landed on the coast of Peru....

The dynastic story of Pachacuteq and his sons is the widely accepted version of Inca history. But unfortunately, certain details only hold up if we ignore numerous contradictory and puzzling references in the Spanish chronicles of the Conquest. In truth, we have no clearcut Inca history, and there are various reasons for this. First and foremost, the Andean peoples had no written language or codices; history and most other cultural information was transmitted orally. Thus, when the Spanish chroniclers collected information from the vanquished Incas, they conducted interviews. Most of these Spaniards spoke Quechua poorly, if at all, and their information was often distorted by the poor quality and the biases of native interpreters. Moreover, their informants were often desperate, for reasons of survival, to ingratiate themselves with their interrogators. And, the Spanish arrived at the end of a fratricidal civil war, when they would inevitably hear many conflicting versions of the Inca rulers.

Finally we have to consider that the Spanish chroniclers were viewing the affairs of a culture vastly different from their own through the narrow optic of crusading medieval Christians, who had recently driven the last of the heathen Moors out of the Iberian peninsula and were inclined to view the native Peruvians simply as more of the same.

Modern structuralist ethnohistorians, exemplified by R.T. Zuidema of the University of Illinois, propose an interpretation of the chronicles which replaces the Inca dynastic succession with a sort of mythic saga of the royal ayllus (clans) of Inca Cusco. In other words, Inca Pachacuteq may or may not have been a historical individual, but primarily he is an archetype, embodying the deeds, attributes, and functions of his Ayllu. These ethnohistorians are saying, in effect, that nothing is truly known about Inca history prior to 1532.

With uncertainties as profound as these prevailing among the experts, the story of the Incas told to visitors is often highly impressionistic, and adorned with the biases and personal obsessions of the teller. Your local tour guide can get away with murder, and does.

Pachacuteq

Pachacuteq was the warrior-king who launched the Inca expansion, around 1438. He was not the chosen heir to the Inca throne, but when the Cusco region was threatened with invasion by the Chancas from the north, he wrested power from his father, Inca Wiracocha—who was preparing to flee rather than fight—and rallied the Incas against their enemies. In two legendary battles he smashed the Chanca threat and began the expansion that transformed the Incas from a regional power into an empire.

Pachacuteq's name is in fact a title, meaning "Transformer of the Earth." His impact on the Andean world was such that he fully earned this sobriquet. He has been compared to Alexander the Great and Charlemagne as one of the great conquering statesmen of history.

He was more than simply a warrior—for he is credited with founding the basic systems of government and administration by which the Inca empire was ruled. All of the famous monuments of the Incas were built, or at least started, during his reign: Sacsaywaman, Pisac, Ollantaytambo, and the rebuilding of the Inca city of Cusco itself. Machu Picchu and the Inca Trail, too, seem to have been a personal project of his. Pachacuteq is also credited with establishing sun-worship as a pan-Andean religion, within a framework of cultural and religious diversity that allowed considerable local autonomy.

During the controversial time of the 500th anniversary of Columbus's landing in America, the mayor and municipal authorities of Cusco responded to Spain's Orwellian "Meeting-of-Two-Cultures" version of the European invasion by building a monument to Pachacuteq, which today towers over the lower end of the city, about halfway between the center and the airport.

As the official monument was being built, a controversial rival Pachacuteq monument was going up on the hillside above it. Legal action blocked the maverick Pachacuteq, and it will probably never be finished. Its sponsor was a wealthy Cusco doctor who claimed Pachacuteq as his personal inspiration. Later, a magical-realist political twist straight from a Latin-American novel brought the doctor himself to power as mayor of Cusco. While in office, Pachacuteq's avatar dispatched bulldozers in dead of night, to rip out nearly all the main square's graceful old native trees—one of many dark deeds that angered his constituents and cost him the next election.

The Pachacuteq tower, with its huge bronze statue, is open to the public. Its faux-Inca stonework—a medley of incompatible styles—raises purist eyebrows, but the panorama of the city and its surroundings from the tower is excellent.

The Inca empire was called Tawantinsuyu—the "Four Quarters of the Earth." Cusco was the heart of it, and its exact center was considered to be the main square of the city. To the north lay the Chinchaysuyu—northern Peru and modern Ecuador; west lay the Contisuyu—the south-central coast regions; south lay the Collasuyu—the altiplano of southern Peru and modern Bolivia; and east the Antisuyu—the unconquered Amazon jungle. From the name of the inhabitants of this region—"Antis"—we get the Spanish word Andes.

Most of Cusco's Inca settlement was clustered on the ridge between the Tullumayo and Saphi rivers. Its tightly-thatched and steeply-pitched roofs gave the buildings an almost spired look. The streets were narrow stone alleys between high walls enclosing courtyards the size of city blocks, where few doorways broke through the long stretches of impeccably-laid stone. Springs and reservoirs in the hills fed water channels which flowed everywhere, bursting to the surface in countless sparkling fountains. The austerity of the stone compounds was softened by crops and flowers growing on scores of watered cultivation terraces which penetrated the heart of the city.

Two huge squares straddled the Saphi river, encompassing the colonial Plaza de Armas, Plaza Regocijo, and a stretch of land that today is covered by buildings. The main square where the cathedral now stands was called the Wacaypata, meaning Weeping Square, supposedly because of the mourning that took place there when a ruling Inca had died. Generating confusion for posterity as always, the Incas also called the main square the Aucaypata –a kind of pun on its other name– meaning the Square of War, because this was also where the ceremonies initiating military campaigns were held. This square was flanked by the palaces of the Inca emperors, one of whom was alive, while the others were mummies, who nevertheless continued to preside over their lineage groups and were consulted through mediums.

West of the Saphi river stood the Cusipata, the Joyful Square, which was where the Inca state held its most spectacularly drunken festivities, and where there was also a barter market at certain times.

When Pachacuteq rebuilt the city of Cusco, he laid it out in the shape of a puma. This animal may have been his personal totem, but in any case it was certainly a symbol of warrior power. The outlines of this scheme can still be seen in the layout of the city center *(see diagram below)*. Sacsaywaman was the puma's head, while the tail stretched most of the way to where the Pachacuteq monument now stands.

Inca Cusco was not a city, in our sense of that word. It was an élite settlement with special ceremonial and administrative functions. There was no bustle of commerce here, no poor district, no garbage and no

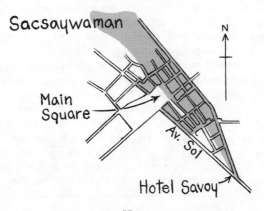

Cusco before the Empire
Archaeology rebuts a legend

Accounts distilled from the oral histories of the conquest tell us that the Inca expansion began suddenly in 1438, as if from nowhere, when the man later known as Pachacuteq rallied the divided ethnic groups of the region against a common enemy, the Chancas, who were invading in force from the north-west. Before this, the legend goes, Cusco was just one more Andean village at war with its neighbors during an extended period of regional conflict which began after the Tiwanaku civilization fell, c. 900-1000 A.D.

According to the story, Pachacuteq defeated the Chancas, massively reorganized the Cusco region, built a new imperial capital, and went on to unite a vast area under Inca hegemony, a task continued by his son Topa Inca. Thus Tawantinsuyu—the Empire of the Four Quarters—was born.

This version of events suggests that Tawantinsuyu was less than one hundred years old when it was overthrown by the Spanish, in 1532. When we contemplate the enormous complex of roads, agricultural terraces and monumental structures in the Cusco region alone, and calculate the time and manpower required to build it, this chronology seems to require a mind-bending suspension of disbelief.

Fortunately for our sanity, recent archaeological work has shattered this traditional view, revealing, for example, that people living as far as 60 kms away from Cusco were under the control of the Incas several centuries before the Chanca war. Furthermore, these groups were incorporated into the early Inca state through peaceful means rather than military conquest. Archaeological survey work conducted directly south of the Cusco valley indicates that incipient state growth began as early as 1100 AD—more than three hundred years before the Chanca war! From this early period onwards there was a gradual consolidation and centralization of social and economic power in Cusco. Archaeological work indicates that the period of early state development in the Cusco region (AD 1100-1400) was characterized by widespread regional exchange, rather than being a time of regional conflict. Recent research has also revealed that the Incas, rather than competing with other ethnic groups, already dominated the local social and political organizations during this early time period, and that Cusco was already the center of economic influence in the region.

Some event indeed took place around 1438 to launch the Incas under Pachacuteq on their career of Imperial expansion, but it was preceded by centuries of regional consolidation over a much wider area, and involving many more ethnic groups, than was previously believed. It is clear that our understanding of Inca history, and the growth of their empire, is still in its infancy.

- Brian Bauer

panhandling on street corners. It was a holy city, the center of the known world. The greatest temple of the empire stood here, the buildings within it devoted to all the Inca deities, and hundreds of regional cults. The chronicler Garcilazo de la Vega wrote that the name Cusco meant "navel of the earth." It was the most exalted public pilgrimage center of the Andes (Machu Picchu was probably more exclusive, and utterly private), and so every ranking citizen of the Tawantinsuyu tried to visit Cusco once in his lifetime.

Despite its importance, Cusco was not the largest city in the Inca empire. The Chimu capital of Chan Chan, near modern Trujillo, was bigger, as was the Inca northern administrative center of Huánuco Pampa, now an abandoned ruin on a desolate plateau in the central highlands. But access to Cusco was restricted and, perhaps to emphasize this point, all non-Incas had to leave the city once a year, in early September, while the Inca nobility performed the ceremony of *sitwa*, a ritual cleansing.

Withal, it was a colorful and cosmopolitan place, because thousands of regional nobility with their families and retainers from all over the empire also lived there. Quechua was the *lingua franca*, but many other languages were spoken in the courtyards, and many varieties of clothing and headdress were worn in the streets.

The Incas built an empire comparable in size to the Roman empire, stretching from the modern Ecuador-Colombia frontier to the Rio Maule in southern Chile; bounded in the east by the Amazon forests, in the west by the Pacific Ocean. Like the Romans, they built their empire largely on the achievements of earlier civilizations. They inherited the accumulated culture and knowledge of more than 4,000 years of continuous civilization in Peru, starting around 3000 B.C., with the early pre-ceramic textile-making and pyramid-building cultures of the coast, such as Waca Prieta and Aspero, whose ruins survive at the mouths of the Chicama and Supe rivers. Every major technical development of the Andes had already occurred before the rise of the Incas: cultivation of potatoes and high-altitude maize, domestication of animals, metallurgy, irrigation, stoneworking, and so on. The Incas took these achievements and added their uniquely refined style of statecraft, their ability to mobilize and rule millions of people over an enormous area of land. They created a powerful cultural synthesis within a strong centralized state, building a pan-Andean, Quechua-speaking culture, whose roots live on tenaciously to this day, though stem and branch have long since been hacked down.

It is worth reminding ourselves that the Incas, and the millenia of Andean culture that preceded them, represent a significant event in human history. Their civilization was brought to an abrupt end, and little of what they created has entered the mainstream of human culture, because they were overwhelmed by a race that was blind to all but the material aspects of their world. But much of what sustained Andean civilization was not material, and the spirit of that ancient way lives on in the hearts and customs of the millions of native inhabitants of the Andes. In this sense it is possible after all that we have not heard the last of the Incas.

CUSCO AND THE CONQUEST

The first Spaniards to see Cusco were three ruffians sent from Cajamarca by Pizarro early in 1533 to speed up the collection of treasure for Atawallpa's ransom. They came and went, leaving posterity no word of their reactions. Not long afterwards, literate Spaniards arrived, and were hugely impressed by the great structures of Cusco. "We can assure your Majesty that it is so beautiful and has such fine buildings that it would be remarkable even in Spain," wrote an early chronicler. The Spaniards arrived as allies to the Cusco-based faction of the Inca civil war, and for a while they had the run of the city. They passed the time looting, extorting treasure and abusing the natives, leaving most of Cusco's buildings undisturbed for more than two years after Pizarro's triumphant entry, on November 8, 1533. But then a much abused native, Pizarro's puppet Inca, Manco II, escaped and returned—puppet no more—leading a massive army of between 100,000 and 200,000 Indians against the Spanish.

Thus began the six-month siege of Cusco—and thus also began the destruction of the Inca city. On May 6, 1536, Manco launched his main attack on the trapped Spaniards. The Indians used slingshots to rain red-hot stones on the city. "They set fire to the whole of Cusco simultaneously and it all burned in one day, for the roofs were thatch," wrote the chronicler Cristobal de Molina. The Spaniards—bottled up in the Inca armory of Suntur Wasi—survived to break out and put down the rebellion. But the glorious Imperial City was left a smoking ruin.

Despite the enthusiasm of some chroniclers and conquistadors for Inca architecture—some even built their mansions in the Inca masonry style *(see Spanish Walls by Inca Masons, p. 74)* —the buildings and streets did not generally suit Spanish taste. Moreover, evidence that the Inca civilization was highly advanced provoked discomfort among the Spaniards; it complicated the task of justifying the destruction. And so the dismantling of Inca Cusco began soon after Manco's rebellion. Inca cut stones were re-used higgledy-piggledy in new construction, while the buildings of Sacsaywaman served as a public stone quarry.

For a few decades after the Conquest, Cusco remained the major city of Peru. It became the focus of conflict during the civil wars between Pizarro's men and a faction led by Diego de Almagro, as the conquerors fought among themselves over the spoils of victory. It was also the headquarters of the Spanish campaign against the last desperate resistance of the Inca Manco and his successors, in their mountain-ringed refuge of Vilcabamba, northwest of Cusco.

But in 1535 Pizarro had founded a new capital at Lima on the coast. Other new cities rose: Trujillo, Arequipa. The focus of power shifted to Lima, and the focus of wealth moved to the fabulous silver deposits which had been discovered at Potosí, hundreds of miles to the south. There was no more loot to be had in Cusco; even the silver route from Potosí had passed it by. Gradually the city faded into relative obscurity.

Events, natural and political, shook Cusco out of its torpor occasionally during the long centuries of eclipse. In 1650 a violent earthquake transformed many of the fine colonial buildings into heaps of rubble. The Inca walls and foundations stood firm. In 1780 the Cusco region came to the shocked attention of the Spanish crown as the scene of an Indian uprising led by the mestizo rebel Tupac Amaru II. The insurrection came closer to succeeding than any indigenous movement since Manco Inca's rebellion, but it was ultimately crushed. Tupac Amaru II himself was put horribly to death in the main square of Cusco. Three decades later there were a couple of premature, abortive creole uprisings against the Spanish, two tremors among the early rumblings of Independence from Spain that were being felt across the continent. But those great political convulsions of the 1820s largely passed Cusco by. Another violent earthquake shook the city in May of 1950. Once again many post-Inca buildings came tumbling down; once again the Inca structures held fast.

Now Cusco was beginning to emerge from the long years of provincial obscurity. In 1948 Hiram Bingham, discoverer of Machu Picchu, had inaugurated a new road built from the Urubamba river up to the dizzying ridge where the ruins of the Incas' lost city are perched.

Overseas visitors began to arrive in Cusco, drawn by the mysterious ruins and intriguing customs of the Incas and their modern descendants—creating a momentum which has continued to build ever since

Recently Cusco itself has become one of the symbols of a new nationalism and a recovered pride in the greatness of Peru's pre-Hispanic heritage. The Peruvian government has channeled millions of dollars into conservation and restoration of archaeological and colonial monuments, better roads and transport services, and new hotels. This has been part of a plan sponsored by UNESCO, which has declared Cusco a World Cultural Heritage site.

THE LAY OF THE LAND

The Incas conceived their city in the shape of a puma. Remembering this, the best place for a good general view of the Cusco valley is the puma's head: the top of the hill of Sacsaywaman. As you face out over the city from this point, east is to your left. There stands the statue of Christ the Redeemer, donated to the city in 1944 by a group of Palestinian refugees, grateful for the city's help. It is a replica of the famous Christ in Rio de Janeiro.

The highest of the jagged peaks beyond the statue is *Pachatusan,* which means Fulcrum, or Crossbeam, of the Universe. It is probably so named because it was considered a critical point on the horizon; viewed from the supremely important location of the Qoricancha, the Sun Temple, the sun rises directly behind this peak on the day of the winter solstice. To the right of the statue lies the broad valley of the Huatanay river, flowing toward its junction with the larger Vilcanota. This is the route to southern Peru and Bolivia—one of the Four Quarters of the Inca empire known as the Collasuyu. There, too, lie the modern suburbs of Cusco, and the airport. The huge snowcapped peak visible beyond the valley on clear days is Ausangate (6384 ms./20,940 ft.) in the Cordillera Vilcanota, about 100 km. distant.

The cryptic "B.I.9" inscribed beneath "Viva el Peru" on the hill opposite stands for Infantry Batallion 9, the local army unit. The adjacent hill to the right bears the Peruvian national shield. These inscriptions can be considered as recent examples of an ancient Peruvian hill-writing tradition dating back to the Lines of Nazca on the Peruvian coast. However, in recent years the practice has gotten utterly out of hand. Now political parties, schools, government ministries, police stations, and every Tomás, Ricardo or Enrique who feels like it, scratch the slogan of their choice over the Andean landscape. Once it was art, now it's an institutional ego-trip.

A little farther to the right (SSW) lies the Huancaro valley, marked by a swathe of eucalyptus trees, that was once the route of the royal Inca highway to the Contisuyu, the western quarter of the empire. The route to the northern quarter—the Chinchaysuyu—ran up the hillside to the right, about due west across the defile of the river Saphi. This is now the route to Abancay and Ayacucho. The highest peak to be seen in the ranges lying in that direction is called Mama Simuna. Directly behind you lie the ranges that separate Cusco from the Sacred Valley of the Incas. Pisac lies to the northeast, in the direction of the old highway to the eastern quarter, the Antisuyu.

PLACES OF INTEREST IN THE CITY
(Each location in this section is given a number, which refers to the numbers marked on the city map, following page)

The Main Square
This square was originally more than twice its present size. It was divided in two parts by the river Saphi (which becomes the Huatanay), which now flows beneath the buildings on the west side of the square, opposite the cathedral. Today's Plaza de Armas is the part that was once called the Wacaypata, the Weeping Square. (One morning in 1997 it really *was* the Weeping Square, when the citizens of Cusco awoke in anguish to the news that, during the night, the city's mayor Raúl Salizar had ordered his bulldozers to rip out nearly all the square's luxuriant

native Andean trees. All their tears could not bring the trees back, and they were replaced by the sparse, pitiful flowerbeds that you see today).

In Inca times this square featured a stone, covered with sheets of gold, known as the Stone of War, where offerings and ceremonies were made at the start of military adventures. This stone gave the square its other Inca name—Aucaypata, the Square of War. There was also an *usnu*, an Inca -tiered platform used during ceremonies, topped by a rounded stone, shaped like a woman's breast and encrusted with gold and jewels. A channel carved around its base carried sacred libations away to the Huatanay river. From here, astronomers observed the position of the sunset in relation to stone towers on the western horizon.

This was the great civic square of the Incas, the site of solemn parades and great assemblies. Each territory conquered by the Incas had some of its soil taken to Cusco to be mingled symbolically with the soil of the Wacaypata, as a token of its incorporation into the empire. The square was reported to have been surfaced with white sand from the coast, mingled with numerous tiny ritual objects of gold, silver, coral, shells and so on. Excavations carried out when the fountain was being restored in 1996 seemed to confirm this report, as they uncovered a set of four tiny llamas made of gold and shell.

Later, converted into the Plaza de Armas in colonial times, the square witnessed many executions, including those of Tupac Amaru, the last Inca, the rebel conquistador Diego de Almagro the Younger, and Tupac Amaru II, the 18th-century Indian leader.

On the west corner of the square stood the *Casana* (1), believed to have been the palace of Wayna Capac, the last all-powerful Inca before the Conquest. Francisco Pizarro occupied the building after his troops entered Cusco in 1533. Little remains today except one corner, now occupied by a travel agency. To the right stood Topa Inca's palace, which became part of Gonzalo Pizarro's share of the conqueror's loot. It was destroyed after Gonzalo's failed rebellion against the Spanish crown in 1548.

The northeast side of the square is dominated by the *Cathedral* (2)—

CUSCO
STREET MAP

*Note: District names (MUNAICENCA etc.)
date from Inca times. They are no longer in
popular use, but are revived here so as to
orientate the reader for a walking tour of
Places of Interest (see text), which takes
the Plaza de Armas as its starting point.*

PLAZA DE ARMAS

PLAZA REGOCIJO

PLAZA SAN FRANCISCO

PUMACURCU

TOCOCACHE

MUNAI CENCA

PUMAC CHUPAN

COLCAMPATA

CARMENCA

QUILLIPATA

PICCHU

CHAQUICHACA

AVENIDA SOL

AV. DE LOS HEROES
(Av. Pardo)

Santa Ana
Railway Station
(To Machu Picchu)

To Puno

To Pisac

To Chinchero

Hours: 10-11.30 and 14:00-17:00 daily (T.T.)—which is built on the site of Quiswarcancha, generally thought to have been the Inca Viracocha's palace, although J.H. Rowe has said that this building was a huge *kallanka* hall. The construction of the cathedral was begun in 1550 and not completed until nearly 100 years later. It contains nearly 400 colonial paintings, including many from the Cusco school, which was prominent in the 17th century. (It may be worth your while to take a guided tour. The cathedral has been under restoration, still incomplete at this writing, and it is likely that some of the paintings will have changed locations). During that period, Cusco painters supplied religious art to the whole of Spanish America, and Cusco paintings can be seen in churches as far away as Santa Fe, New Mexico.

The sacristy contains an exceptional Crucifixion, attributed to Van Dyck. Oddities to look for from the Cusco school: a painting of the last supper by Marcos Zapata showing Christ and the Apostles about to dine on guinea-pig (guinea-pig was the main course at sacred feasts in Inca times); a painting depicting a noticeably pregnant Virgin Mary (in the third alcove from the end, on the left); a flock of cherubs conceived by the Indian artist as flightless, and therefore clinging desperately to the curtains. In the first chapel, to the left behind the main altar, there is a

KEY TO CITY MAP

1. Palace of Wayna Capac (remains)
2. Cathedral
3. Chapel of Jesus María
4. Chapel of El Triunfo
5. House of the Chosen Women (Aqllawasi)
6. Jesuit Church (La Compañía)
7. Palace of Sinchi Roca (remains)
8. Church of San Cristobal
9. Palace of Manco Capac
10. Admiral's Palace (Inka museum)
11. House of Borja
12. House of Cabrera
13. House of the Serpents
14. Seminary of San Antonio de Abad (Hotel Monasterio)
15. Palace of Inca Roca (Museum of Fine Arts)
16. House of Maldonado
17. Church of San Blas
18. House of Concha
19. Santo Domingo/Qoricancha
20. Monastery of La Merced (museum)
21. House of Valleumbroso
22. Church of Santa Clara
23. Church of San Pedro
24. Central Market
25. House of Garcilaso de la Vega (Regional Historical museum)
26. Monastery of San Francisco (museum)
27. House of Pumas
28. House of Peralta
29. House of Silva
30. Church of Santa Teresa
31. Santa Ana (Machu Picchu) railroad station

recent painting of Pope John Paul II's visit to Cusco in 1985, when he crowned Paucartambo's image of the Virgin of Carmen at Sacsaywaman.

On a wall to the left of the main altar is a historically interesting painting of the Cusco earthquake of 1650, which severely damaged most of the colonial buildings in the city. The colonial Cusco that we see today was largely built after that date, and its artistic sponsor and inspiration was Manuel Mollinedo y Angulo, archbishop of Cusco from 1673-1699. This cleric was a wealthy art lover and patron from Madrid, who donated much of his fortune to the rebuilding of Cusco, and sponsored the famous local artists, Diego Quispe Titu, and Tomás Tuirutupa. He was fond of Cusco's Corpus Christi festival, and helped to make it famous. Mollinedo y Angulo figures in two of the celebrated 17th-century paintings of the Corpus Christi, which are owned by the archbishopric but regrettably no longer on public display in their art museum.

Among the art treasures are the "Señor de los Temblores"—the Lord of the Earthquakes *(see Calendar, p. 46)*—set upon 26 kilos of solid gold studded with a galaxy of precious stones. The main altar is a single piece covered in sheets of beaten silver (aptly described by the historian Luis E. Valcarcel as "baroque at its very worst"). However, the carved wooden choir facing it is particularly fine, featuring carvings of the saints.

In one of the cathedral towers lives María Angola, a huge bell cast in 1659 whose deep knell is said to be audible 40 km. away. This bell, the largest in South America, is supposedly named for a black woman who tossed 25 pounds of gold into the crucible, thus ensuring success after two previous castings had failed. There is a local legend that an Inca prince was walled up in one of the towers when it was built, and that when the tower falls the Inca will emerge to claim his birthright and free his people. After the earthquake of 1950 thousands of believers waited hopefully for the towers to collapse, but despite severe damage they remained standing, and were later repaired. In April 1986 Cusco suffered another severe earthquake, which again damaged many of the

A Quiet Walk through Cusco

The city's barely-regulated growth has left many of Cusco's streets intolerably noisy, crowded and polluted with diesel fumes. However, San Blas and San Cristobal are still pleasant to stroll through. For a downhill walk that takes you through the center of Cusco on pedestrian-only streets (except at the Plaza de Armas and Maruri), start on *Saphi*. Climb partway up the steep steps of *Amargura* then turn right onto *Qoricalle*. At the end turn down *Procuradores*, cross the *Plaza de Armas* and continue on down *Intik'ijllu (a.k.a. Loreto)*, turn left on *Maruri* then right on *Romeritos*, cross *Zetas* with Santo Domingo church on your right, and continue down *Ahuacpinta* all the way to the end. Descend the steps to the right, and you will see the main post office on *Avenida Sol*.

city's colonial buildings, including the cathedral.

Attached to the main building on both sides are two smaller churches. On the left as you face the cathedral is *Jesus María* (3) and on the right *El Triunfo*. The first is comparatively recent, dating from 1733. El Triunfo, however, is historic.

El Triunfo is built on the site of *Suntur Wasi* (The Roundhouse), the main Inca armory where the Spanish were trapped during Manco Inca's siege in 1536. When the Incas burned the city the thatched roof of Suntur Wasi caught fire, but then mysteriously went out—an event which came to be seen as a miracle. Titu Cusi, son of Manco, witnessed the siege and later stated that the Spanish had black slaves stationed on the roof to put out the flames. But long before his account was written, the "miracle" had inflated into a vision of the Virgin Mary extinguishing the flames, accompanied by Saint James (Santiago) on horseback, spreading terror among the Indian hordes. Miracles acquire an irresistible momentum, and this one has passed into legend. The Spanish subsequently broke out and recaptured Sacsaywaman, ending the siege.

El Triunfo –The Triumph– was the first Christian church in Cusco, built to commemorate the victory and the miracle of 1536. The church has two inscriptions referring to the miracle, and a painting depicting it; also a statue of the miraculous "Virgin of the Descent."

To the right of the cathedral on the adjacent side of the square stands a colonial arcade behind which you can see a long Inca facade, interrupted by the doorways of modern restaurants, and a bank. This was the *Acllawasi* (5), the House of the Chosen Women. Its righthand wall is the longest surviving Inca wall in Cusco, leading away from the square for the entire length of *Intik'ijllu street (a.k.a.) Calle Loreto*, a pedestrians-only street. Here lived the fabled "Virgins of the Sun" (as the Spanish misnamed them), and the Inca's concubines. They were dedicated to religious service, and wove exquisite garments of vicuña and alpaca for the Inca (which were worn once and then burned), brewed his chicha, and made other objects for his personal use. Certain among them were chosen to bear his children.

Tradition says that at the time of the Conquest a mighty condor fell dying into the patio of the Acllawasi after being attacked by a hawk. This ominous sign was later interpreted as a prediction of the death of Tawantinsuyu at the hands of the Spanish. Fittingly, after the Conquest part of the Acllawasi became the convent of Santa Catalina, home of a cloistered order of nuns; a small and dwindling group of them occupies it to this day.

The great church to the right of the Acllawasi is that of *La Compañía* (6). This building stands on the ruins of *Amarucancha*—the Serpent Courtyard—which was the palace of Wayna Capac, the last Inca to preside over a united, untroubled empire. Its walls run parallel to Acllawasi along the west side of Calle Loreto, and they contain a fine walled-in colonial entranceway bearing the two carved serpents which give the building its present-day name. There are also fine niches inside the school courtyard and inside the *Hostal Loreto*.

La Compañía –the Company– is named for its builders, the Company of Jesus, the Jesuits. Its construction became the subject of a terrible wrangle between the Jesuits and local ecclesiastics, because its sheer size and grandeur, not to mention its location, seemed a direct challenge to the primacy of the cathedral. The controversy went on for years and its reverberations reached Madrid and Rome. Although the first structure was destroyed before completion by the earthquake of 1650, work was begun afresh, and the final arbitration of Pope Paul III, against the Jesuits, came too late—the building was almost complete. All the local clergy could do was to have the side entrances kept back from the square and embargo the casting of a great bell designed to rival María Angola.

The church's altarpiece is a vast tableau of gilded woodwork punctuated with saints and angels, a classic of its kind that, when lit, fills one's entire field of vision with a mighty panel of shimmering gold.

Notable works of art in the church are the scene from the life of St. Ignatius Loyola, attributed to the Cusco artist Marcos Zapata; the "Cristo de Burgos," a Crucifixion effigy of agonized realism located by the main altar; and the documentary scenes evoked in two paintings, one on either side of the main door. These show the marriages of Doña Lorenza Idiaquez of Cusco to Beltrán García de Loyola (right), and of Martín de Loyola to Doña Beatriz Ñusta, granddaughter of Manco Inca (left). Martín de Loyola was the man who pursued and captured Manco Inca's son, the last Inca, Tupac Amaru. These paintings are of great historical interest for their depiction of contemporary detail. Both the bridegrooms, incidentally, are related to St. Ignatius, founder of the Jesuits, which may have something to do with why the paintings are there in the first place. Also interesting is a painting (inside left, by the door) of St. Ignatius Loyola, hero of the Counter Reformation, scourging heretics labeled Luther, Calvin, etc.

The buildings and arcades on the fourth (SW) side of the square occupy land that formerly opened onto the Incas' Cusipata, the Square of Festivals, and are built on top of the Saphi river.

Towards Colcampata (Storage Place)

Some of the most attractive streets of old Cusco wind through this sector. Try walking up the pedestrian-only street of *Procuradores* (Tax Collectors), and continuing along *Qoricalle* (Gold Street). Soon it is hard to believe you are only two blocks from the main square of a busy city.

Uphill, parallel to Procuradores, runs *Suecia*. The buildings on the right conceal the remains of *Cora Cora* (7), the palace of Sinchi Roca, the second Inca. This building was captured by Manco Inca during the great rebellion, and from this salient Manco's troops directed a withering hail of slingshot fire and arrows upon the Spanish in Suntur Wasi. Looking into one or two patios you can glimpse the great stone walls of Sinchi Roca's palace.

Parallel to Suecia, yet farther uphill, runs *Resbalosa* (Slippery Street). Walking up this steep street past *Quiscapata* (Spiky Place), you arrive at the main road to Sacsaywaman, opposite the steps leading to the church of *San Cristobal* (8). The puppet Inca, Cristobal Paullu Inca became–outwardly, at least–a devout Christian, and dedicated this church to his patron Saint.

The church itself is unexceptional; it pales next to the great retaining wall of *Colcampata* (9), which flanks the adjacent square. According to folklore, Colcampata was the palace of Manco Capac, the founding Inca. This lower wall has eleven great niches the size of doorways.

The remains of Colcampata itself are located above this wall and considerably farther back into the hillside. You can reach this ruin by following the main road uphill from San Cristobal church, and turning through the gateway on the left just past the lefthand curve in the highway. About 50 meters along the drive to the right stands an ancient doorway, the remains of the palace where Paullu Inca and Carlos Inca held court after the conquest. The foundations of the building are still visible among the eucalyptus trees. Just behind the one standing entranceway is an enigmatic stone, about 1.20m high, which appears to be carved in the shape of a frog or toad. Each year in September the ruling Inca would plant the first corn of the empire's new season at this spot. The harvest from this ritual planting would later be used to make sacred chicha for the highest rituals.

The fine Spanish mansion next to the ruins is also historic. It is said to have once belonged to Lope de Aguirre, the mad conquistador portrayed in Werner Herzog's 1972 film *Aguirre, Wrath of God*, which was shot on location in Peru. The house also served briefly as headquarters for Simón Bolívar during the wars of independence. It is now a private residence.

Towards Pumacurcu (Puma's Spine)

The *Admiral's Palace* (10) stands on the corner of *Ataud* (Coffin) and *Tucumán*. How an Admiral of the Waves came to have his home 11,000 feet above sea level is not on record. The house dates from the early 17th century, and originally belonged to Admiral Francisco Aldrete Maldonado. The coat-of-arms over the doorway is that of the second owner, the Count of Laguna. The first, according to the story, was a man so arrogant and self-important that he would begin his prayers, "Holy Mary Mother of God, our relative..." He is said to have been found hanged mysteriously in this very courtyard after roughing up a priest who came to complain of an injustice.

The building was badly damaged in the 1950 earthquake but has recently been restored and a modern annex has been added. It is now the Inca Museum, belonging to Cusco's main university *(see Museums, p. 45)*. The place is a veritable palace, with an enormous courtyard surrounded by miniature profiles of Francisco Pizarro next to that of Queen Isabel of Spain. The stairway is guarded by ferocious creatures sculpted in stone: a three-toed lion (his head was knocked off by the quake, but later repaired), and a hideous, cloven-hoofed...something. The corner window overlooking the street has a central column which, seen from outside, is carved in the shape of a woman's head and naked torso. Seen from inside, however, the figure is that of a bearded man.

Opposite the Admiral's Palace is the *House of Francisco Borja* (11), one of the Viceroys of Peru. It is now a girls' school.

Spanish Walls by Inca Masons

According to the archaeologist J.H. Rowe of U.C. Berkeley, much of what is normally taken to be Inca stonework in the city of Cusco is not so at all: it is transitional stonework done after the conquest by native craftsmen in the service of Spanish masters. The Spanish thought well enough of Inca architecture to imitate aspects of the style in their own buildings.

Examples of this abound throughout the city center: the House of Serpents (13), the House of Valleumbroso (21), the House of Pumas (27) *(numbers refer to the city map, p. 66)*, the north wall of Hatun Rumiyoc street, the east wall of Romeritos street, and many others.

How do we distinguish Inca from transitional construction? Well, with rare exceptions, it is not Inca if: the wall is not battered (inclined inwards); there are different grades and colors of stone mixed in the same wall; a join is located directly above another (sloppy construction); or the height of the stone courses is irregular, instead of diminishing progressively from bottom to top. And it very likely isn't Inca if the wall has motifs such as snakes and pumas carved in relief onto the stones.

Very few genuine Inca doorways, and none of the principal ones, have survived in Cusco. The best surviving Inca interior doorway is in the Qoricancha (19) between the temples buildings on the west side of the interior courtyard. The best exterior doorway is a half block away at Romeritos 402. There is another at Choquechaca 339, and that's it. Any other Inca-like doorways you see in Cusco are just that: Spanish in the Inca style. The notable surviving Inca walls in the city center are at the Qoricancha, and in the streets of Ahuacpinta, Herrajes, Q'aphchik'ijllu (a.k.a. Pasaje Arequipa), Santa Catalina Angosta, and Loreto.

Parallel to Ataud, a little up the hill, is *Purgatorio* (Purgatory). Just beyond it stands the *Plaza de las Nazarenas*. To the left as you face the Plaza coming from this direction stands the *House of Jerónimo de Cabrera* (12), founder of the coastal city of Ica, on the coast of Peru, and later the city of Córdoba in Argentina. Across the Plaza is the *House of the Serpents* (13), named after the numerous snakes carved in relief onto its masonry. This is a typical "transitional" structure, built by Inca masons working for Spanish conquistadors. The house is said to have belonged to Mancio Sierra de Leguizano, who claimed to have looted the famous golden disc of the sun from the Qoricancha, and then lost it the same night at dice. This must have been empty boasting, since Francisco Pizarro ensured that all the captured Inca treasure they found was melted down into bullion before distributing it, and some chroniclers claimed that the sun disc was spirited away by the natives, never to be seen again. In any case, Sierra's story caught on and gave rise to a Spanish expression in use to this day: "to gamble away the sun before it rises."

Running down the righthand side of the House of the Serpents is a narrow alley, named *Siete Culebras* (Seven Snakes) after the carved walls. A tunneled arch runs across the alley connecting the building to the chapel of the old *Seminary of San Antonio Abad* (14), which is now the opulent quarters of the Hotel Monasterio.

Towards Tococache (Salt Cave—probably the Incas mined salt here at one time)

The *Museum of Art* (15) *(see Museums, p. 45)* is located in a historic building, which according to folklore was the palace of Inca Roca, the sixth Inca. The massive Inca wall of the palace runs, almost intact, the length of *Hatunrumiyoc* (The Street of the Great Stone), and is also well preserved along the rear and the south side of the building. Hatunrumiyoc street is named for the famous 12-angled stone which features prominently about halfway along the megalithic wall (and also on the label of every bottle of Cusqueña beer). The stone is renowned for its size and for the perfection with which its twelve corner-angles fit the neighboring blocks of masonry. Some writers have speculated on a symbolism in the number of angles—one for each month of the year, for example—but there is no evidence for any special significance. Twelve angles in one plane is by no means a record for Inca masonry. The local historian Dr. Victor Angles (no relation) mentions a stone with no fewer than 44 angles in one plane at the ruins of Torontoy, near Machu Picchu.

High up on the wall of Hatunrumiyoc, at the eastern end, is a section of what looks like Inca masonry, built in regular courses of dark grey andesite, which contrasts sharply with the greenish dioritic porphyry and the polygonal style below. This upper course is actually a classic exampe of transitional masonry, built shortly after the Spanish conquest.

The colonial building erected on these walls once belonged to the Marquis of Buenavista, and later became the Archbishop's Palace. Subsequently the church dedicated part of the building as an art museum. Behind this building stands the *House of Diego Maldonado* (16), one of Pizarro's band of conquistadors. Following the direction of Hatunrumiyoc downhill to *Choquechaca* then straight up the *Cuesta de San Blas*, you come to the *Church of San Blas* (17). Founded in 1562, this is a small adobe building, unremarkable except for its extraordinary carved pulpit. This pulpit, dating from the late 17th century, is unsurpassed in the Americas, and is sometimes claimed to be the finest piece of wood-carving in the world. Starting at the base of this elaborate cedarwood work, carved from a single massive treetrunk, we find eight agonized heretics groaning under the weight of the pulpit. Above them are seven ghastly chimera, looking like masks from Greek theater. Winged angels and baroque columns support the cornice of the pulpit, below which are five figures: the four apostles and the Virgin Mary. The backdrop is dominated by the figure of St. Thomas. The canopy is alive with figures: the nine doctors of the church, numerous seraphim bearing the implements of the Crucifixion, and at the very top the figure of St. Paul. Under St. Paul's feet sits a human skull, which is thought to be that of the woodcarver who created this remarkable work. There is some dispute as to this man's identity; most often the carving is attributed to one Juan Tomás Tuirutupa, an Indian leper who was a protegé of the art patron, Bishop Mollinedo y Angulo.

San Blas square, where the church is located, was remodelled during the administration of Daniel Estrada, a very popular local mayor who became renowned for his propensity to build fountains everywhere. Here stands one of the largest of his fountains. On Saturdays there is a handcrafts market in the square.

The streets around San Blas have some repute locally as an artists' district. There are many small workshops, studios, and galleries in the area *(see Shopping, p. 27)*. Local folklore has it that this area was the artists' district even during Inca times, when the area was filled with gold- and silver-smiths from Chimor, and potters, painters, armorers and carvers from throughout the empire. The streets preserve much of Cusco's colonial charm, and most of them are pedestrians-only. Some of the street names are wildly colorful: *Atoqsayk'uchi* (Where the fox got tired); *Siete Angelitos* (Seven Little Angels); *Siete Diablitos* (Seven Little Devils); *Saqracalle* (Demon Street); *Pantaqcalle* (Confusion Street); *P'aqlachapata* (Bald men's place); *Pasñapakana* (Young girls' hiding-place); *Miracalcetas* (See stockings). Much has been done in recent years to make San Blas more attractive for tourists, and it is a very pleasant place to stroll around. Be careful at night, however, since thieves are still prevalent.

Towards Munaysenca (Pretty Nose)

On the street called Santa Catalina Ancha stands the probable former *Palace of the Inca Tupac Yupanqui* (18), part of which became the house of José de Santiago Concha in colonial times. Stout royalists, the Conchas occupied the house throughout the colonial era, and Martín Pio Concha was the last colonial governor of Cusco before Independence. The House of Concha is especially noted for its fine balconies. It now serves as a police station. The rear of Tupac Yupanqui's palace, running along *Calle Maruri*, is largely intact, though punctuated by post-Inca doorways which open onto colonial patios and shops. The Inca name for this building was *Pucamarca* (Red Settlement).

Adjacent to Maruri, also in the block formed by Pucamarca, stands a well-known local building, the House of the Four Busts. It is named after the four Spanish nobles carved in relief over the doorway. Traditionally these are held to be the four Pizarro brothers, though there is no historical evidence to support this. The building is now the Hotel Libertador.

Towards Pumac Chupan (Puma's Tail—the area corresponding to this part of the city, according to the puma configuration conceived by the Incas)

Following the streets of *Intik'ijllu a.k.a.Loreto* and *Pampa del Castillo*, you arrive at the convent of *Santo Domingo* (19). This church is built upon the remains of the fabled *Qoricancha*, the Court of Gold (some local guides I spoke with lately suggested the the name may actually have been *Qorik'ancha*, meaning Resplendant Gold), the most famous temple of the Americas. Visits: Mon.-Sat. 08:00-17:00; Sun. 2-4pm. The Dominicans have taken over the administration of this site, and there is now a separate entrance fee, whose ticket states (wilfully missing the point, one feels): "Welcome to Santo Domingo, Peru's first Dominican Convent."

Only three Spaniards ever saw the Qoricancha in its full glory. These men were sent by Pizarro from Cajamarca, where the Inca Atawallpa was being held prisoner, to speed up the collection of the royal ransom. They were among the roughest of Pizarro's unlettered soldiery, and their appreciation of this wonder of the world was confined to awe at the sheer quantities of gold they found there. With their own hands (the horrified Indians refused to help) they prised 700 gold sheets weighing 4 1/2 lbs. each from the walls. They reported an altar weighing 190 lbs. and a ritual font lined with 120 lbs. of gold. Aside from these financial details they left no account of the Qoricancha.

The first looters took only the largest and most accessible pieces. Members of Pizarro's main party later recalled a plethora of precious objects: a field of maize made with silver stems and leaves, and ears of gold; golden llamas, figurines, jars and pitchers. All these exquisite treasures ended up in the crucible; nothing survived.

The first three conquistadors did not remove the holiest religious symbol of the empire, the golden disc of the sun, though they reported its existence. Subsequently it seems to have vanished—taken, presumably, before the main party of Spaniards arrived. In 1553 Cristobal de Molina wrote, "The Indians hid this sun so well that it could never be found to the present day." In *The Conquest of Peru*, William Prescott tells us that the disc was positioned to catch the morning sun and throw its rays into the gold-lined temple, filling it with radiant light. There was a silver disc of the moon as well, in keeping with the Incas' parallel worship, and we may infer that this was set to cast moonlight into a silver-lined temple of the moon. Aside from these two principal temples there were shrines to Thunder and Lightning; to the Pleiades and other stars; to Venus; and to the Rainbow. There were also chambers to house the *wacas* , or sacred objects, of conquered tribes.

The splendor of this temple is beyond imagining today. It housed 4000 priests and attendants. Religious observance was constant. Offerings to the gods and the Inca's ancestors were made each day. The original temple enclosure stretched hundreds of meters, all the way down to the confluence of the Tullumayo and Saphi rivers, close to where the Hotel Savoy now stands. At this spot the accumulated ashes from a whole year's sacrifices were cast into the waters each January.

One vital aspect of the Qoricancha, however, has since been largely forgotten. It was the Incas' principal astronomical observatory. The Inca caste of *Amautas* (learned priests) included a sect of *Tarpuntaes* —effectively, the royal astronomers. Their task was to study the celestial bodies, note the advance and retreat of the sun, fix solstice and equinox dates, predict eclipses, and so on. This function was vital to everything from sacred rituals to the planting of crops. Early chroniclers tell us there were once great monoliths called *sucancas* standing on the mountainous horizons of the Cusco Valley at strategic points visible from the Qoricancha, marking the azimuths of the winter and summer solstices, as well as the critical dates for the planting of crops.

The system was yet more complex. The Qoricancha was the hub of a kind of conceptual wheel—called the *Ceque* system *(see The Ceque System of Cusco, p. 109)*. Each waca on the system had its day of the year, and was cared for by a specific Cusco Ayllu, or clan. So the ceques were an integral part of daily life in Cusco, and the movements of the heavens were an integral part of ordinary consciousness. Familiarity with the Quechua zodiac is common among Peruvian campesinos to this day.

The monastery of Santo Domingo, which was built over the ruins of the Qoricancha, obscured most of this archaeological jewel until 1950, when the earthquake fortuitously felled much of the Spanish building and laid bare the inner Inca walls which you can see today. Some questionable restoration has been carried out here (close inspection will reveal what is original and what is recent; newly-cut stones, for example, display chisel marks at the edges). Nonetheless, the surviving walls of the Qoricancha represent the finest Inca stonework in existence. The stone font in the central courtyard is the same one whose gold lining so excited the first conquistadors, but it has been substantially reworked to Spanish design. To your left as you enter here stand two lesser shrines against the wall that runs along Ahuacpinta street. These possibly housed the hostage idols from around the empire. No explanation exists for the three holes bored through the wall at floor level between these rooms, but speculation has it that they were used for channeling away ritual chicha or the blood of sacrificial animals. (In 1996 the Dominicans who own the monastery of Santo Domingo took control of the site. They have signposted the different locations within the temple, and some shameless individual, who should be working on a tabloid newspaper, has designated this area the "Sacrifice Room," and installed a square, colonial-era reworked Inca stone—*upside down!*—which visitors are presumably supposed to think was an Inca sacrificial altar).

The two rooms to the right of the main courtyard are believed to have been the temples of the Moon, and of Lightning, although, as is so often the case, this is folklore, not historical fact. The Sun Temple itself has entirely disappeared, but the surviving outer wall is one of the most famous Inca structures in existence, an ovoid, tapering construction whose perfection of line has amazed architects and laymen alike ever since the conquest. This stucture is actually best seen from outside the building, from the street of Pulluchapata.

Between the terraces of the Qoricancha and Avenida Sol stands a park which was built in the early nineteen-nineties. A small subterranean museum whose entrance is on Avenida Sol houses some of the artifacts that were unearthed there during the attendant archeaological excavations.

Towards Picchu (Hilltop)

A block from the Plaza de Armas, walking west along *Mantas*, stands the church, convent and museum of *La Merced* (20)—Hours: 08:00-12-00 and 14:00-17:00. The entranceway of the monastery (to the left of the church) contains two intriguing paintings from colonial times. The painting on the left portrays the brutal ethos of the conquest in all its gory actuality. Mounted and armored Spaniards battle the fierce Araucanian Indians of Chile; among the horsemen, a white-cloaked Mercedarian friar wields his lance, which is tipped with a deadly steel-pointed crucifix. Overhead, celestial warriors led by the bloodthirsty St. James (a.k.a. Santiago, patron of Spanish warriors against the Moors, and virtually the god of war in the medieval Christian pantheon), are busy performing miracles on behalf of the Spanish; the arrows fired by the Araucanians have all turned in flight and are falling on the Indians themselves. A meeting of two cultures, indeed. The painting to the right shows the first missionaries of the Mercedarian order being clubbed and roasted to death by those same heathens, while a more successful group makes converts in the foreground. In the second lobby, another interesting painting depicts a damned soul in hell being devoured by zoömorphic demons. At the bottom is a list of his complaints about life in hell.

The cloister is a fine piece of Spanish architecture, surrounded by a large mural depicting the life of San Pedro de Nolasco, founder of the Mercedarians. On the far side of the cloister is the small museum of religious art. Here you find what is probably the best little collection of old paintings in Cusco, among them a Rubens scene of the holy family. There is a rich variety of opulent religous vestments, including an unusual item—a tunic bearing three crowned skulls, representing the King, the Pope and the Bishop; reminders that nobody is immortal.

Here, kept behind a double set of steel bars, is the famous monstrance (a vessel used for displaying the communion Host), which is a solid gold extravaganza four feet high, encrusted with diamonds and pearls. (Because of the distance imposed by the bars, you need binoculars to observe the details). Note the huge pair of pearls in the center, uniquely matched to form the body of a mermaid.

From the cloister you can walk through to the church itself. There are several plaques here to commemorate the conquistador Diego de Almagro, the first conqueror of Chile, later executed, whose bones lie in the vaults below. The church contains some bizarre examples of religious art: to the right of the altar a decapitated San Laureano, spouting blood, holding his own head and being helped out of his difficulties by two rather lovely archangels; left of the altar, an ancient sage being carried bodily along by angels while profoundly lost in a good book; at the back of the church are two paintings of cherubs, apparently performing surgery on the Sacred Heart of Jesus; and near the opposite wall, in a glass case, an effigy of the child Jesus surrounded by votive offerings such as toy planes, motorbikes and racing cars.

Follow Mantas away from the main square, to *Marquez*, and you come to the *House of the Marquis of Valleumbroso* (21) on the left side. The grandiose portal of the old Cusco mansion is a magnificent example of Spanish construction in the Inca style. The columns and the upper lintel are obviously Spanish, but the inner doorway itself is very Inca-influenced masonry. But notice that the sides are vertical, not trapezoidal, and that the double-jamb is recessed on the inside, not the outside; these

A Song of Cusco

People in the Andes sometimes say that there are several kinds of music: sublime music, good music, ordinary music, bad music, and Mexican music. This unkind jibe arises from a certain natural pride in the Andean musical tradition. The music of the Quechua and Aymara people, descended from the citizens of the Inca empire, has lodged itself deep in the souls of generations of musicians throughout Latin America. (Only Spain and Africa have had comparable impact here.)

The music is both sad and lively. Tunes like the *huayno* are charged with this paradox; the rhythm makes you want to dance, the melody tears your heart out. It is impossible to say now what the music played in Inca times sounded like. For example the lament, the tragic quality underlying the piping of Andean flutes— was that present in the glory days before Pizarro, or was it born of the horror of the conquest? No one can say.

We do know, however, what instruments Inca musicians used. Pre-Columbian peoples had not developed stringed instruments; there were only wind and percussion. The most common of the percussion instruments still in use today are the two types of drums, the *wankar* (also known as the *bombo*), a big side-drum that gives the bass-line to most Andean bands, and the *tinya*, a little hand-drum, traditionally played by women. For ritual and magic purposes the drum is played with seeds, chilis, etc. inside it. Also common are small cymbals and bells, and dried seed-pods or sheep's hooves, worn around the wrists and ankles.

The ancient wind instrument most popular today is the *quena*, the ubiquitous Andean flute, which originally used a pentatonic scale, but nowadays is tuned to the familiar western chromatic. Its heart-piercing sound first reached most Euro-American ears on Simon and Garfunkel's reworking of "El Condor Pasa", a famous tune in Peru (S & G made up the lyrics).

Then there is the *antara*, and the *zampoña* or *siku*, which are different versions of the familiar bundle of bamboo tubes that we call "Pan pipes". Examples of these made from ceramic and dating from early Peruvian prehistory have been found. It has a haunting and breathy sound. The Antara is a solo instrument, tuned to the pentatonic scale. The zampoña, is an intriguing example of Andean "dual complementarity"—in a traditional setting the complete instrument is made up of two separate bundles, considered to be the male and female halves of the instrument, which must be played by two people to make the full scale. Thus the traditional siku melody is played as a dialogue between a pair, or many pairs, of musicians (to visualize this, imagine two pianos, one with only the black keys, and the other with only the white, playing one piece of music). Modern city musicians "cheat", by holding both halves of the instrument together and playing them as one instrument.

Three of the most popular and characteristic instruments in Andean folk music—the guitar, harp and *charango*—are stringed, and therefore European imports. However, two of them have been completely transformed in their Andean incarnations. Instead of the massive frame of the European version, the Andean harp is light and portable. It can be played by a walking—or even a drunkenly staggering—musician. It has a sound-box to give it volume, and it is tuned to the diatonic scale.

The little *charango* is a hybrid of the mandolin and the bandurria. The sound-box is often made from the shell of some unfortunate armadillo. Let it be known!—the ones with a wooden sound-box are much better—for the music *and* the armadillo.

Visitors to Cusco should be aware that all the locally seen groups—no exceptions—play a highly modified and commercialized form of Andean music. It is hard to hear authentic traditional music that has not been adapted to foreign tastes, unless there is a rare performance by one of the groups Imasmari, Arte Sikuri, or Cruz de Mayo. *Taki Andean Music Museum*, Hatunrumiyoq 487, #5, is the latest brave effort to preserve the authentic tradition in the city of Cusco. Thurs. & Sat. events of music & dance.

Many Cusco bars and restaurants feature music from the Peruvian coast. It is easily distinguishable from the highland variety. The musicians use guitars and, for percussion, a cajón—simply, a box with a round hole—on which a player sits and beats out a greater variety of sound than you would believe possible.

In the local clubs the group Expresión is noted for an adventurous approach to Andean folk; Amerinka and Metáfora are also good. Andean Rock is played locally by the groups Apu and Keromarka. Coastal music is played by Son Peruano.

Some places where you can hear local music are listed on page 27.

(Thanks to Román Vizcarra for new information for this section.)

features identify the door as a Spanish construction. The building is now the Cusco School of Fine Arts.

Continuing in this direction along the south side of *Plaza San Francisco* you pass under the colonial archway of Santa Clara, coming to the *Church and Convent of Santa Clara* (22) on your left. This is a cloistered nunnery—the oldest in Peru—but it is possible for early risers to visit the church, which is chiefly noted for an altar set with thousands of mirrors. The entrance is on the side street of Concevidayoc.

One more block brings you to the *Church of San Pedro*(23), located directly opposite the *San Pedromarket* (24). The church was built with stones taken from an Inca structure which was situated just up the hill. The main entranceway bears the coat-of-arms of the Spanish crown.

The main market of Cusco (24) is a place not to be missed by the visitor. Lamentably, this imperative must come with a warning: the market is heavily infested with the contemporary pest *Turistus pickpocketus*, along with related species *T.bagslashia* and *T. camerasnatchus*. (For species behavior and pest control information see *Miscellaneous Information, p. 47)* The uphill section consists of stalls where tourist goods and souvenirs are sold. But this area is the least of it, as far as local life is concerned. The main food market is a great tin-roofed hall opposite the Santa Ana (Machu Picchu) railway station. Hundreds of stallholders—mainly women—sell every imaginable item of food: spices, fruits, meat, vegetables, plus coffee and tea from Cusco's northern jungle. Here you see the prolific variety of produce grown in the multiple climatic regions of Peru, which range from rainforest through desert and temperate climes to frozen wasteland. The market is also a social world of its own: the vendors' children play hide-and-seek among the stalls; women arrive from distant villages to barter grain or potatoes for items ranging from salt to sewing needles. There are stalls for hot meals, others for fruit juices (neither section recommended for unconditioned stomachs, however); inhabitants of the market never need to leave it by day. The surrounding streets are cluttered with more stalls: an area for pots and pans here, one for primus repairs there.

There is an order in all this chaos. Inevitably it invites comparison with the well-oiled stainless-steel world of a Euro-American supermarket, where the only person you speak to is the cashier. Don't miss it.

Towards Quillipata (Place of the Sparrowhawk)

Opposite the Hotel Cusco stand the graceful colonial arches of the *House of Garcilaso de la Vega* (25), the mestizo chronicler. This elegant building was severely damaged in the April 1986 earthquake but has been restored and is now the home of the Regional Historical Museum *(see Museums, p. 45)*. Following *Calle Garcilaso* uphill from this corner leads you to the wide open spaces of Plaza San Francisco. On the opposite side stands the *Church and monastery of San Franciso* (26)— Claimed opening hours: Mon-Fri 07:00-12:00 and 13:00-16:30; Sat. 07:00-12:30; actual opening hours: anyone's guess, at this writing. The monastery has been closed, undergoing restoration for many years, but the work is now almost complete, and plans are to re-open it to the public as a museum in June, 1999. It has a magnificent collection of colonial paintings, surviving in excellent condition, including a Last Judgement (with scenes surpassing Hieronymus Bosch for macabre cruelty) by the famous Cusco painter Diego Quispe Tito, and Flemish renaissance-influenced works by Marcos Zapata. The cloister of the monastery is a superb example of colonial architecture, with paintings of incidents from the life of St. Francis of Assisi around its courtyard. Many of the ceilings are decorated with elaborate and colorful frescoes. At the head of one stairway is an enormous painting, nine meters by twelve, of the Franciscan family, crowned with saints, coats-of-arms and rubrics, representing a total of 683 people.

Off the courtyard are two sepulchres containing macabre arrangements of bones and skulls, some pinned to the walls to form the lettering of morbid homilies ("What you are, I once was; what I am, you will be"). Via the stairs you reach the choir, which is interesting for its carved wooden panels (featuring cohorts of slaughtered saints), and the fascicule, a huge cylindrical device of wood inlaid with ivory, for displaying religious texts and hymns to groups of seated monks. There is also a 17th-century German organ, in reasonably good working order. All in all, one of Cusco's finest religious buildings.

Outside, the Plaza San Francisco also provides the interested visitor with a nice crash course in basic Andean botany. The square has been planted entirely with native Andean shrubs, trees, flowers cacti and crops, many of them labeled with both Quechua and scientific names. The cultivated Andean grains such as Quinoa and Kiwicha can also be seen there during their growing season.

On the street of Santa Teresa, number 385, you find the *House of Pumas* (27), an Inca-style transitional-period doorway with six animals, probably pumas, carved in relief upon the lintel. At the intersection of *Santa Teresa* and *Siete Cuartones* stands a colonial mansion, the *House of the Counts of Peralta* (28). Opposite this house, set back from the street, stands the Inca-walled *House of Diego de Silva* (29), now a girls' school. The Viceroy Francisco de Toledo watched from these windows as his victorious troops returned from Vilcabamba in 1572, dragging with them the captive (and soon to be executed) last Inca, Tupac Amaru.

Next to this house stands the *Church and Monastery of Santa Teresa* (30), also built on Inca foundations. The balcony high up on the corner with Saphi was once used by the colonial authorities for making civic announcements and hearing public complaints. This church is not open to the public on any regular basis, but if the door is open, take a look. The interior is one of the prettiest in Cusco.

CHAPTER TWO

OUTSIDE THE CITY

Walks and Tours Close to Cusco

The most interesting and accessible area for walks and taxi-tours close to the city lies roughly in the arc between northwest and northeast of Cusco. Here squats the massive ruined structure of Sacsaywaman, along with other well-known ruins and shrines close to the paved highway to Pisac. The nearby hills are criss-crossed with pathways. Most are gentle enough for the average weekend hiker, yet there are tremendous views, and the entire countryside is dotted with fascinating places to discover and explore: Inca dams, roadways, shrines, carvings, walls and terraces; abandoned colonial brick kilns; grottoes, caves and waterfalls.

SACSAYWAMAN

This site stands on a hill looming over the city to the north. The limestone blocks in the three tiers of outer walls which form the perimeter of this awe-inspiring ruin are the vastest of any Inca site—yet even these enormous stones are fitted with that extraordinary Inca perfection. Every visitor should see this.

The name has been variously translated as "Speckled Falcon" and "Royal Eagle," and also (taking the name to be a corruption of the Quechua words Sacsa Uma) as "Speckled Head." This last interpretation refers to the idea that the city of Cusco was laid out in the form of a puma, whose speckled or tawny head was the hill of "Sacsa Uma."

This ruin can be taken in as part of a popular tour that includes three other ruins close to Cusco (*see below*), or visited very easily on its own. It lies about half-an-hour's walk or ten minutes by taxi from the city. There is no public transport. The walk uphill passes Colcampata (City Map, #9); follow the main road until you come to a ticket kiosk and signboard announcing the ruins. A footpath (steep but not drastic) leads you up to the east flank of the ruins, along the valley of the Tullumayo river. Entry is by the US$ 10 group ticket, which is also valid for the three ruins mentioned below.

The origins of Sacsaywaman are uncertain. It is commonly attributed to the period of the Inca Pachacuteq, the man essentially credited with founding the Inca empire. Prescott, in *The Conquest of Peru*, states that 20,000 men were employed in its construction over a period of fifty years. But these figures have been supplied, like so much of Inca history, by the imagination of Garcilaso de la Vega, a chronicler justly honored for his literary talent, but suspect on many points of historical detail.

Sacsaywaman is usually described as a fortress, chiefly because a great battle was fought there between the Spanish and the Incas in 1536. The defensive aspect may have been considered by the architects, but it was more than simply a military structure. The Incas did not divide their world into different functions as we do. Such a large center as Sacsaywaman clearly had various functions. It was an important religious site; some have pointed to the zig-zag configuration of the outer walls as evidence that the structure was a temple to the god of lightning, an important Inca deity. Others assert that the zig-zags represented the teeth of the conceptual puma whose body was the city of Cusco, and whose head was the hill of Sacsaywaman. Of course, since things could have many different meanings simultaneously in the Inca mind, these two ideas are not mutually exclusive. The chronicler Cieza de León refers to Sacsaywaman as a "Storehouse of the Sun," where all manner of goods were stored. The huge complex of buildings on the hill, now almost entirely gone, probably also served as an administrative center, with its adjacent storehouses.

In *The Conquest of the Incas*, Hemming tells us that the largest stone block in the mighty outer walls of Sacsaywaman stands 8.5m high and weighs 361 tons. The three parallel zig-zag ramparts that clad the north side of the hill stretch for more than a thousand feet, in 22 salients, perhaps designed to make an attacker expose his flank. For structural strength, the most massive stones are set at the apexes of the salients. This is one of the most astounding megalithic structures of the ancient world.

The early Spanish noted a veritable labyrinth of buildings on the summit, with room enough for the estimated five thousand troops who garrisoned it during Manco Inca's rebellion. The hilltop was crowned with three great towers, whose foundations can still be seen, named Muyucmarca, Sayacmarca and Paucarmarca.

For hundreds of years after the conquest, until the 1930s, Sacsaywaman served as a kind of pre-cut stone quarry for the city of Cusco, so it is not surprising that the site has been denuded of the smaller stones that once covered the hilltop. Only the mighty outer walls were too massive to be looted. With all the buildings gone it will never be possible to settle archaeologically the question of Sacsaywaman, and what purpose it served.

All of the structure survived the first years of the conquest. Pizarro's party entered Cusco unopposed in 1533, and lived there securely for more than two years. They were caught totally unprepared by the rebellion of Manco Inca which exploded in 1536. Sacsaywaman was lightly-garrisoned, and fell quickly to Manco's troops, and thereafter they used it as a base from which to rain fire and arrows upon the city and launch sorties against the beleaguered Spaniards. The bitter struggle for these heights became the decisive military action of the conquest. Manco's failure to hold Sacsaywaman cost him the war, and the empire.

It was in May 1536, after weeks of siege, that the Spanish cavalry under Juan Pizarro broke out of the city and charged northwest into the hills beyond the Saphi river, whose valley lies to your right as you face the city from Sacsaywaman. Reaching the tablelands above the city, they wheeled east and doubled back through the hills, to capture the rocky knoll, known today as the *Rodadero*, opposite the fortress.

From this knoll the Spanish made repeated attacks across the level plaza against the walls of the fort throughout a full day. Late in the afternoon Juan Pizarro, half-brother of Francisco, was mortally wounded by a slingshot. "They buried him by night so that the Indians should not know he was dead, for he was a very brave man, and the Indians were very frightened of him," recalled the conquistador Francisco de Pancorvo in later years.

The conquistadors were violent, lawless men—often too much so to live comfortably in their own country. Their greed and ambition frequently led them to disaster. Of the conquering Pizarros, Juan was the first to die. Each of these four bastard half-brothers from Estremedura, a hardscrabble region of Spain, came to a relatively sticky end. Hernando was incarcerated at the instigation of political rivals who accused him of provoking Manco's rebellion, and spent twenty years rotting in a Spanish jail (albeit a gilded cage; he lived like an imprisoned drug lord on his share of the loot from the conquest). The egregious Gonzalo, Manco's chief tormentor and provocateur, was executed in 1548 for high treason after rebelling against the Spanish crown. Francisco himself, the leader and chief strategist of the conquest, was assassinated in Lima in 1541 by embittered rivals from the Almagrist faction, which had been defeated by the Pizarros. Only a younger cousin, Pedro Pizarro, died respectably in bed, after writing his memoirs of the conquest.

The day after Juan's death was a critical one for the entire Spanish occupation of Peru. The whole country was in open insurrection against the invaders. All settlements except for Lima and Cusco had been overrun or abandoned. All three Spanish columns dispatched from Lima to relieve the highland city had been massacred to the last man. Everything now hinged on this action at Sacsaywaman. If the Spanish in Cusco failed to take the fort they were doomed; nearly all their slender forces were concentrated on this exposed hilltop, and there could be no easy escape to the city.

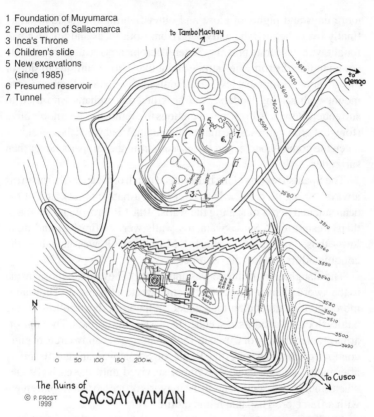

1 Foundation of Muyumarca
2 Foundation of Sallacmarca
3 Inca's Throne
4 Children's slide
5 New excavations
   (since 1985)
6 Presumed reservoir
7 Tunnel

to Tambo Machay

to Qenqo

to Cusco

The Ruins of
© P. FROST
1999
SACSAYWAMAN

Main Source: INC, Cusco

As the attacks continued throughout the day, 5000 fresh Inca troops arrived to reinforce their comrades. Meanwhile, "in the city the Indians mounted such a fierce attack that the Spaniards thought themselves lost a thousand times." But that evening the Spanish assaulted Sacsaywaman with scaling ladders, seizing the outer walls and driving the defenders into the fortified complex dominated by the three towers. After two more days and nights of close and bitter fighting, the conquistadors finally overwhelmed the native garrison. Both Incas and Spanish had fought with desperate bravery. Several chroniclers recall an Inca noble commanding the fort who "strode about like a lion from side to side of the tower on its topmost level. He repulsed any Spaniards who tried to mount with scaling ladders. And he killed any Indians who tried to surrender." Gonzalo Pizarro was anxious to capture this Inca noble alive (for what grim purposes we may well imagine), but when the tower was taken the commander leaped to his death from the ramparts rather than surrender.

The Spanish reports of the battle made much of their own heroism (as always, giving no credit whatsoever to their native allies), and of the near-suicidal perils of scaling the walls. But J.P. Protzen notes that at their western end, Sacsaywaman's walls were unfinished and quite low—thus, vulnerable to attack. Most likely it was here that the conquistadors broke the defences.

The slaughter in the battle was appalling. "They put all those inside to the sword, there were 1500 of them," wrote a Spaniard. Thousands more had died defending the citadel. In the grim dawn following the battle, flocks of condors descended to feast on the corpses. The coat-of-arms granted the city of Cusco in 1540 bears a tower and a circle of eight condors commemorating the Battle of Sacsaywaman and its grisly aftermath. This melancholy symbol survived until the early 1990's, when "indigenist" sentiments in the mayor's office led to its replacement with a fierce pre-Hispanic feline motif.

In 1982 rains caused a section of the outer walls to subside, revealing the hastily-buried remains of eleven high-ranking Inca warriors who must have died in this battle.

The destruction of Sacsaywaman began after the defeat of Manco's rebellion. The outer walls remain—too massive, perhaps, for the Spanish to destroy. But the complex of towers and buildings was razed to the ground. There was nothing to be seen of them until Luis Valcárcel carried out excavations there in 1935, to commemorate the 400th anniversary of the conquest. Today one can see the round foundations of Muyucmarca, a tiered, cone-shaped tower (*Muyu* = circular shape in Quechua) which once had a great cistern and a system of conduits to feed water to the garrison, the remains of which are clearly visible. So, too, are the foundations of Sayacmarca, a rectangular tower, identifiable by two large altar-like bases in the center, which were probably great stone supporting-columns. Beneath the towers ran a warren of tunnels connecting the fort to the outer walls. To this day many fantastic legends are told about Sacsaywaman concerning labyrinthine tunnels of enormous length into which people descend, to be lost forever, or to emerge, gibbering mad, clutching items of Inca treasure.

The rocky knoll which the Spanish first captured was covered with carved and stone-clad surfaces, for what purpose we don't know. There is a kind of stepped dais with finely carved, flat surfaces, overlooking the so-called esplanade, which is known informally as the Inca's Throne; it would seem a good place from which to review parading troops, except that it does not directly face the esplanade; it is angled toward the south-east. At the rear of the knoll you find the "children's slide"—natural grooves in the glacier-scored rock, worn smooth by

The storming of
Sacsaywaman
May, 1536

generations of children, and more than a few grown-ups. This puzzling geological formation is apparently a "slickenside," the result of two rock strata grinding against each other with such pressure that the rock melts, leaving smooth grooves where the lower stratum has been left exposed.

Beyond this area stands a huge ovoid construction which was uncovered by the local INC, beginning in 1985. This sector is called Suchuna. The structure is believed to be the remains of a reservoir that supplied water to the Cusco. Around its northern and eastern edges stand the remains of its associated ritual baths and shrines. Remains of ritual offerings were found here during excavations particularly quartz crystal, and pink spondylus shell from the coast of present-day Ecuador. This type of offering is commonly associated with the veneration of water in Inca religion. Suchuna must have been an important religious site, because, according to the chronicle of Pedro Pizarro, the Spanish went to the trouble of destroying and burying it.

To the north of the road that runs past this point lies a maze of carved rock outcrops and caves, typically puzzling pieces of Inca work, in which outcrops of bare rock have been sculpted into endless variations.

The Stones of Cusco

People have always marveled at Inca stonemasonry—the famous "Inca fit," so snug that one often cannot slip a razorblade into the joins between stones that often weigh many tons. No civilization of the Old World took so much trouble with stone, and consequently none matched the accomplishments of the Andean masons.

Many bizarre and fantastic theories have attempted to explain how these wonders were performed. Colonel Fawcett, the eccentric early-20th-century explorer, published a tall tale that has been on the lips of tour guides ever since. In his book *Exploration Fawcett* he claimed the Incas possessed an herb from the Amazon capable of dissolving stone. Awestruck early Spanish chroniclers, on the other hand, claimed that the natives had enlisted the aid of demons. Nowadays the identical

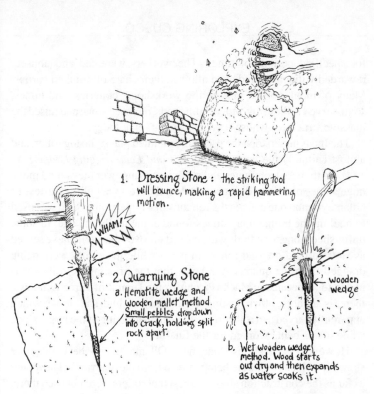

1. **Dressing Stone :** the striking tool will bounce, making a rapid hammering motion.

WHAM!

2. **Quarrying Stone**
a. Hematite wedge and wooden mallet method. Small pebbles drop down into crack, holding split rock apart.

wooden wedge

b. Wet wooden wedge method. Wood starts out dry and then expands as water soaks it.

psychology operates in reverse: now it was not demons but "gods" (extra-terrestrials) who built the things. Either way, according to this thinking, those primitive Incas couldn't have done it themselves.

Although the Incas did not have the hard steel tools necessary for rapid chiseling, nor the engines and draft animals that Old Worlders would have used for shifting 100-ton rocks, they did have a vast mass of surplus labor, due to the legendary efficiency of their agriculture. They also had a social system capable of channeling these energies into great public works projects.

In Inca society, taxes essentially were paid in labor. The rulers created a system of conscription known as *mit'a*, whereby communities from throughout the empire sent labor contingents to work for the state

97

for specified periods of time. The workers were fed and housed, rewarded with cloth, and even allowed their share of drunken parties. Many of them worked in weaving workshops, potteries, and mines, some served in the army, others built roads, quarried stone and raised the massive structures whose remains we marvel at today.

The Incas understood the use of the inclined plane, the log roller, and almost certainly the lever *(see Levers and Leapfrogging Ladders, p. 144)*. With these techniques and sufficient manpower they could move huge stones over long distances. Below the west wall of the fortress of Ollantaytambo one can see the remains of a huge ramp which was used to haul up the tremendous stones found at the top of the site. In some unfinished stones one finds wide carved grooves that could have served as slots to hold greased rollers in place while the stones were being dragged from the quarry. We know that the principle of rollers was understood, because at Machu Picchu, by the Temple of Three Windows, there is a large block resting on a small cylindrical stone which apparently served as a roller to facilitate maneuvering of the larger stone while it was being worked for the final fit.

However, excavations done near Ollantaytambo beneath "tired stones" —blocks that were being moved from the quarries but never got as far as the construction site—suggest that rollers were not used there; the stones were simply dragged along prepared roadbeds.

There is a subtle, less obvious explanation of how the Incas were able to move vast stones. Their society was highly unified and well-nourished, they did not use slaves, their labor force was not reluctant, and their mightiest structures were dedicated to the deities which everyone worshipped. Thus an undivided focus of human energies may have accomplished what seem almost superhuman feats to we individualistic moderns.

To quarry stones the masons made a starting cut along a natural weakness in the rock, probably using hard stone such as hematite as a tool. Then wedges were used to widen the fissure until the rock broke away from the main mass. The wedges were made either of another, harder stone, which they drove in by pounding, or wood, which split the rock by expanding when soaked in water.

One of the "tired stones" of Ollantaytambo— sitting to the right of and slightly above the modern road to Quillabamba, just beyond the outskirts of Ollantaytambo—shows clear evidence of how the masons were shaping it, and also re-cutting it because of an accidental fracture.

An interesting discovery has been reported from the quarries at Rumicolca, 35 km. from Cusco, which supplied much of the andesite used in the construction of the city. A modern quarryman says he found small round pebbles at the bottom of a crack in a half-split rock that was in the process of being quarried. These pebbles would have had a ratchet effect, dropping down and preventing the crack from closing again after it had been fractionally opened by a blow on the wedges at the top *(see illustration, p. 97)*.

The Inca masons dressed stones into the smooth, perfect shapes required for building by simply pounding on the stones repeatedly with another, harder stone, chipping and flaking away the worked surface. This method is not as laborious as one might think, because a skilled worker can get a rhythm going, such that the hammerstone will bounce back into his hands at each blow, allowing a rapid, relaxed drop-and-catch technique to eat away the face of the worked stone at a surprising rate. Using this technique, J.P. Protzen, a leading researcher into Inca stoneworking, turned a shapeless lump of andesite into a smooth cube about 25 cm. along the edge in a space of only an hour and a half.

Evidence that the Incas used such a technique is visible everywhere. Even the finest of their masonry is covered with tiny pockmarks made by this pounding process. This technique, incidentally, helps to account for the deeply recessed, or beveled, edges of the blocks in Inca walls. It is hard to get a sharp, right-angled edge using stone hammers, because the corners tend to break off.

The intermediate stage between splitting rock and fine dressing may have called for a rough-cutting process whose nature has not been determined. However, a partially-cut block examined by the author at

Phuyupatamarca on the Inca Trail was apparently being cut by the same pounding process used for fine dressing.

One characteristic of existing Inca walls is that the load-bearing (i.e. horizontal) joins of the stones are always made to fit perfectly over their entire surface, whereas the vertical joins are usually perfectly joined to a depth of only a few centimeters from the outer surface. Often mud and rubble has been used to fill up the internal gaps. If the Incas had possessed some easy, magic technique for fitting stone they would not have resorted to a labor-saving method like this.

The techniques described above were not simple or easy; they were immensely laborious, especially when working with huge stones. The mind reels when one considers the time and painstaking work invested in structures like Sacsaywaman. But these stoneworking feats do not require supernatural explanations. The most convincing proof that the techniques employed were neither mysterious nor extra-terrestrial rests in the fact that much of the "Inca" masonry in the city of Cusco was actually done after the Spanish conquest *(see Chapter One)*. The masons were working for Spanish masters to a different design and with declining quality, but the style of workmanship is still unmistakeably Inca.

The Spanish themselves did not lack the technology to perform such work; nor do we today. What we lack are other traits that the Incas did have: endless patience and a profound spiritual reverence for their working material, the stone itself.

(The author is indebted to Dr. Jean-Pierre Protzen for most of the above information.)

Scribing and Coping...answer to an ancient riddle?

At the annual meeting of the Institute of Andean Studies at Berkeley, California in 1987, the architect Vincent R. Lee proposed an ingenious solution to the problem of how the Inca masons achieved the legendary precision of their stonework. The idea is based on a method traditionally used to fit the corner joints of log cabins, known as "scribing and coping."

The modern "scribe" is an instrument like a draftsman's compass, used to mark the upper of two corner logs with the exact profile of the lower one. It uses a leveling-bubble to maintain a constant spatial relationship between the lower log and the cutting-mark on the upper one. Lee shows that the leveling-bubble can be replaced with a plumb-line, to create a similar artifact well within the technical capabilities of the Incas.

The "cope" is the term used by log cabin builders for the cut which is made in the upper log. In an inversion of this technique, Lee proposes, the Incas cut the upper stone first, and then used a scribe to trace a perfect replica of the cut face on the lower stones, pounding away (or "coping") the excess stone with hammers, as described above. The basic principle involved is the same as that used for duplicating door keys.

This operation requires (a) that the cut stone be fixed immovably in place above the one to be cut, which lies beneath it; (b) that the cut upper face is open and free of obstructions; and (c) that there is enough space in between the stones for the masons to use the scribe while cutting the lower stone. Considering the mass of some of these stones, this would seem the hardest part of the operation. Lee suggests that massive tree trunks were used to form a "trestle" structure, to support the stones from either side *(see illustrations, p. 102)*. Log trestle structures were formerly used to build railroad bridges, and are enormously strong. If true, this theory might explain the otherwise baffling indentations and knobs on the surfaces of Inca walls, which could have been used to hold these diagonal props in place.

The theory also helps to make practical sense of the deeply recessed joints in virtually all Inca stonework: the beveled profile allows the mason's scribe into position, where a right-angled edge might block it.

The "scribing and coping" technique represents a vast improvement over any "trial and error" method of lowering stones into place and lifting them again to perfect the joint, since, according to Lee, the stones could be cut and fitted perfectly in one operation.

However, sceptics (J.P. Protzen among them) regard this theory as far too hypothetical. No specimen of its principal artifact—an Inca "scribe"—has ever been found by archaeologists, and they consider the "trestle" support for vast stones unrealistic.

(A detailed account of the scribing and coping theory appears in Vincent R. Lee's paper *The Building of Sacsaywaman*; *see Bibliography*.)

1. Pre-cut stone is moved into place

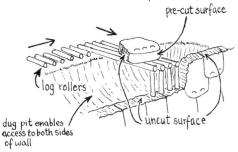

pre-cut surface

log rollers

dug pit enables access to both sides of wall

uncut surface

2. Stone is immobilized in place

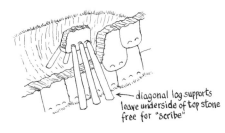

← diagonal log supports leave underside of top stone free for "scribe"

3. Hypothetical Inca "scribe"

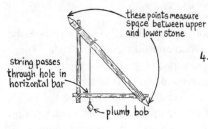

these points measure space between upper and lower stone

string passes through hole in horizontal bar

← plumb bob

4. Scribe is used to measure, as lower surface is cut

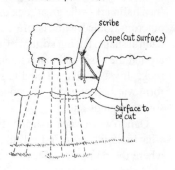

scribe

cope (cut surface)

Surface to be cut

5a. How the stone is lowered into place

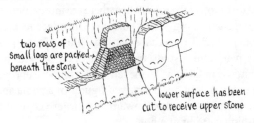

two rows of small logs are packed beneath the stone →

lower surface has been cut to receive upper stone

5b. Upper stone is set onto lower stone

Upper stone is tipped back and forth; each time a layer of small logs is removed from below.

two rows of small logs

QENQO (Zig-Zag)

Following the road leading northeast for about 2 km., you come to the ruins of Qenqo, lying below the road embankment to the right. These are not precisely ruins, for Qenqo is one of the finest examples of that Inca hallmark—the great rock carved in situ. It is an eroded limestone outcrop, riddled with fissures, all artfully carved to utilize the rock's natural shape. Facing north we find an amphitheater with 19 niches built around the base—all that remains of a high wall—centered upon a tall rock. It was perhaps a phallic symbol or a sitting puma—its original form was obliterated by the conquerors—and was evidently a focus of some religious cult.

Qenqo was a waca, a shrine. Inside its caves we find large niches and what looks like an altar. Early chroniclers mention caves around the city where the mummies of lesser royalty were kept in niches along with gold and precious objects. This was almost certainly one of them.

Stone steps lead to the top of the rock, where there are more enigmatic carvings: the zig-zag channels (p'aqchas) that give the place its name, which served to course chicha, or perhaps sacrifical blood, for purposes of divination; and a pair of thick studs, reminiscent of the bollards used to tie up a ship—purpose unknown. To the left (west) of these uprights, on the edge of the outcrop, look for the carved figures of a puma and a now-headless bird, perhaps a condor. Towards the eastern edge of the rock stands a foot-high carving of a house.

Qenqo Chico, the outcrop just downhill from Qenqo is also heavily carved on top and is surrounded by a fine retaining wall.

Note: There have been robberies around Qenqo, especially inside the passageways. The victims are often solitary tourists or small groups assaulted at quiet times when the ruins are deserted. Be alert.

PUCA PUCARA (Red Fort)

This small site stands to the right of the highway about 6 km. beyond Qenqo. It is misnamed—it was not a fort. More likely it was a tambo, a kind of post-house where travelers were lodged and goods, animals, etc. were housed temporarily. The Spanish chronicler Bernabe Cobo states that Tambomachay *(see below)* was the hunting lodge of the Inca Pachacuteq, but since there are no signs of dwellings at that site perhaps he was referring to Puca Pucara, which is close by.

The last ruins in this circuit stand just a few hundred meters up the road.

TAMBOMACHAY (Cavern Lodge)

This place is popularly called the "Baño del Inca"—the Incas's Bath. It is a rather finely preserved example of a site for ritual bathing and perhaps a water cult. We know that the Incas revered water as one of the principal elements of life, and they frequently practiced devotional ablutions. Here, where a spring emerges from the hillside, the Incas built a series of three waterfalls, painstakingly channeling them through fine stone courses. Doubtless the site was far less bare and stark in former times than it is today. It was probably surrounded by trees, shrubs and ornamental gardens.

Note an element of mystery in the location of the spring itself. The slope behind it is simply not high enough or large enough to provide so much water; one assumes that it comes underground from the mountain opposite, via a U-shaped natural conduit.

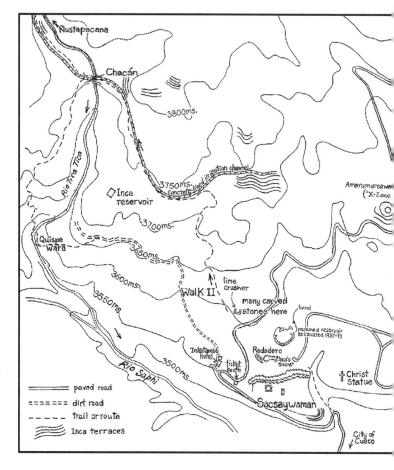

Map labels:
Nustapacana
Chacán
3800ms.
Río Tica Tica
3750ms. concrete-lined irrigation channel
Inca reservoir
Amarumarcawasi ("X-Zone")
3700ms.
Quispe wara
3650ms.
3600ms.
3550ms.
Walk II
lime crusher
many carved stones here
tunnel
presumed reservoir (excavated 1985-7)
Inkatambo Hotel
ticket booth
Rodadero
Inca's Throne
Christ Statue
Río Saphi
3500ms.
Sacsaywaman
City of Cusco

Legend:
—— paved road
=== dirt road
- - - trail or route
∿∿∿ Inca terraces

TWO HALF-DAY WALKS NEAR CUSCO
Note: the best way to follow these routes is to use the map above.

You can wander at will in the hills north of Cusco without getting lost. The country is open, and major landmarks are always in sight. Here are two suggestions for walks that make a convenient round trip, easily done in half a day, allowing plenty of time for looking around, and well-

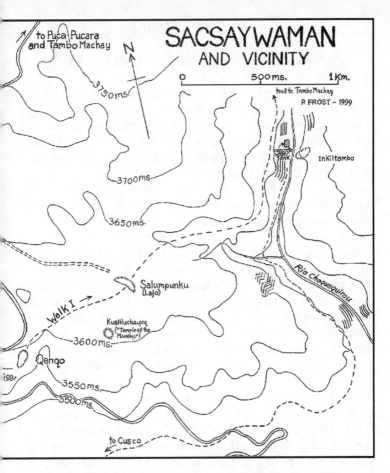

SACSAYWAMAN
AND VICINITY

to Puca Pucara
and Tambo Machay

N

0   500ms.   1 Km.

trail to Tambo Machay
P. FROST - 1999

3750ms.

3700ms.

3650ms.

concrete
water
tank

Inkiltambo

Rio Choquequirau

Salumpunku
(Lajo)

Walk I

Kusilluchayoq
("Temple of the
Monkeys")

3600ms.

Qenqo

3550ms.

3500ms.

to Cusco

laced with interesting places to explore and scenes to photograph. Each
starts from a point on the highway which can be reached by taxi. The
walks take a bit longer if you embark from Cusco itself. Refer to the
introduction of this book for a few general remarks about hiking around
Cusco. Be sure to carry a compass on the hikes mentioned below.

*Note: For a longer hike starting near Qenqo and finishing at Huchuy
Cusco, see Chapter Three.*

WALK I. WACAS, CEQUES AND SOLSTICES

Start at *Qenqo*. Get your bearings *(see Lay of the Land, p. 63)*. A path leads off from just above Qenqo, uphill through a eucalyptus grove, with some houses on your right. You are heading roughly east with your back to Cusco. Stay below the paved road, which curves uphill to the left at this point. Emerge onto open pasture. Head for a large rock outcrop in front of you, slightly to the right. This outcrop is a waca known as *Salumpuncu* (also *Lajo*, or the *Temple of the Moon*). There are two significant caves in this outcrop on the south side, and an immense fissure running right across it, through which one can walk. The cave near the southeastern end of the rock, about halfway up, is the most intricately carved. The battered outlines of snakes and a puma carved in relief on the rocks are still clearly visible at the entrance. Inside the cave there are mummy-niches, and a kind of altar onto which sunlight falls through a fissure in the rock above. The author has been told that this altar is bathed in a pool of direct moonlight at midnight on the full moon closest to the winter solstice. There are other carvings to be found on the top of this great rock. Salumpuncu (a.k.a. Lajo) can be reached by car from the main road to Tambomachay, over a rough track. Taxi drivers will take you.

Stand atop the waca with your back to where you came from. You see a small stream below, and a wide footpath leading away beyond it E.N.E. This is the old Inca road to Pisac. Follow it as it winds up and around the right flank of the hill. The trail pulls to the left, passing some low rock outcrops on your right, and crosses from a small valley into another larger one. Walk about one kilometer from Salumpunku. There is a new eucalyptus plantation to the right of the trail which now obscures the view across the valley, but if you walk downhill through these trees you will reach open meadows where you can see the remains of well-preserved ancient terraces, on the far side of a stream. The rock outcrop of *Inkiltambo* stands just to the right of these terraces. On the near side of the stream there is a small concrete water reservoir just

The Ceque Lines of Cusco

Inca Cusco encompassed one of the most extensive and complex ritual systems history has seen. Known as the ceque system, its center was the Coricancha, the hub from which 42 lines, or ceques, radiated like the spokes of a wheel. Stretched along these lines lay at least 328 *wacas*, the shrines of Cusco's sacred landscape. Some were natural features of the land, such as springs, rock outcrops, caves and lakes; others were constructed sites such as houses, walls and water channels which were associated with events in Inca mythology.

Most of our information on the ceques comes from a Jesuit priest, Bernabé Cobo, writing in 1654, more than one hundred years after the conquest. The record is incomplete, and it is difficult today to understand the full scope of the ceque system and what it meant to the Incas. But, in typical Inca fashion, it seems to have functioned simultaneously on multiple levels, ranging from mundane matters such as marking boundaries between local *ayllus* and the organization of the irrigation system, to keeping the ritual calendar and making celestial observations. Several of the shrines marked locations on the horizon where the sun would rise or set on important ritual days, such as the June and December solstices.

How the ceque lines looked on the ground — or even if they were visible at all — is impossible to tell today. Some may have been simply conceptual, with only the *wacas* along them appearing as features of the landscape. But others would have been visible on the ground, because they were ritual pathways which people walked along on certain days.

Historical references suggest that the ceque system may have extended far beyond the boundaries of the Cusco region. The Cusco lines were surely the largest system, but they may have linked up with other line systems radiating from local centers, probably with fewer lines and *wacas*. Indeed, "ritual radiality" seems to have represented a core concept in pre-Hispanic Andean religion. Traces of other ceque systems exist today, and in remote parts of the altiplano of southern Bolivia and Chile indigenous people still walk ritual lines and venerate shrines located on them.

One very important ceque line ran far beyond Cusco, 150 air kms. south-east, ending at the pass of La Raya, the divide between the Urubamba and Lake Titicaca watersheds. Each year at the time of the winter solstice the Inca priests walked this entire line, making offerings to the *wacas* along it.

On certain rare occasions, such as the investiture of a new Sapa Inca, or when Tawantisuyu was beset by natural calamities, a vast ceremony called the Capac Cocha was held. Priests set off from the Aucaypata with offerings to *all* the *wacas* along the ceque lines of the empire — a process which must have taken months to complete. This was one of the few times when the Incas practiced human sacrifice at certain designated *wacas*.

One question that remains open is whether ceque systems existed in Andean culture before the rise of the Inca empire. The famous Nazca lines, dating from more than one thousand years before the Incas, bear certain similarities, but they radiate from many different centers, not just one, as did Cusco's.

- Brian Bauer

across from Inkiltambo. If you find you have reached the end of the eucalyptus grove you will see an open, rocky area to the right of the trail, just before you reach a tiny cluster of adobe houses, the hamlet of Chilcapuquio. From here you can make your way steeply down into the valley, where you will see the aforementioned terraces.

Inkiltambo has several deep carved niches, which probably housed the ancestor mummies of the *Ayllu* that tended this shrine. The remains of carved water channels and a ritual bath can be seen below the rock on the western and southern sides. On top there is a carved fissure with two deep niches set where the tunnel narrows into a crack. On the evening of the equinoxes the sun can be seen to set dead center in this crack.

From Inkiltambo, turn downhill and follow the stream running down the *quebrada* (ravine) of *Choquequirau*. Pick up a trail on the righthand side of the stream. Soon you come to some old kilns, dating from colonial times, that were used to make roofing tiles. Lower down you pass more of these, tucked under a cliff, which are in use today as dwellings. Beyond this point you find a trail that leads up the righthand valley sides to a magnificent view across the Huatanay valley to the town of San Jerónimo. The trail rises through a notch in a ridge to your right, and you find yourself abruptly on the outskirts of Cusco.

Take the dirt road that traverses the hillside toward the city. Cross the paved road, follow it to the right, about 100 meters, to pick up the path again. You pass the waca called *Titicaca*, above you to the right. This waca has been christianized—adorned with a cross and chapel. Titicaca is on a line of the Cusco ceque system, the winter solstice line. Interestingly, in Inca legend the sun is born in Lake Titicaca; and the sun is likewise born, in astronomical terms, in the line of the solstice, which perhaps accounts for the name of the waca. As you see Titicaca above you the path forks. Take the upper fork. Pass *Mesa Redonda* (Round Table), the Spanish name for yet another waca (Cusco teems with them). This one features a large flat rock, the "Round Table" of the name. Continue downhill and you emerge onto a Cusco city street. From here it is a short walk to the center.

WALK II. DAMS, CAVES AND AQUEDUCTS
(see Map, p. 106)

Start from Sacsaywaman. A paved road runs around the northern perimeter of the ruins. As you walk up this road from Cusco past the Sacsaywaman ticket booth, you come to a sharp righthand curve. Leave the road at this point and pick up a sunken pathway between two fields, which heads due north. After about 50 m. you will see a high stone wall with four openings in it, and an adobe house above it—dead ahead, and about 500 m. from the road. From here it looks vaguely Inca, but it is in fact part of a modern lime-crusher; the openings are chutes. As you pass below and about 50m to the left of the crusher, there are numerous trails to follow; choose one that stays high and keeps ascending—but keep the hilltops to your right. You pick up traces of an Inca roadway, which runs to the left of the main modern track. When you come upon a modern concrete-lined irrigation channel, follow it upstream. *Finding this channel is the key to reaching Chacán*— because it flows directly from that location.

About 2 km. from Sacsaywaman the aqueduct meets the valley of the river Tica Tica at a place where a great natural barrier straddles the gorge. This is called *Chacán* (Bridge-place). The aqueduct runs across the top of this unusual geological formation, while the stream itself runs beneath it, some 30m below.

Early chroniclers mention several dams on the rivers above Cusco, and this may have been one of them. Each year in our month of January, when the flood waters were peaking, the Incas would break the dams above Cusco. The ashes of the whole year's sacrifices would be thrown into the river Huatanay below the Temple of the Sun. Then, in a ritual called Mayucati ("following the river") young men would chase the ashes downriver all the way to Ollantaytambo, a distance of at least 100 km.

At the top, above the aqueduct, stands a rock which has been carved and fitted with stone walls, now mostly destroyed. This was probably another of Cusco's wacas. Just after crossing the natural bridge you can descend just a few meters to the right, and cut back towards the cliff edge. Follow a broad fissure descending onto a natural balcony within a cave, partially carved by the Incas, which looks down into the mouth of the river-tunnel below. Here, the Tica Tica runs through a huge, tapering cave underneath Chacán. It starts out about 10 m. high, and narrows to a bit more than one meter where the stream exits. Those who like to indulge their inner child can walk through this tunnel, crouching as they emerge and getting their feet a bit wet. But *don't* try this if the river is running strong; check the stream's exit as you arrive from below.

If you wander upstream for a kilometer or so above Chacán, you will pass Inca platforms, fine terrace walls and a rock shrine by the water's edge, before reaching another ravine at the small ruins of *Ñustapacana*.

Returning to Chacán, walk downstream along the righthand (west) side of the river. Stay high, about 150 m. above the river, for about a kilometer, until you pass above high bluffs on either bank. Here the ravine widens, and you will see a large eucalyptus plantation on the opposite (east) bank of the river. (But remember—trees can be cut down! If the grove has been logged since this writing, you should be able to see numerous tree stumps, and a grassy motor track, about the width of a truck, that currently is hidden by the trees.) Descend to the river opposite this plantation, and cross (this is easy—there are plenty of big rocks). You come to a great stone, carved on all sides, with remains of a walled enclosure and a water duct on the left bank of the stream. Overlooking the stream you find a stepped-pyramid shape (a common religious motif in the Andean cultures) cut into the rock, about 2.5m high. In the center of it, notice the rounded outline that remains where some carved Inca symbol, now defaced, once overlooked the water. This waca is called *Quispe Wara* (Crystal Loincloth). Just downstream on the right bank you will find a snaky channel cut into the ground rock, which was probably used for ritual divination, like the smaller ones at Qenqo.

About two hundred yards downstream there is another section of high quality Inca structures, walls and channels, and a bridge across the river—all part of this same shrine complex.

To return to Cusco, climb straight up the hillside on the left bank of the stream at Quispe Wara, until you pick up a narrow motor track that winds gently downhill about 2 km. You will pass the Inkatambo Hotel on your left. Turn left immediately beyond it, and after 100 m. you reach the paved highway at the tight curve just downhill from Sacsaywaman.

The Celestial Andes

One source of the well-regulated order of the Inca empire was its calendar system. Based on a complex integration of solar, lunar, stellar and even biological cycles, the Inca calendar provided an orderly basis for all aspects of Inca life. Agricultural and herding activities, the celebration of state and provincial rituals and the performance of public works for the Inca, were all coordinated with clockwork precision by calendar specialists in Cusco and in other administrative centers throughout the empire.

The astronomical knowledge of the Incas derived from regular, naked-eye observations of celestial events. Astronomical cycles were probably preserved on the knotted-string recording devices called quipus. The center for the collection, storage and interpretation of the astronomical information, and for the coordination of provincial calendars throughout the empire, was Cusco. Stone towers, or pillars (called *sucanca*), were set up at the appropriate places on the horizon around Cusco to mark the points of sunrise and sunset on the days of the solstices, the equinoxes and days when in Cusco the sun stood straight overhead, in the zenith, at noon (October 30 and February 13). Observations of moonrise and moonset at the horizon (solar) pillars, as well as the recording of the phases of the moon, were combined with the solar observations to provide month-like units of time and an overall greater precision in the annual calendar.

The Inca knowledge of the stars and constellations was as rich (and as complex) as that of any other ancient civilization. The morning and evening stars (Venus) were recognized and named and were accorded a special room for their worship in the Coricancha. The principal stars and constellations of the Incas were located within or near the Milky Way; the Inca called this bright path of stars *mayu* ("river"). In Inca cosmology, the "river" of the sky had its earthly counterpart in the Urubamba river, along which are located Pisac, Ollantaytambo and Machu Picchu. According to their vision, the two great rivers of the Inca universe, the Milky Way and the Urubamba, were joined at the edge of the known universe in the waters of a great cosmic sea which encircled the earth. The Milky Way was thought to have its source in the cosmic sea, from which it took water into the sky. As the Milky Way passed through the sky at night, it deposited moisture in the sky which fell to the earth in the form of rain, replenishing the waters of the Urubamba river.

The Incas recognized two major types of constellations along the mayu, the celestial river. One type, similar to the constellations of western Europe, traced familiar shapes in the sky by conceptually joining together neighboring bright stars. These constellations included such shapes and objects as bridges, storehouses, crosses, and animals. For example, the constellation which we know as Scorpius was considered by the Incas to represent a great serpent (the tail of Scorpius) which was changing into a condor (the head of Scorpius). One of the most important constellations of the Incas was the cluster of stars known to us as the Pleiades, in the constellation of Taurus. The Pleiades were considered to be a "storehouse" (colca), and they were observed regularly to help determine the times of planting and harvesting the crops.

The other type of constellation identified by the Incas was called yanaphuyu ("dark cloud"). These constellations, virtually unknown in traditional European astronomy, are seen in the dark spots and streaks which cut through the bright path of the Milky Way. The "dark clouds" are explained by modern astronomy as fixed clouds of interstellar dust within our galaxy which block our view of stars in the direction of the dark spot. These deep black, seemingly amorphous clouds in the Milky Way took shape in the Inca imagination as a veritable menagerie of Andean animals; these include a snake, a toad, a tinamou (a partridge-like bird), a mother llama with her suckling baby stretched beneath her, and a fox. The dark cloud constellations can best be seen when the Milky Way stands more or less overhead and when there is little or no light from street lamps or the moon.

- Dr. Gary Urton

NOTE: We are not speaking only of the dusty records of a long-lost culture here. Much of the above information was compiled from interviews with modern-day campesinos , who are still using many of the elements of this system. For more information see Gary Urton's book *At the Crossroads of the Earth and the Sky*, U. Texas Press, 1988.

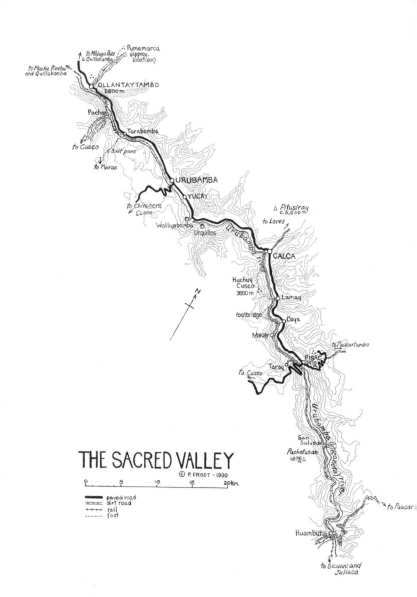

THE SACRED VALLEY

© P. FROST - 1999

0	5	10	15	20 Km.

————— paved road
∿∿∿∿∿ dirt road
←+←+← rail
- - - - - foot

116

Chapter Three

THE SACRED VALLEY

Pisac-Calca-Yucay-Urubamba-Ollantaytambo

The river which rises at the pass of La Raya, 150 air km. southeast of Cusco, runs through the very heartland of what was Tawantinsuyu, the Inca empire. There was an important Inca shrine at La Raya where the valley begins, and 300 km. downstream towards the eastern frontiers of the Inca realm, lay the sacred center of Machu Picchu. In between stood many of the most famous sacred or elite Inca sites, such as the temple of Viracocha at Raqchi, the ruins of Pisac and Huchuy Cusco, the royal palaces at Yucay and Urubamba, the imposing settlement of Ollantaytambo, and the string of ceremonial centers along what is now known as the Inca Trail.

The river which the Incas called Willcamayu, the sacred river, had its celestial counterpart in the Milky Way, a key element in Inca cosmology which they also called Mayu, the River, and which was oriented along the same southeast/northwest axis as the Willcamayu during the southern summer.

(Note: Some confusion arises around the name of the river, owing to the Quechua custom of naming rivers by sections. In Inca times the whole river was called the Willcamayu. Today it is usually called the Vilcanota upstream of Pisac or Huambutío, and the Urubamba lower down, but there is no precise point where the name changes.)

Today when people speak of the Sacred Valley they are generally referring to the stretch between Pisac and Ollantaytambo, a broad and gently sloping river plain 500-600m. lower than Cusco. This valley was undoubtedly a key area of settlement to the Incas; its combination of agreeable climate and fertile plains bestow an unusual abundance for the high Andes. Here the Incas sculpted the mountain flanks with vast contour terracing and irrigation works, also channeling the main river between stone walls, which today have largely disappeared.

Today this is still a bounteous agricultural region supplying the city of Cusco with much of its table fare, particularly fruit, vegetables and corn. The white corn of the Sacred Valley, with its huge, fat kernels, is a major export crop of the region—popular in Japan as a toasted snack, for example—and it is said that nowhere else, in Peru or the rest of the world, does this variety of corn grow to such size and quality.

The Incas were attracted not only to agricultural wealth, but also to natural beauty, placing ceremonial sites and royal estates—such as Pisac and Machu Picchu—in the most dramatically scenic locations imaginable. The Sacred Valley is a corridor through one of the most glorious mountain landscapes in the world, its lush green floor walled in to the north by the dark granite crags and gleaming snow peaks of the Urubamba range, to the south by a more arid, rolling mosaic of russet earth and yellowed grassland, which is interrupted by verdant ravines and stretches of soaring, red cliffs that tower five or six hundred meters above the wandering ribbon of the Urubamba river.

The Valley, as it is known simply in Cusco, also was, and still is, the route to the forest regions to the east, and therefore an area with access to the fruits and plants of the tropical lowlands, which the Inca nobles were privileged to consume (most importantly the coca leaf, vital to rituals, festivals and daily pleasure). And during the formative period of the Inca state it was probably a strategic buffer region, protecting Cusco from the incursions of the Antis, the fierce jungle tribes who raided the highlands from time to time.

Being at a lower altitude than Cusco, the Valley is a warmer and less physiologically stressful environment for the visitor. It is also very convenient for visiting many of the best-known attractions of the Cusco region, including Machu Picchu. Pisac is only 45 minutes from Cusco by paved highway, and Urubamba is about 1 1/4 hrs. Since local transport and hotel services have improved greatly, some people now choose to base themselves in the Sacred Valley during their visit to the Cusco region.

Pisac is usually taken as the starting point of visits to the Valley, because this is where the main road from Cusco crosses the Vilcanota (downstream, the Urubamba) river. There are, however, a few points upstream worth seeing as well. To include this part of the Valley in your visit, take the road east-southeast from Cusco *(see Chapter Seven)* along the Huatanay valley and turn left to double back northwest down the Valley at Huambutío. (River rafting is popular here, and it makes a very pleasant and easy half-day trip in the dry season—*see General Information, p. 31).* This route to Pisac adds about 25 km. to the journey, and for reasons of time is best left out if you are planning to visit Pisac, Ollantaytambo and points between in a single day.

The journey from Huambutío downriver takes you through an impressive gorge of red sandstone cliffs, hung with long beards of Spanish moss. The road is a windy lane (being widened and paved as this edition goes to press), following the Vilcanota River—a beautiful drive. About 20 km. downstream you come to Huanca. High on the mountain to your left is the shrine which once a year, on Sept. 14th, becomes the scene of an enormous pilgrimage for thousands of believers in the miracle of "El Señor de Huanca" *(see Calendar, p. 46).*

At Pisac the road crosses the river, the valley widens, and you reach the point from which most tours begin.

See *Provincial Towns (p. 36)* for services, hotels, transport etc.

PISAC

The direct route from Cusco—33 km.—is the road that winds over the mountains north of Cusco, past Sacsaywaman and the other three ruins described in Chapter Two. Beyond Tambomachay it crosses a pass and drops down into a broad basin, passing through the village of Corao, where there is a small handcraft market. Beyond Corao the road skirts some abrupt plunges and offers magnificent views as it winds down into the Valley. Far below you to the left as you enter the Valley lies the village of Taray; lower down you get a superb view of the modern village of Pisac, and the majestic ruins and terraces on the mountain spur high above it.

The Inca terracing systems were used mainly for the cultivation of maize, considered a prestige crop, and at sacred sites grown for the preparation of the *chicha* used in ritual libations. Maize has a long growing season, which in the highlands must be shortened as much as possible by irrigation, to protect the crop from frosts. Other Inca staples—potatoes and quinoa—were grown successfully without irrigation, and at higher elevations.

Notice the arrow-straightness of the Urubamba river below you, in contrast to the disorderly meanders farther downstream. The Incas walled in the entire river to conserve agricultural land, and this part of the work has survived—3.3 km. of it, the largest pre-Columbian canal in the Americas.

Modern Pisac is a picturesque Andean village, typical except for the huge, spreading *pisonay* trees that dominate the central square. (But the lovely *pisonays* of the Urubamba valley, including these ones, are being choked to death by an overgrowth of epiphytes.) The village is best known for its Sunday Market (now also held on Tuesday & Thursday), which draws hundreds of tourists each week. In spite of its popularity the market retains some of its local character, at least in the part where villagers from miles around gather to barter and sell their produce. The tourist section is a mixed bag of handcrafts—the same things you see in Cusco, but sometimes at lower prices. Pisac has a sizeable cottage ceramic industry. Pots, mugs, ashtrays and beads etc. are quite cheap.

One of the attractive features of the Sunday market is the colorfulness of the local people: different dress from different areas, and all in Sunday best. After Mass—usually at around 11 am—the mayors from the local villages leave church in procession, dressed in their best ponchos and mushroom-shaped hats, and carrying silver-embossed staffs of office. Their attendants blow prolonged blasts on conch shells to clear a way through the crowd.

Worth visiting is the old bakery on Calle Mariscal Castilla, just off the main square, with its huge adobe oven. The bread is excellent.

The *Ruins of Pisac* cling to a mountain spur, a condor's nest of a place far above the Valley. If the name "Pisac" ever had a specific meaning it has since been lost. However P'isaca, the name of one sector of these ruins, refers to a kind of Andean partridge. Pisac ruins are filled with wonderful examples of Inca stonework and construction, set in a stupendous location. The complex seems to feature some example of almost everything the Incas did in terms of architecture, defense, religion, agriculture, roads and residential construction. Altogether, it is one of the most spectacular Inca sites in the Cusco region. For those who are fit and like to exert themselves, it is well worth the effort of scrambling and climbing up the west flank of the mountain to reach them from Pisac village. For softer adventurers, an equally impressive way to see them is to take the road from the village which loops up the Chongo valley, east of the ruins, to within about a kilometer of the Intiwatana temple sector. The highway is used almost exclusively by tour buses, but taxis and combis to the ruins are often available for hire by the Pisac bridge. An advantage of this option is that you can hike into the ruins along a spectacular Inca pathway, through gateways and tunnels, experiencing as you walk a crescendo of stunning views of the Valley and Mount Pachatusan, to the south, beyond the river. Entrance to ruins is by T.T.

Pisac confronts archaeologists with an enigma almost as baffling as Machu Picchu. It is the largest fortress-city-temple complex of the Incas, and one of the largest of ancient America. And yet the early chroniclers mention no word of it. The Spanish knew of its existence, of course; the ruins are visible for miles around. In spite of its awe-inspiring natural defenses, the Incas made no stand here against the

Spaniards. During Manco's rebellion the Inca made his headquarters at Calca, some 18 km. down the Valley, and later retreated to the terrifying fortifications of Ollantaytambo, even farther away from Cusco. Perhaps he felt that Pisac was uncomfortably close to Pizarro's cavalry in Cusco; that the gentler northeast flank might give way under a Spanish cavalry attack; or that a wide encircling movement to seize both Paucartambo and the Valley itself would leave him hopelessly bottled up in Pisac, with no escape route.

It is possible to interpret Inca Pisac as a classic *pucara*—a huge defended area into which the population of a wide area could retreat in times of military threat. The redoubt was layered with agricultural terraces which served the dual purpose of feeding the city and ringing it with perilous defensive walls. Several springs secured the *pucara's* water supply, so the defenders could endure a siege indefinitely.

However, the construction of Pisac has been attributed to the ubiquitous Inca Pachacuteq, whose "royal estate" it was, and this may place it in a different category altogether—a more enigmatic one, since little is know about the role of Inca royal estates. With all its high-status temple architecture, the elaborate visual design of the approaches and surroundings, and its ritual use of water, Pisac can easily be interpreted as essentially a ceremonial center, like Machu Picchu.

A synthesis of these two possibilities is probably closest to the truth: that Pisac started out as a border stronghold controlling the approaches to Cusco from the eastern lowlands during the formative period of the Inca state, and that later, under Pachacuteq, it acquired its ceremonial and administrative dimensions. Most of the Inca structures we can see there today were those built by Pachacuteq during the imperial Inca period, including most of the superb ceremonial structures, which rank among the finest Inca architecture in existence.

Visiting the ruins (see map, p. 124)

On Foot: Take the footpath which leaves directly from the village square and climbs through steep terracing. Partway up the terraces the footpath forks. The left path takes you up the (relatively) gradual slope of the Quitamayo (Risky River; a possible reference to the climb, which would be risky indeed if hostile Inca troops were hurling boulders down from the cliffs above); it bypasses the southern sector of the ruins and leads you straight up to the temple sector. The righthand trail makes a very steep ascent through the defensive terracing of Huimin. One way to visit on foot is to climb via the Quitamayo to the temples (1-2 hours), then descend through Huimin on the southern tip of the spur.

By Road: There are two main pathways one can take to reach the Intiwatana sector. Both are clearly visible from the roadhead for part of their ways. It is possible to take either of these routes and return to Pisac village on foot *(see South of Intiwatana, below)*, thus obviating the need for and expense of having your transport wait for you.

The *upper pathway* requires fitness and a reasonable head for heights. It begins at the northeast sector of the ruins—to take this path, have your transport deliver you to the end of the highway turn-off at Qanchisracay, the highest part of the ruins *(see map, following page)*. A good option is to take this trail, and return to the road via one of the lower trails *(see below)*, sending your driver on down to wait for you at the lower car park.

After a short walk from the roadhead to the ruins sector of Qanchisracay, you come to a platform with a superb view onto the magnificent agricultural terraces and the Urubamba valley below. Follow the trail that begins here, traversing the mountainside to your right. You can see the Inca road ahead of you as it curves around to your left (south), rising and falling along the heights near the top of Pisac's mountain spur. It is a well preserved Inca road that, in the space of a kilometer or less, gives you a full taste of what the Inca Artist-engineer could accomplish. It has a massive gateway, steep stone stairways, sections where the path exists only by virtue of an artful stone buttress built into a sheer rock face, and a tunnel made by enlarging a natural fissure where the cliff overhangs the vertical, and even the Incas could not extend the trail. Finally this path emerges onto a steep crag with a

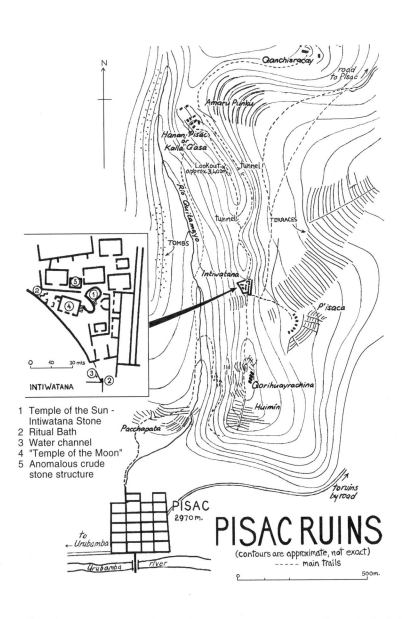

N

Qanchisracay

road to Pisac

Amaru Punku

Hanan Pisac or Kalla Q'asa

Lookout approx. 3,400m.

tunnel

Río Quitamayo

tunnel

TERRACES

TOMBS

Intiwatana

P'isaca

INTIWATANA

1 Temple of the Sun –
  Intiwatana Stone
2 Ritual Bath
3 Water channel
4 "Temple of the Moon"
5 Anomalous crude
  stone structure

Qorihuayrachina

Huimín

Pacchapata

0   40
     20 mts

to ruins
by road

PISAC
2970 m.

to
Urubamba

Urubamba   river

PISAC RUINS

(contours are approximate, not exact)
----- main trails

0   500m.

fine view over the temple complex of the Intiwatana.

The *lower pathways* require some fitness, too, but these routes are almost risk-free. Have your transport take you to the small parking lot at the road's end, some 100 vertical meters below Qanchisracay. Two converging trails lead toward the ruins and the Intiwatana. If you intend to return this way, take the higher one, and return on the lower one. You descend a stairway and then follow the eastern slopes of the mountain, climbing gradually. On the way it passes two defensive gateways, characterized by a double bar-and-niche arrangement at the rear of the door-jambs. This was apparently a system for securing the door-piece (separate, not attached by hinges) by means of a lateral rope, or bar.

The great expanse of terracing below you—still partially cultivated today—perhaps enabled the city to feed itself, or may have been dedicated to the production of maize specially for the making of chicha for ritual use, or for sacrifice. The path turns steeply uphill as you reach the sector known as *P'isaca* (Tinamou, a kind of Andean partridge). This cluster of buildings is thought to have been the home of the ruling elite, because of its proximity to the temple, and the quality of its constructions.

Just above P'isaca stands a small ritual bath, which lies at the bottom of a long water-chute leading down from the principal bath in the ceremonial area of Intiwatana. The P'isaca sector has suffered some very questionable reconstruction work, which is immediately obvious to even the least practiced eye.

Intiwatana.. Whichever route you choose to take on the ascent, you will emerge at the temple sector of *Intiwatana* (Hitching Post of the Sun), noted for and named after the large rock topped with a small stone pillar (1), a great carving of many parts and elements. Here you find the finest stonework of the ruins, and some of the finest Inca masonry in existence, comparable to the enclosures of the Qoricancha *(see Chapter One, p. 78)*, but well preserved and much closer to its original appearance. It was an astronomical observatory, like all Inca temples.

Points of interest are a liturgical bath (2) at the south end of the complex, with descending steps, and what seem to be carved hand-holds for hauling oneself in and out. The bath is fed by a water channel (3), easily traced past the four carved waterfalls (characteristic of Inca structures, and often referred to as "fountains") to the west face of the spur, where it can be seen cut into the side of a vertiginous cliff face. The building next to the Sun Temple is thought to have been the Temple of the Moon (4) because of its important location. One rough little building at the center of the complex (5) offers an interesting contrast in stonework. It is the only structure whose door faces north; the others face south or west. Perhaps this crude room was for servants, unfit to witness holy proceedings. Another suggestion is that this was an earlier sanctuary that was left intact when the later, more imposing temple was built.

South of Intiwatana: A trail leads over the jagged spine of the ridge, a steep but interesting route back to Pisac village through the fortified district of Coriwayrachina (Gold Sifter). Here you find towers for observation and/or communication, and, below, a series of impossibly steep terraces, perhaps erected for defensive purposes. On the east flank of the spur here you can see a string of six identical structures that served as community storehouses, another feature of Inca city planning.

North of Intiwatana: A staircase path leads up the mountain spur. It forks after about 100 paces. Take the lefthand path, and after another 100 paces you come to a small area of fallen structures where the ancients carved a wide throne; hence its name, *Tianayoq* (Throne-having).

A trail leads up from the Intiwatana sector and then traverses the east flank of the mountain. After about 300m the trail returns to the top of the ridge. The spur rises steeply in front of you. There is a tower perched on a tall rock at right, and a platform with another building stands around the cliff to the left. From here the main trail climbs a steep stairway to the right, and as you ascend it you meet a set of worn steps—quite hard to see—that climb straight up the spur. This is a steep and rocky climb which leads through a tunnel to the very summit of the ridge.

The main trail is wider and easier to follow. (This is the *upper pathway* described above, but in the opposite direction.) Both trails bring you out to *Kalla Q'asa* (Parrot Pass; perhaps named for the daily migrations of parrots from the jungle, across the ranges to the northeast; they cross these passes at dawn, returning at dusk). This was the most heavily fortified sector of Pisac, since its access was the easiest. The remains of great encircling walls can be seen.

As you take either of these trails, notice how the Incas wrapped the mountain flanks above you in stone cladding laid so artfully and sinuously that it is hard to tell where nature ends and culture begins.

The western pathway. Another route back to to Kalla Q'asa from Intiwatana involves retracing your steps and descending the western flank of the mountain from the Intiwatana. It is possible to follow a rough path upstream, parallel to and just below the aqueduct that once fed the ritual baths. In places this aqueduct was cut into a sheer face, and at one point it flows along a stone buttress with two breaks in it which must have been spanned by hollowed-out log sections. Just beyond this point the aqueduct crossed the Quitamayo canyon, presumably by means of another log section. A gracefully rounded and perfectly preserved buttress which once supported this bridge stands there on the far side of the river. Continuing along this path you will come to Kalla Q'asa, where excavations have revealed a chain of ritual baths.

The cliffs opposite the spur of Pisac, across the Quitamayo gorge, constitute the largest Inca cemetery known to archaeology. Bodies were walled up into the faulted caves of this sheer face with adobe and stone. The cliffs are now pockmarked with hundreds of holes where daring grave robbers plundered the tombs. Every grave has been looted, and yet the site has never been excavated for scholarly purposes. Perhaps mountaineering skill and nerve are more common among thieves than archaeologists.

A Soft Adventure
*Taray to Coya, Lamay, Calca or Wayllabamba,
along the south bank of the Urubamba.*

An old, unpaved road leads downstream along the tranquil south (left) bank of the Urubamba. It winds along the base of the mountains, passing crumbling colonial haciendas and picturesque villages, allowing serene views of the astonishing mountain scenery, and carrying little traffic. It is also fairly flat, in contrast to most Andean trails, so it makes an excellent walking or bicycling route (see *General Information, p. 33,* for bicycle rentals) for the leisurely visitor who likes to amble and enjoy.

Another advantage is that there are several bridges across the Urubamba along the way (at Coya, Lamay, Calca and Wayllabamba), which give quick access to the main highway on the north bank, so you can make your trip as long or as short as you want. A bus in either direction can be picked up quickly during daylight hours (flag them down anywhere), or one could rent a taxi or minibus with driver, and have them wait at an appointed bridge to pick you up. If you are staying at one of the main hotels in the Sacred Valley the staff can arrange this for you, and among several people this can be quite cheap.

Don't expect to find food or lodging on this trail.

How To Do It

As you arrive in Pisac coming from Cusco, take the unpaved motor road leading to the left just before the road bridge over the Urubamba. You pass first through Taray, about 1 1/2 km. from Pisac. About 8 kms further downstream the village of Coya stands on the main highway, across the river to your right, and here is the first footbridge. Going just this far makes for an easy half-day walk, or a short bike ride.

The next footbridge is at Lamay, about four kilometers walking distance downstream. Shortly after Coya, you reach the very pretty Andean village of Macay. The road divides, one branch descending to the right and skirting the village along the flats near the river, the other continuing along the base of the mountains until it reaches the narrow, high-walled and labyrinthine footpaths leading through the village itself. Take either route, but don't take the road leading up the mountain slopes to your left, just before Macay.

If you choose not to cross the river at Lamay, the next bridge is about 7 km. distant, at Calca—a level walk beneath towering red cliffs with the snow peaks of Pitusiray and Sawasiray up ahead.

Calca to Wayllabamba is a pleasant hike or rugged bike ride (since most of this route is not a motor road), that eventually takes you past the rapids of Huarán and through the village of Urquillos, ending up in Wayllabamba, where there is a road bridge. But this hike is longer than the previous sections—at least 18 km. total—and finding the route is sometimes more difficult. Be careful about 2 km. beyond Calca, where a rising trail to the left should be avoided.

CALCA

Calca, 18 km. down the highway from Pisac, is the principal town in the Valley, though not from the visitor's point of view. The town's layout incorporates two main squares, a distinctly non-Spanish feature, which adheres to the town's original Inca layout. Manco Inca established his headquarters here during the great rebellion of 1536. Spanish cavalry seized the town with characteristic boldness at the beginning of the campaign, but abandoned it hastily when they learned that their rear, Cusco itself, was threatened with imminent attack. Later the town was captured again, this time by a column of Diego de Almagro's men, just back from a disastrous expedition to Chile. Manco's troops drove them out, and harassed them as they forded the Urubamba, but they joined up with their compatriots in Cusco, and subsequently pursued Manco all the way to his refuge in Vilcabamba.

The modern town has some lovely gardens and orchards and is pleasant to wander through, though there are no specific points of interest to visitors.

YUCAY

A further 19 km. beyond Calca on the main Valley highway brings you to this picturesque village—once again with two main squares, dominated by *pisonay* trees like those of Pisac. The squares resemble English village greens, and at Christmas time they become the scenes of an esoteric local festival that features masked dancers and characters similar to medieval mummers.

The surrounding lands were granted to the puppet Sapa Inca, Sayri Tupac (son of Manco II), after his emergence from Vilcabamba. The story goes that this captive Inca behaved ungraciously towards the Spaniards at the banquet marking the occasion of his land grant, pulling a thread from the tablecloth and declaring angrily that his estate in Yucay stood in proportion to the lands of his Inca forefathers as this one thread to the entire cloth. (Sayri Tupac did not survive long in Spanish-occupied Peru—dying in mysterious circumstances, possibly poisoned, a few years after leaving Vilcabamba). The remains of Sayri Tupac's palace can still be seen in one of the village squares, an interesting example of post-Conquest Incan architecture.

There are also remains of fine Inca masonry on the other side of the Plaza. Yucay was an important "royal estate" before the coming of Pizarro, and the agricultural terraces just behind the village to the north constitute one of the finest surviving Inca agricultural systems in the Cusco region—well-preserved, and still in use.

HUCHUY CUSCO

A One- or Two-Day Hike

Huchuy Cusco is a fascinating Inca site spread over several hectares of a small plateau commanding a magnificent view of the Urubamba valley, about 5 km. upstream from Calca, and 800m. above the valley floor. It is believed to have been the royal estate formerly known as Caquia Jaquijahuana. According to myth the Inca Viracocha built this settlement after conquering the previous inhabitants by setting fire to their town with a stone thrown from his golden sling. He later fled to this place from Cusco, when the invading Chancas threatened to overrun the Inca capital, around 1438. After the Conquest the Spaniards found the mummy said to be that of Inca Viracocha here.

The ruins are part stone, part adobe. There is a fine *kallanka*—the "great hall" type of building common at Inca royal and administrative settlements—some 40m long. This building looks onto a great esplanade buttressed by terracing, which might have been used for parades and games. There are signs of a post-Inca "transitional" occupation here, during which fine-dressed stones were used to build cruder houses in the Inca style. There's also a Spanish-style reservoir, partly built of fine Inca stones.

Note the use of horizontal wooden struts inside the corners of some buildings. These were previously thought to be an Inca anti-seismic construction technique, but they apparently don't serve this purpose, since the corners of Inca buildings are actually their strongest feature. The true purpose of these struts remains a mystery.

How to get there: On foot only. The shortest way is from Lamay, on the main Valley highway *(see map, p. 116)*, about 3 hours. A new footbridge across the Urubamba has been built at this village, and a new trail leads up to the ruins. Most of it is reasonably easy climbing, except for the last part, an extremely steep zig-zag up a narrow ravine. The total vertical gain is about 800m. Horses can sometimes be rented in Lamay to make this an easier day-trip.

There are two major hiking routes to Huchuy Cusco from the direction of Cusco. It is best to take two days, and camp at Huchuy Cusco; as one-day hikes, these are strenuous and leave little time for viewing the ruins. *Note:* it is best to have a compass to follow these routes. For both routes, refer to the map on opposite page.

ROUTE ONE

Starting near Cusco, this is a beautiful hike through open country with spectacular views. It's about 24 km./15 miles (max. elevation: 4300m/14,100 ft.) to Huchuy Cusco, plus another 3 km./2 miles down to Lamay. You can reach the ruins in one long hard day, or in an easy day and a half with an overnight camp. But there's little water on the plateau north of Cusco, so if you camp along the way, expect a side trip to collect it. Huchuy Cusco itself has fine, well-watered campsites.

The Walk: Start at the weirdly-named "X-zone," about 500m beyond Qenco on the Pisac highway (you can also start at Tambomachay; this is shorter, but the route is harder to find). A dirt road signposted Kusilluchayoq leads off to the right; you take the road almost opposite, leading to the left. Walk about 100m. On the right stand some farm buildings. Follow a footpath leading behind the buildings, to meet a rough track heading north, which curves around to the east as it tops a rise. Here you glimpse the Pisac highway to your right, again. The trail turns almost due north once more, and becomes the old Inca highway to Calca. Traces of it are visible.

After climbing gently for about 4.5 km. you come to a stone-lined Inca irrigation channel, which parallels the trail for about 800m. (You may also see traces of the old telephone line to Calca, replaced by microwaves, whose poles have now mainly been pulled up and put to other uses by the local campesinos.) Now you are ascending a steep, narrow valley, which forks at the top. Stay on the righthand side of the left fork to reach a pass at 4200m. Descend to your left around the head of a draw and climb, veering slightly northeast around a gentle summit, to a second pass at 4300m. Here you look

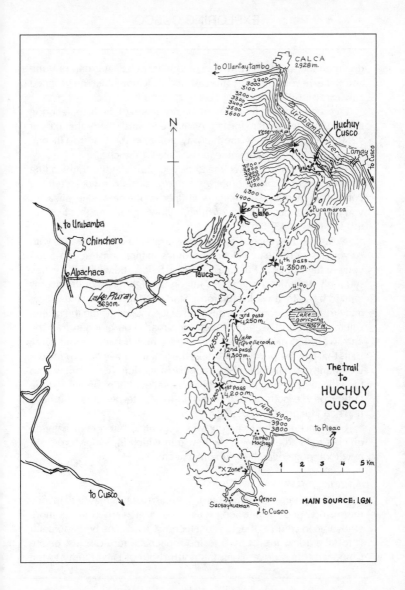

to Ollantaytambo
CALCA
2.928 m.

2900
3000
3100
3200
3300
3400
3500
3600

Urubamba river

Huchuy
Cusco

Reservoir

Lamay
to Cusco

3700
3800
3900
4000
4100
4200

4300
4400

N

Pucamarca

to Urubamba

Chinchero

lake

Alpachaca

Tauca

4th pass
4,360 m.

4100

Lake
gorricocha
4067 m.

Lake Piuray
3.690 m.

3rd pass
4,250 m.

4500

Lake
Quellacocha
2nd pass
4,300 m.

1st pass
4,200 m.

4400

altos 4000

3900
3800

to Pisac

Tambo
Machay

"X Zone"

0   1   2   3   4   5 Km.

MAIN SOURCE: I.G.N.

Qenco
Sacsayhuaman
to Cusco

to Cusco

The trail
to
HUCHUY
CUSCO

down on the small, shallow lake of Quellacocha. A group of stone corrals lies beyond the lake to the east, and in clear weather snowcapped Sawasiray (5600m) is visible 18 km. due north.

Descend the high trail around the north end of the lake, ignoring a fork which leads off to the left. Ascend eastwards to another pass at 4250m. This is roughly the halfway point on the way to Huchuy Cusco. Off to your right you can see Lake Qoricocha.

Cross the shallow draw ahead of you and take the trail leading northeast over the next ridge. As you cross this rise you see three conical adobe boundary markers grouped on the next ridge, ahead of you to the northeast. Head for them, following the trail that leads to this last pass at 4300m.

Now take the trail leading northeast down the valley ahead of you. As you descend, the trail clearly becomes an Inca construction. Soon you see the village of Pucamarca ahead. Below the village the valley suddenly becomes a ravine. A bluff on the right bank of the river is topped by an Inca-walled platform. Skirt the upper part of the village and cross this platform, then descend a steep stairway into the ravine. After a section of well-preserved Inca road, you emerge from the narrowest part of the ravine, crossing to the left bank. Avoid rising trails that can tempt you here—take the trail that traverses around the west flank of the mountain, and come to a startling vertical view onto the village of Lamay in the Urubamba valley, 800m below. A little farther on the path leads through an Inca gateway, and you have reached Huchuy Cusco.

Until recently the route out was via Calca, but now it is much quicker to head east down the new trail which ultimately crosses a new footbridge over the Urubamba at Lamay.

ROUTE TWO

This hike starts near Chinchero. You can reach Lamay, and thence return to Cusco, in one long day, if you start early, but it's more enjoyable to camp at the ruins of Huchuy Cusco. The best approach is to take a taxi from Cusco to the Alpachaca turn-off, just before Chinchero, then drive along the north shore of Lake Piuray to the trailhead at the village of Tauca. This will save two hours of tedious road walking (and, I repeat, it's a long day). Total walking time from Tauca to Lamay is about 5 hours, without including time for resting and exploring.

Just at the entrance to Tauca you see a narrow walled path which forks away from the road to the left. Start walking here. There is a big, jagged peak dead ahead, and the trail passes to the right of it, ascending a valley which heads northeast. Follow this valley to its end in a broad cirque, ringed by craggy peaks. The trail curves upward to the right (east), ascending to a pass on the east side of the cirque, which is marked by two prominent stone cairns. On clear days the view from this pass is stupendous, with the Qoyllur Rit'i and Vilcanota ranges, including Ausangate (6384m./20,940 ft.), visible more than 80 air km. away, to the E.S.E. It takes about 2 hours to reach this point from Tauca.

From this pass the trail traverses away to the left (north), following the contours, with a small lake far below to the right. After about half an hour you reach another pass, with superb views of Illawaman (a.k.a. San Juan or Chicón—5530m./18,140 ft.) and Siriwani (5400m./17,712 ft.), a mountain whose view is generally blocked by Illawaman from the more accessible points around Cusco.

Cross this pass and descend into the broad basin below, continuing down as it narrows into a ravine. At this writing the trail is fairly choked with vegetation, but passable. The trail crosses a stream and descends on the left bank. Stay near the stream and you will not get lost. After about 45 minutes you come to Inca terraces and, lower down, straddling the stream, a ruin which was once the gateway to Huchuy Cusco.

It takes about 45 more minutes to reach Huchuy Cusco from this point. The ravine widens and deepens dramatically just after these ruins. The trail crosses to the right bank, but only briefly. As you return to the left bank, stay more or less level, avoiding trails that climb steeply to the left. (Be careful here, it is easy to get lost). You arrive at a small overgrown plateau and, looking over the edge of it, you see a truly stunning view: the ruins of Huchuy Cusco on another small plateau way below, and beyond them the Sacred Valley and the village of Lamay, about 1000 vertical meters below you.

Here the trail doubles back to the right, and zig-zags down the side of the gorge, finally crossing the stream again before reaching Huchuy Cusco. Take what time you can to enjoy these ruins and their stupendous location. It takes about 1 1/2 more hours to reach Lamay. The trail (very steep in places) can be picked up by descending from the ruins diagonally to the right.

URUBAMBA

Three km. beyond Yucay. This attractive town lies at the center of the Valley, where the road from Cusco descending from Chinchero crosses the Urubamba river. It makes a good base from which to explore the area for those with time to spend a night or two in the Valley.

The center of Urubamba is pleasant to wander around in. Notice the town's coat-of-arms on the wall of the town hall. It bears a puma, two wriggling snakes, two *pisonay* trees, and the royal fringe of the Inca. Its only non-indigenous motif is the double-headed eagle of Spain. On the western outskirts of the town you will find a magnificent avenue, lined with towering *pisonays*. They bloom in colors of flame and scarlet in spring-time—around September/October.

OLLANTAYTAMBO

21 km. from Urubamba, 2800m elevation. The road follows the north bank of the river. On the south bank you see the railway halt of Pachar, where the rail route from Cusco joins the Urubamba valley. Past this point, both sides of the valley are increasingly lined with Inca terracing, part of the Ollantaytambo settlement, and there are the remains of two strategic fortifications, located at narrow choke-points between mountain and riverbank, on each side of the Urubamba. During the Spanish assault against Manco Inca's forces at Ollantaytambo in 1537, the Spanish noted that they were obliged to ford the river twice to avoid these obstacles.

Ollantaytambo is said to be named for a local chieftain—Ollantay—who had a forbidden love for one of the daughters of his sovereign, the Inca Pachacuteq. Ollantay rebelled and was crushed, and his story passed into Inca legend, then later became the subject of a popular 17th-century Spanish play which is performed occasionally to this day. According to John Hemming (in *Monuments of the Incas*) the "tambo" of the name refers not to the usual lodge or resting place, but to the tribe which inhabited this area before the Incas imposed themselves.

Historical records say that the entire Inca site of Ollantaytambo was a "royal estate" of the Inca Pachacuteq, which would account for the fine stonework to be seen everywhere, and the quality, abundance and scale of the ceremonial architecture.

The town stands at a strategic spot, the northwestern end of the gentle Sacred Valley, where the river begins to plunge steeply toward the Amazon and the Valley gradually narrows to a gorge. In previous editions I wrote that Ollantaytambo defended Cusco against incursions by the jungle tribes to the north-west, and protected the critical pass above Pachar, leading up the Huarocondo ravine and across the Pampa de Anta, directly to Cusco. However, J.P. Protzen, the man who has done much to enlighten us in the matter of Inca stonework, proposes another theory in his detailed study of Inca Ollantaytambo *(see Bibliography, p. 260)*. He observes that the principal defenses are laid out on the *eastern* outskirts of the settlement, which implies that the main threat lay from the direction of Cusco. Interesting. He suggests that these defenses were built during Manco Inca's occupation of the town during the Inca rebellion of 1536, but after the fall of Sacsaywaman in May of that year. More on this later.

The town

One of the most interesting aspects of the modern town is its street plan. It is the only Inca settlement still inhabited in Peru that has survived pretty much as the Incas laid it out hundreds of years ago, with many people still living in Inca buildings. Seen from above, the settlement is laid out in a form often used by the Incas, a trapezoid. The central area bordering the main square forms the wide base-line, and the streets narrow away uphill. Each block was a pair of *canchas*, self-contained enclosures housing many people, each with just one exit to the street. Some of the Inca names of the blocks survive. To get the best idea of how the town must have looked in Inca times, walk along the west wall of the town, just above the river Patacancha. This street is bounded by the rear walls of several long *canchas*, with narrow streets between them leading onto the central thoroughfare of the town.

Following the main street eastward out of the principal square leads you out of the village along a road known as the "Avenue of the 100 Windows," named for the niches (actually 72, by my count) along the wall. The street is a post-Conquest construction built over the site of a huge barrack-like structure whose long wall is all that remains.

The ruins

Just across the Patacancha from the town lies a great open yard known as *Mañaraki*, beyond which a ruined gateway gives onto the towering terraces and defensive walls of the main ruins, the impressive temple structure of Ollantaytambo. The terraces are known as *Pumatallis*, while the main complex above them is known simply but misleadingly as the Fortress. As with Sacsaywaman, this name has stuck to the place because a battle with the Spaniards was fought here, but in fact the structures seem to be principally ceremonial in character.

The battle took place at Ollantaytambo during Manco Inca's rebellion in 1537. The siege of Cusco had dragged on, despite the fall of Sacsaywaman, and Hernando Pizarro decided on a bold stroke to break the stalemate—to kill or capture the Inca himself, thus ending resistance as effectively as the Spanish had, in seizing and executing Atawallpa four years earlier in Cajamarca. Manco was quartered with most of his army at Ollantaytambo, having abandoned the more vulnerable base of Calca. Pizarro marched "with 70 horse and 30 foot, and a large contingent of native auxiliaries." Evidently the Spanish knew nothing of the layout at Ollantaytambo, presumably never having visited it despite 2 1/2 years of occupation at Cusco, for Pedro Pizarro later wrote, "we found it so well fortified that it was a thing of horror..."

The Spaniards arrived before dawn, stealing up to the main gateway below the eastern terraces in hopes of catching the garrison asleep. "But thousands of eyes were upon them, and as the Spaniards came within bow-shot a multitude of dark forms rose suddenly above the rampart, while the Inca...was seen on horseback in the enclosure directing the operations of his troops." (Prescott, *The Conquest of Peru*)

The Spaniards were shocked by the violence of Manco's resistance. Squads of archers from the jungle wreaked havoc among the cavalry beneath the walls; boulders, javelins and slingshots added to the destruction, and the Spanish were forced to retreat. Manco had a further unpleasant surprise for Pizarro's men. Diverting the river Patacancha through prepared channels, he inundated the plains below the fortress, swamping the Spanish cavalry in mud and water up to the horses' bellies. In neutralizing the Spaniards' most terrifying and unanswerable weapon—the horse—Manco nearly succeeded in trapping and massacring this expedition, but the Spaniards fought their way to the river and forced a crossing, then battled their way back to Cusco.

J.P. Protzen suggests that in fact this action was fought about a kilometer east of Mañaraki, below the terraces which face the modern visitor who drives into Ollantaytambo from the direction of Urubamba. Several eyewitness accounts of the battle match the site perfectly. The defenses from that direction are indeed formidable. The Spanish would first have had to take two Inca outposts which fronted the Urubamba river at places where only a narrow gap remained between the river and the cliffs—either that, or ford the Urubamba (which, according to the historical accounts, is what they did). Then they would have had to storm the great wall of eleven terraces that still stands today, to the right of the Inca bridge. In this scenario, the plain below these terraces is the one that was flooded by Manco Inca.

These powerful eastern defenses, which are hard to explain in terms of the Inca Tawantinsuyu period, may have been built by Manco Inca during his occupation of 1536-37. Unless, that is, they were built by the mythical chieftain, Ollantay, who is said to have rebelled against Pachacuteq.

When Diego de Almagro's expedition returned from Chile in 1537, the balance of arms was tipped overwhelmingly against the rebel Inca. An expedition of 300 cavalry was dispatched against Ollantaytambo, and Manco, seeing that the odds were now hopeless, abandoned the fortress and retreated to his historic last stand in the mountainous fastness of Vilcabamba.

Ollantaytambo appears in the history books one last time before it vanishes into the long night of the colonial era. In 1539 Spanish troops returning from an expedition against Vilcabamba were billeted at Ollantaytambo. The campaign had been a qualified success; the Spaniards had not succeeded in capturing Manco Inca, but they had loot, and they had with them the captive Coya, Cura Ocllo, wife and sister of Manco Inca. Francisco Pizarro himself arrived on the scene, hoping to negotiate Manco's surrender. When Manco refused to negotiate Pizarro vented his anger on Cura Ocllo. She was stripped naked, flogged and then killed with arrows. So that Manco should understand fully what had happened, Pizarro had her body tied to a raft and floated down the Urubamba to be discovered by the Inca's men downstream.

In the Ruins. (T.T.) Beyond the entrance yard of Mañaraki (1) you meet a steep climb of more than 200 steps through fortified terracing known as Pumatallis.

At the top of these stairs is an impressive double-jamb gateway, of singular and elegant design (2). This was apparently to have been the main entrance to the Sun Temple, but—like much of the Ollantaytambo complex—neither it nor the access stairway behind it were ever finished. The polygonal stonework around this gate and the terraces immediately below it display a feature unique to Ollantaytambo: a small lobe at the bottom of many stones projecting into the rising joint below it, which gives it a subtly fluid appearance, contrasting remarkably with the massive linearity of the nearby Sun Temple. The reason might have been structural; there is other evidence *(see below)* of an impulse to ensure that the vast blocks would stay in place and last for all eternity. Or perhaps the virtuoso masons were simply adding playful and aesthetically pleasing grace notes to the facade.

To the left of the gate stands the remains of a building known as the Temple of Ten Niches (3), a long structure, also of fine stonework, with the outer wall missing.

The best-known and most impressive part of the ruins is the huge unfinished structure faced by a wall of six enormous monoliths of rose colored rhyolite, above and to the left of the stairs. This structure is popularly called the "Temple of the Sun" (4). It is the best location at Ollantaytambo for observing the sun, although we do not know that the structure was intended for that purpose. It is unique among Inca structures in that the massive stones are straight-edged, with none of the deep beveling and polygonal jointing seen at other megalithic sites, and separated by narrow spacers made of smaller stones, fitted with the usual Inca perfection.

These huge stones were once faced with designs carved in relief. The step motif so common in Andean symbolism is clearly visible, as are the outlines of zoomorphic figues, perhaps pumas, now too defaced to be identified.

This sector is deeply puzzling to archaeologists. J.P. Protzen describes it as "...a very rough sketch of things to come. Yet the sketch is so provocative that it leaves one in suspense, trying to catch a glimpse of the splendor of the masterpiece that will never be." The six monoliths seem to have formed part of the stunningly perfect retaining wall of a great platform. But the other two sides display not stunning perfection but rough construction of recycled blocks, some of them laid on their sides instead of upright, widely spaced and filled in with

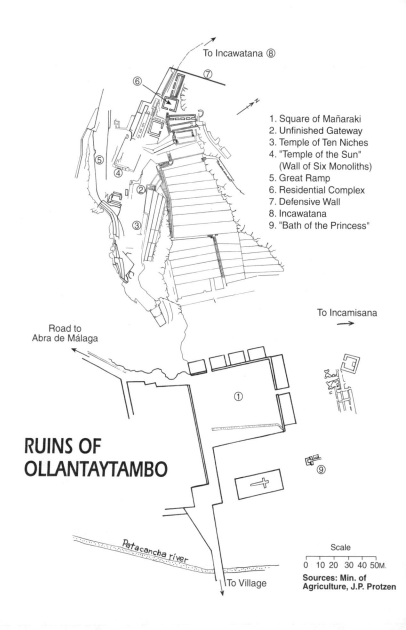

To Incawatana ⑧

⑦

⑥

⑤

④

②

③

1. Square of Mañaraki
2. Unfinished Gateway
3. Temple of Ten Niches
4. "Temple of the Sun"
   (Wall of Six Monoliths)
5. Great Ramp
6. Residential Complex
7. Defensive Wall
8. Incawatana
9. "Bath of the Princess"

To Incamisana

Road to
Abra de Málaga

①

RUINS OF
OLLANTAYTAMBO

⑨

Patacancha river

To Village

Scale

0 10 20 30 40 50M.

Sources: Min. of
Agriculture, J.P. Protzen

rubble—blocks that were originally intended for some other configuration.

Scattered around the plaza in front of the monoliths are stones standing on temporary platforms, finished stones with a brilliant polish on their inner faces, and stones with T-shaped grooves cut in one face— all testimony to the obsessive perfectionism of at least one phase of construction. The T-grooves would have been coupled with similar cuts on an adjoining block, then filled with molten bronze to key them firmly together—as if they weren't sturdy enough already. Some Inca structures wear both suspenders and a belt, as if the builders intended them to outlast the end of the universe. One theory goes that when the bronze contracted as it cooled, it pulled the two adjacent stones together, tightly closing any gap that remained between them. The technique is also observable in a few scattered stones at the Coricancha in Cusco, and is very much in evidence at the ancient pre-Inca ruin of Tiwanaku at Lake Titicaca. This has led some observers to propose a connection between these two sites, so very far apart in both time and geography. However, J.P. Protzen, who has studied both sites, says the two stonework styles are in general very different.

It appears that different phases of building and perhaps different architects succeeded each other. There are many other signs of remodelling and radical changes of plan at Ollantaytambo. Something happened to interrupt the whole project—perhaps the Inca civil war, perhaps the Spanish conquest, perhaps a rebellion of the inhabitants, as has also been suggested. Or perhaps it was simply the death of Pachacuteq, whose estate this was.

To the left of the six monoliths, on the south side of the plaza, stands the head of the great ramp (5) which was built for hauling blocks up to the site. From here you can look W.S.W. 3.5 air km. across the Urubamba valley to the source of the rhyolite blocks, the quarries of Cachicata, located in a great rockfall at the foot of *Yana Urco* (Black Mountain). Some 50 huge stones lie abandoned between the ruins and the quarries of *Cachicata*. This is an aspect of Ollantaytambo especially

Levers and Leapfrogging Ladders
A Theory of How They Moved the Stones

While working for a television documentary on Easter Island, intrepid architect and ancient mystery-cracker Vincent R. Lee came up with some new ideas as to how pre-industrial engineers moved huge stones into tight places. To test his theories, he built a 17m long, scaled-down replica of the ramp at Ollantaytambo, and then tried moving a thirteen-ton stone up it, rotating it 90 degrees at the top of the ramp. Using a combination of a sled, a ladder-type roadbed, and levers, he accomplished this feat successfully in two hours with a crew of only 26 people.

The assumption about ancient stone-moving techniques has generally been that the stones were placed on sleds, which were then hauled over log rollers by large teams of people pulling on ropes. In practice, however, rollers tend to slip out of alignment easily and are difficult to work with in field conditions. Moreover, this method could not have worked at the top of a steep ramp like the one at Ollantaytambo, where the ramp ended in a sheer 16 m. drop-off; there would have been nowhere for the hauling team to stand.

With enough people, almost anything can be dragged across open country. In fact, excavations near Ollantaytambo beneath an abandoned stone which never reached the construction site, revealed that over long distances the Incas probably dragged the stones over prepared cobblestone roadbeds by brute force, without using either rollers or sleds. The stones were rounded off on the underside, so they would not dig into the ground.

However, when working on steep slopes and in tight spots the amount of space available for the work crew is drastically reduced, and the problem then becomes how to apply force to the object you are trying to move. The Incas must have had an Archimedes somewhere in their history, because they appear to have understood that the way to do this was with levers.

Vincent Lee placed his trial stone on a sled, and levered it forward along a kind of ladder, which was greased with lard, and laid flat on

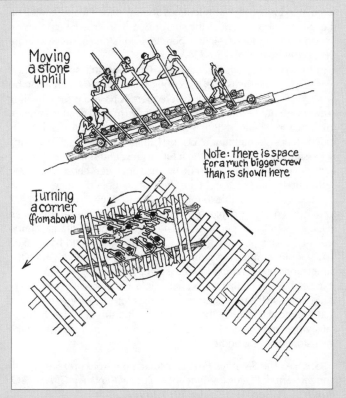

the ground as a roadbed. Sections of ladder were "leapfrogged," to make the roadbed continuous, and the "rungs" were used as points of leverage by people standing on the sled, or on top of the stone. The stone could be rotated, simply by levering forward on one side of the sled, and/or pulling back on the other. If the stone started to slide back downhill it could easily be stopped, using one or two of the levers as brakes.

The gain in mechanical advantage (ratio of exerted to applied force) was immense; Lee calculates about 1:3 for a man standing on the ground; 1:5 if he rides the sled; 1:7, 1:8 or more if he stands on the stone. The added weight of people on the stone or sled was more than offset by the increased leverage.

One of the details that leads Lee to suspect that such a method was used by the Incas was the configuration of the Ollantaytambo ramp itself. Right at the top, where there is no room for a hauling crew, one would expect the builders to have made a gentler gradient, to allow for the added difficulty of raising the stone. Instead, it gets much steeper, a daunting 25%, or 1 in 4. Lee reasons that, having necessarily dispensed with the hauling crew and shifted exclusively to the lever method at that point, the Inca engineers chose to get their stones up the last section in the shortest possible distance.

Lee's crew was able to move its 13-ton stone (plus about 1 1/2 tons of sled and people) up its own 25% incline—moving an average of 450 kilos per person! The largest stone at Ollantaytambo weighs 52 tons; following those calculations, it would have taken 101 people to move this stone up that ramp—a number which the dimensions of the ramp would easily have permitted.

Lee has shown that it is both possible and efficient to move very large stones in the described manner. Of course, this does not prove that the Incas *did* move them this way. But this is by far the most satisfying theory to date—the only one to cover all the bases of the Inca stone-moving riddle.

Source: The Sisyphus Project: Moving Big Rocks up Steep Hills and Into Small Places, by Vincent R. Lee, with Nancy G. Lee, P.O. Box 107, Wilson, Wyoming 83014;1998.

worthy of our admiration; the stones were dragged about 6 km. overland from these quarries. Somehow the Inca engineers maneuvered the blocks over the steep banks and across the surging current of the Urubamba river. Then they hauled them up the long ramp, the remains of which are most clearly seen from the fields between the ruins and the river. Near the bottom of this ramp, a few feet from the modern road, lie three so-called "tired stones"—huge masonry blocks on their way from the quarries which never reached their destination. They are partly finished, and one has marks showing clearly the Inca method of splitting stone

Above the temple is a complex of cruder buildings (6), apparently a residential complex, and beyond that, a massive outer wall (7) protecting the fort on the gentler west slope of the mountain. The wall and houses were built with far less care than the nearby temple, and may date from the later period of Manco's Inca's brief occupation. A path leads through its one gateway and up the mountain to a walled site (8)—not visible from the main ruins—which tradition calls variously *Incawatana* (Place of Tying up the Inca) or *Intiwatana*. This name is certainly recent, post-Conquest. There are four man-sized niches side by side, each with holes bored at about the right height for tying up the wrists of a seated man, hence the popular name. But it is mere racy speculation to suppose that the site was used in this way.

If they did tie people up here they certainly gave them a wonderful view. The niches face south through a narrowing of the Urubamba gorge known as *Wayrajpunku* (The Wind-Gate) to a magnificent sweep of Wakay Willka (a.k.a. Verónica) (5750m).

The floor of the Patacancha Valley below the ruins is worth exploring. Just off the entrance yard at the foot of the terraces, behind the church, is the *Baño de la Ñusta* (9), the so-called "Bath of the Princess," a fine example of Inca sculpture in bedrock—featuring the ubiquitous step-motif in three dimensions—and an adaptation of the environment to form a small waterfall, which was probably a place for ceremonial bathing.

Upstream from here along the left bank of the river the base of the cliffs has been tooled and scrolled with artful carving, much of it bedding work for walls which are no longer there, or were never actually built. About 300m along the cliffs stands a small site called *Incamisana* (a Quechua-Spanish hybrid word meaning Place of the Inca's Mass). It was clearly a shrine of some kind. There is a deep bath here, fed by a channel that has been cut into the rock of the cliff face. Extensive digging done throughout this area in 1981/82 has unearthed a series of baths, water channels and shrines cut into the rock.

The mountain that looms over the Patacancha on the opposite side of that valley is called Pinculluna (Mountain of Flutes). You can see a string of ruined buildings clinging to its steep slopes. Various interpretations of these buildings are bandied about: they are "a jail," "a school," and (surprise!) "Houses of the Virgins of the Sun." Closer inspection reveals that the buildings have no internal niches (always found in Inca housing), and no water supply. They are long and narrow with openings set high in the uphill wall and others low in the downhill wall. The late Ollantaytambo sage Robert Randall, demonstrated that the buildings were granaries. The upper openings were used to tip in the grain, the lower ones to remove it. Horizontally across the mountainside to the right are some smaller, square structures which were also storehouses, these ones of a dark, windowless design intended for potato storage. The inaccessible location high on a windy hill is logical, because the coolness and ventilation would help preserve the stored food. The yellowish tinge to the walls of these and other buildings at Ollantaytambo comes from a hard coating of sun-baked clay with which the walls were adorned.

Explorer's Note: the quarries of Cachicata are worth a visit for those curious about Inca technology, and make an excellent day-hike. They are located 700 to 900 meters above the valley floor, about 3.5 km. southwest of Ollantaytambo as the crow flies, and can only be reached on foot. Cross the river at the bridge upstream from Ollantaytambo village, and follow the foot trail downstream. It eventually climbs the mountainside to the quarries. The Inca access road to the quarries is fairly well preserved. There is also a slide that was used to shift the stone blocks down the mountainside to the river.

High on the mountainside three quarries lie within a radius of about 500m. Here the Incas took advantage of two huge rockfalls to supply themselves with loose stones of great size. Many partially worked,

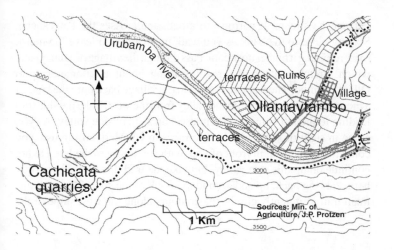

abandoned blocks can be seen, along with numerous *chullpas*—small burial towers. . At the west quarry, the highest of the three, there are some extraordinary "needles" cut from the fine-grained gray granite of that site: almost 7m long and only 40 by 40 cm in cross section, they bear no sign of tool marks. How they were extracted and what their purpose was remains a mystery.

Pumamarca

This is a small, nicely preserved Inca ruin, about 2 1/2 hours walk from Ollantaytambo up the Patacancha Valley. The high surrounding wall with its numerous zig-zags suggests a fort. But, as in the case of the Ollantaytambo ruins, all the food storage structures are located outside the walls. Does this make sense if the building was a fort? Puzzling. There is a nice kallanka-type building within the walls and the overall layout is classic Inca. The stonework is "pirca" style—uncut fieldstone set in adobe.

How to Get There: Follow the road leading northward along the western edge of Ollantaytambo village (not the ruins), parallel to the

Patacancha stream. It narrows to a path and crosses the Patacancha. Staying close to the bank as you walk upstream, you leave the motor road, rejoining it higher upstream. Pass through the village of Munaypata, which stretches along the road, starting about a kilometer from Ollantaytambo. The last two houses in the village back onto the base of a mountain spur that juts into the valley from the west. Take the side trail leading to the left behind these houses, up a small side valley. As you come in sight of some fine Inca terraces to your left, still in use, you come to a stone wall in front of you with a gateway to the left. Do not continue on up this side valley, but take the trail that turns sharp right here, curving back, up and around the flank of the spur. Stay with this main trail as it gently climbs the contours along the west slope of the

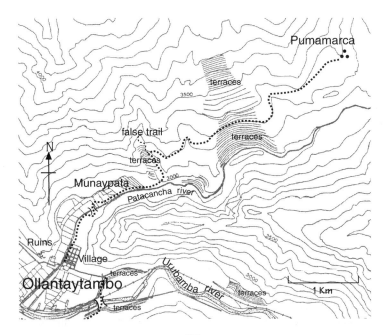

Patacancha Valley. You will pass through many hectares of well-preserved Inca terracing along the way, and as you come to a place where the steep hillside eases into a small sloping plateau you see Pumamarca atop the ridge to your left. This hike takes about five hours round trip, not counting time spent at the site.

Chapter Four

THE INCA TRAIL

A Hike Through the Incas' Lost Province

The whole of Peru was once criss-crossed with Inca and pre-Inca highways. They were paved with thick interlocking blocks of stone, and varied in quality and width. On the plains and rolling uplands they might be as much as six meters wide; in the mountains, less than a meter. Sometimes they followed the valleys, but just as often they traversed the high mountainsides, tracing impossible pathways and following narrow ledges above the bottomless gorges of the Andes. The trails were built for men on foot, and lightly-burdened llamas. Frequently their gradients gave way to stairways, tunnels and long zig-zag trajectories down steep faces.

Most of these highways were useless to the European invaders. Horses balked at the steps and got stuck in the tunnels. Carts and carriages could never pass. The roads of the coast and the valleys became colonial highways, which were allowed to deteriorate in a way the Incas would never have accepted, but kept in use. Many are roadways to this day. But the highland trails were abandoned to the natives, mostly to crumble and vanish over the centuries—even though many an Andean footpath quite suddenly becomes a staircase of huge, carefully-laid slabs, worn down by generations of mules and herders, but still solid, enduring.

One such trail followed the gorge of the Urubamba river. The main highway turned north out of the valley just downstream from Ollantaytambo, to cross the Panticalla pass leading to the jungle settlement of Amaybamba. Perhaps this was the only highway still in use by the time of the Conquest, for the Spaniards never discovered the

153

The Early Days

History tells us that the route known today as the Inca Trail was discovered by Hiram Bingham during his explorations of 1915. Today we are prone to believe that the trail, and the Urubamba gorge below it, had lain deserted, buried in forest, for the previous four centuries. We may also imagine that the names Machu Picchu, Wayna Picchu and so on were unknown to the rest of Peru until Bingham's discovery.

Not so. A church document of 1728 states that "over 900 souls inhabit the stretch of river between here and Guaynopicho [Wayna Picchu] who lack any form of spiritual administration." I have in my possession a copy of a map drawn about 30 years prior to Bingham's journey, by the explorer Antonio Raimondi. Clearly marked and in their correct position are the words "Cerro Machu Picchu." Bingham must have used this map in his explorations, and it is strange that he never acknowledged the importance of Raimondi's cartography to his work.

Did the Inca Trail itself lie abandoned during those long centuries? Again, no. Through the last century of colonial rule and the first of independence the area downriver from Machu Picchu became a center of great sugar and coca plantations. They distilled cane alcohol, on which taxes were levied as it moved along the official route to Cusco, via the Abra de Málaga. However, moonshiners evaded taxes by hauling illicit "trago" on muleback up the Aobamba (the valley you see below you from the ruins of Sayacmarca, which joins the Urubamba near the modern hydro-electric plant, just west of Machu Picchu), joining the Inca trail at the Pacamayo, between what we now call the 1st and 2nd passes. The heavily-laden and sharp-hoofed mules must have eroded the Inca road, which probably explains the complete absence of Inca paving stones from Km. 88 to the Pacamayo valley, and the good state of preservation thereafter (*the "Inca" paving on this first part of the trail is in fact recent construction, added since 1990 - Ed.*).

So it was only the section of the Inca Trail from the Pacamayo northeastward that remained mostly overgrown and unused. Pacamayo, aptly enough, means "hidden river." Even so, this trail was not unknown. According to Old Zavaleta, everything that has been discovered, along with much that outsiders have not yet discovered, was already known to the inhabitants of the region.

Old Zavaleta used to live on the south bank of the Urubamba at the point now known as Km. 88. Several generations of his family owned most of what is now the Machu Picchu Historical Sanctuary, until the Agrarian Reform of 1969. Even after losing most of his land he was a force to be reckoned with on the river. When he became fed up with all the gringos wandering across what was left of his land, he put an axe to the wooden bridge spanning the river. Later he replaced it with an *oroya*—a steel cable with pulley and metal basket—and charged a fee for using it. Many a hiker found himself dangling high above the river, engaged in a fierce but futile debate with an inebriated Zavaleta over the price of arrival on the south bank. On those days when he was too indisposed, or away from the homestead, there would be no *oroya* at all, for he kept it padlocked. A mass of hikers and porters would pile up on the banks of the sacred river, Waiting for the Man... After a lengthy legal battle the INC put an end to the problem by building the footbridge we use today.

While re-reading Hiram Bingham, let us remember that in his day walking the trail to shortly beyond Phuyupatamarca was a relatively easy task, but no one at that time managed to reach Machu Picchu. There were one or more tunnels on this section which had completely collapsed, and Bingham's men could not find their way around them. Eventually they completed this section by walking back from Machu Picchu, discovering Intipunku in the process.

-Alberto Miori

trail that continued on down the valley to a point where it is becoming a gorge and will soon be a canyon. The Incas built a string of settlements onward from here down the right bank of the Urubamba, and pushed secondary highways down both sides of the gorge far beyond Machu Picchu. But at the spot named *Qoriwayrachina* (Gold Sifter)—now better known as Kilometer 88—the main Inca highway crossed the river and turned southwest up the gentler valley of the *Cusichaca* (Bridge of Joy). This was the royal highway to Machu Picchu—the famous Inca Trail.

The route was rediscovered by Hiram Bingham in 1915 when he returned to Peru to make further studies and clear the ruins at Machu Picchu. His guides took him to other ruins to the south and east. He discovered traces of an ancient road linking the city to a string of lesser settlements in the direction of Cusco. The highway was traced and explored in more detail in 1942 by the Viking Expedition, sponsored by the Wenner Gren Foundation. Its leader, Paul Fejos, made important discoveries—most notably the stunning site of Wiñay Wayna—and published his conclusions in the United States.

By this time the trail had ceased to be the exclusive territory of archaeologists and scientists. A handful of rugged travelers each year were struggling along its 50 or so kilometers, a trail far more overgrown and difficult to follow then than it is today. And in the years since, the Inca Trail has become a celebrated and popular hike, known to backpackers all over the continent. There are thousands of Inca trails, but there is only one Inca Trail.

Why? Few relatively short hikes in the world can offer such variety of scenery, so many staggering views, such a mix of jungle and high sierra. Certainly no other walk known to man will lead you along an ancient highway from one secluded ruin to another, each in a breathtaking setting, each almost perfectly preserved, offering shelter, solitude and views that no pen or camera can ever adequately record. And of course, no other hike in the world ends with a climactic descent into Machu Picchu.

Walking this trail it is impossible to doubt that the entire experience was planned — there was nothing happenstance about the stunning combinations of scenic and man-made beauty. The Incas wanted those who walked this way to reel in awe as they crested the passes and rounded the corners. They designed the trail like a dramatic narrative, with a series of troughs, slow build-ups and climaxes, each greater than the last, until the stunning finale, when travelers look down from Intipunku upon Machu Picchu, shining on its stone isthmus between two great peaks, far above the Urubamba river.

The Inca Trail and Machu Picchu are rarely, if ever, considered in this light: as a complete work of art — perhaps because there is no work of art in our civilization on anything approaching this scale. And yet it can be argued that it *was* a work of art, rather like a gothic cathedral, with its intended purpose: to elevate the soul of the pilgrim on the way to Machu Picchu. In this author's view, the Inca Trail to Machu Picchu was a pilgrim's route; its destination, a sacred city.

Machu Picchu Historical Sanctuary

The Machu Picchu Historical Sanctuary was created by Presidential Decree in January of 1981, as an area of 32,592 hectares to form part of the National System of Conservation (now the National System of Natural Areas Protected by the State) under the administration of the Ministry of Agriculture, "in co-ordination with" (details unspecified) the Ministry of Education—referring to the National Institute of Culture (INC), which is responsible for the conservation of archaeological sites. After numerous bureaucratic changes in the ensuing years, the agency inside the Ministry of Agriculture now managing the Sanctuary is the National Institute of Natural Resources (INRENA). The founding decree declares the territory of the Sanctuary, in formal Spanish, to be "intangible," "imprescriptible," and "inalienable," meaning in essence that no part can be altered, sold or transferred.

In 1983, at Peru's request, it was designated by UNESCO as both a natural and cultural World Heritage site, one of only two such in the western hemisphere (the other is Tikal, in Guatemala).

Conserving the Inca Trail

The sites along the Trail have been some of the most valuable remaining for the study of Inca settlement patterns, land use and daily life, since, like Machu Picchu, they were never found by the Spanish. But since then, alas, they *have* been found by archaeologists—architects, more accurately—whose life's work is to restore, reconstruct and prettify everything they can get their hands on without even first allowing adequate study or recording of the things they are about to completely transform. In many cases the visible consequence of this Theme Park mentality is that partly-tumbled ruins, draped with mosses, lichens, orchids and bromeliads, are turned into sterile structures that appear to have been built yesterday—which, in a sense, they were.

In recent years use of the Inca Trail has swollen to flood proportions. Thousands of hikers now walk the trail each year, and this figure does not include the hordes of guides, cooks and porters who accompany the commercial groups. Littering and the rampant accumulation of trash has become a serious problem. Ruins have been damaged by hikers' campfires and by people who clamber thoughtlessly over their walls. Meanwhile the borders of the Protected Area are threatened by the encroachment of farmers who are clearing the forest at an alarming rate with slash-and-burn-agriculture, destroying wildlife habitat and killing animals that threaten their crops or livestock. In recent years, forest fires—some deliberately set by farmers, others started by careless hikers—have threatened ruins sites and become a dire threat to the environment.

The problems are not being ignored, but it has proven difficult to create a coherent administration policy for the park. The major problem has been that no fewer than ten government agencies have some form of jurisdiction or interest in the area (the INC, INRENA, COPESCO, ENAFER, ElectroSur the Regional Government, the Municipality of Aguas Calientes, the Ministries of Agriculture and Transportation, and MITINCI—see list of abbreviations for translations), and none of them has overall authority. However, the INC, being the sole beneficiary of the gate at Machu Picchu, and principal beneficiary of the Cusco tourist ticket, is the Godzilla of local insitutions, and acts more or less unilaterally. Getting all the agencies to act in accord has been akin to achieving a peace settlement in the Middle-East. Still, in late 1998, goaded by a UNESCO threat to place Machu Picchu on its list of endangered sites, the authorities adopted a Master Plan for the management of the park.

Recently the Finnish government negotiated a debt-swap worth more than six million dollars with Peruvian conservation authorities, intended to address the crisis-level conservation problems of the Machu Picchu Historical Sanctuary. This program is being watched with great interest by national and international agencies, as a possible model for future conservation action. If successul, it will have cut through one of the thorniest political thickets in Peru.

Park Rules: **Don't**: litter; fell trees; light open fires (camp stoves only, to protect the fragile forest); remove stones from or otherwise damage ruins; remove plants; kill animals. Camp only in designated campsites, never in the ruins. Remember, the Machu Picchu park is a sanctuary: for ruins, for wildlife, for trees and flowers—and for you. Please treat it that way.

Preparing to Walk the Trail

In fair weather, the trail can easily be walked by any reasonably fit person in three days. However, when you load onto that person a backpack, tent, stove, sleeping bag, food for three days, camera, clothes and a copy of *One Hundred Years of Solitude*... how fit is reasonable? There are some tough climbs and three passes above 3700m/12,000 ft. Porters are often available in Wayllabamba near the beginning of the trail *(see below)*, but unfortunately this cannot be relied upon. If in doubt, contract the services of a Cusco guiding company *(see Adventure Tours, p. 29);* the cheaper ones carry only the food, tents, and communal equipment, but if you pay a bit more they will carry everything, except you.

Quinoa: The Little Grain That Could...

Quinoa (*chenopodium quinoa*, pronounced KEEN-wa) is a species of pigweed which grows in the high Andes, resisting drought and frost, requiring little attention. Of the three staples (maize, potato and quinoa) that sustained Andean civilization it's the least known and consumed today. Yet it is by far the most nutritious. Today it's being hailed as the "miracle grain" and "the sacred food of the Incas," and people are beginning to consume it in the industrial nations. It contains about twice the protein of the usual grains, with an amino acid balance similar to that of milk—with none of the cholesterol. It is also high in unsaturated oils, calcium, iron, phosphorous, vitamin E and several B vitamins.

Until recently quinoa was a subsistence crop, grown in the highland communities of Peru, Bolivia and Ecuador, and ignored by urban consumers. It grows about 1.5 meters (5 feet) in height, and when ripe produces tiny seed in large clusters which turn deep red, purple or gold, according to variety. Nowadays the grain is processed into different forms: into flour (harina), flakes (hojuelas), and pearl (perladas), all available in Cusco grocery stores. The flour and flakes are particularly useful for camping trips. Try pancakes made from quinoa flour, or the flakes (can be mixed with oats or wheat to give it texture) for a hearty porridge that cooks fast.

Weather: The best months are May through September. April and October are transitional months, sometimes with fine weather; November through March, count on rain (be prepared anyway); January and February—yuk! At any season rain most often falls late in the day, so start early to make good time. Local lore holds that the best weather occurs in the last few days before full moon. In the author's experience this is indeed true.

Solar radiation is extremely powerful, due to the high altitude and the tropical latitude. Dehydration is a common problem; use plenty of sun-block, and drink plenty of liquids.

Quinoa Pancakes for Breakfast and Trail Food

Dry ingredients can mixed together ahead of time and stored in a plastic bag for the trail; then just add water, egg, fruit & oil.

For 10-12 medium pancakes:
1/2 cup quinoa flour (harina de quinoa tostada)
1/4 cup wheat flour (harina de trigo)
1/4 cup corn flour (harina de maíz)
1/2 cup dried milk powder (leche en polvo)
1/2 teaspoon baking powder (polvo de hornear)
1 tablespoon sugar [more for sweeter pancakes] (azúcar)
1 cup water (agua)
1 large egg (huevo grande)
1 tablespoon oil (aceite)
Chopped dried or fresh fruit and/or trail mix

Mix ingredients in the order given. Cook in a frying pan or griddle that has been oiled slightly. I have also added quinoa flakes or cornmeal to vary this no-fail recipe for nutritious and delicious breakfasts and trail lunches. I make double or triple the batter needed for breakfast, adding fruit for the breakfast pancakes, then adding trail mix or nuts to the rest which I cook for lunch or trail snacks.

- Carol Stewart

At any time of year there can be biting blackflies on certain stretches of the trail (particularly from Km. 88 past Wayllabamba).

Equipment: Keep it light. This is a rugged hike, with lots of steep climbing. The following items are essential:

Backpack	Complete change of tough clothing
Sleeping bag	Sweater and jacket; something warm
Ground pad	Towel
Tent	Broad-brim or peaked hat
Rainwear	Toilet paper

Knife	Collection of plastic bags
Flashlight	Sunglasses
Matches	Washkit
Water bottle	Insect repellent
Hiking boots	Sun block
	This book

Food: There is nothing available on the trail. Some people travel light by eating only cold food and leaving the stove behind. If you think you can manage on cold rations for up to four days (sometimes longer in very bad conditions), here are some items obtainable in Cusco worth taking:

Dried fruit (raisins, bananas, figs, prunes, apples)

Cheese

Chocolate

Dried meat (charqui)

Crackers

Brazil nuts (castañas)

Tinned sardines, tuna, corned beef, paté, frankfurters

Small pancakes make a good, not-too-bulky substitute for bread, and stay fresh longer; quinoa flour makes excellent, nourishing pancakes *(see recipe, preceding page)*

Salami, ham, etc.

Quince jelly—sold in a solid block; not runny

Hardboiled eggs

Note: A 35mm film cannister makes an excellent container for a shot of your favorite after-dinner liqueur. Tape the lid.

If you do plan to cook, definitely take a stove—fires are forbidden. Locally-sold pressure stoves are a bit heavy—lightweight camping stoves are best. You can rent one of these in Cusco, but remember to test it before taking it on the trail. Camping Gas cannisters are available in Cusco. If you have a white gas stove, you can buy white gas *(benzina)* in pharmacies or hardware stores *(ferreterías)*.

Nature on the Inca Trail

In the tropical Andes, altitude is biological destiny, and small changes in the former produce radical transformations in the latter. The Inca Trail starts in arid cactus-and-agave valley-floor habitat on the approaches to Km. 88, at 2,600m.; it ascends the farmed and lusher Cusichaca side valley, then climbs steeply through the enchanted *polylepis* woodlands of the humid Llullucha streambed, encountering a brief belt of Andean dwarf forest before flattening out onto the treeless *puna* grasslands of Llulluchapampa, at around 3,600m. Then, more climbing, through ever sparser vegetation, to the first pass, at 4,200m. On down to the Pacamayo valley, where there is a denser *polylepis* woodland, then, after more *puna* grassland and the second pass, the hiker reaches the rolling stretches of the trail that border the fringes of the high altitude cloud forest, at 3,400m.— a zone of nocturnal fogs, made temperate by increasing proximity to warm air rising from the Amazon lowlands. After Phuyupatamarca, the seemingly endless descent to Wiñay Wayna and then Machu Picchu takes you through ever-changing layers of cloud forest, finally reaching zones rich in tree ferns, in the last stretch before Intipunku.

Scientists have recorded 374 bird species in the Sanctuary (nearly 5% of all known species), most of which may be seen along the Inca Trail. Patallaqta, the Llullucha valley, and the stretch between Sayacmarca and Phuyupatamarca are particularly rich in bird life (though you have to *look* for them in the woods, and use binoculars— they do not usually fly in your face). The high altitude grasslands are excellent for viewing Andean raptors, like the Black-chested buzzard eagle, the mountain caracara and the aplomado falcon. Condors are rare, but sometimes seen.

Ground animals are rare, too, though white-tailed deer are not uncommon. The barrel-chested Andean deer (taruca), is much rarer. Vizcacha, the rabbit-sized Andean rodent, may sometimes be seen leaping around areas of jumbled rockfall—near the waterfalls in the upper Pacamayo, for example—while the jewel in the crown of wildlife sightings along the trail is the Andean bear—a highly-endangered cloud-forest species, whose continued survival in the Sanctuary is in doubt.

Plant *aficionados* will find bewildering variety—some 250 species of orchid have been identified in the Sanctuary, along with countless bromeliads, begonias, mosses, ferns, and others, too numerous to list. Orchid specialist Benjamín Collantes found 59 species of orchid, including ten new to the Sanctuary and three new to science, while simply walking along the banks of the Urubamba river from Km. 88 to Km. 104.

See Bibliography , p. 260, for field guides

If carrying a liquid fuel stove, fill the tank, and carry extra fuel in a plastic bottle; carry alcohol for priming, and wires for cleaning the jet. Now you can carry a more varied larder. In addition to the above:

Oatmeal	Noodles (rice takes too long to cook)
Quinoa and kiwicha flakes	Powdered milk
Cracked wheat	Tea, coffee, Milo, cocoa
Semolina (Semola, in spanish)	Sugar
Packet soups and cubes	Salt and pepper

First Aid Kit: Basic items include:
Antiseptic ointment or liquid
Bandage, cotton and gauze, safety pin
Band-aids
Aspirin, or stronger painkiller
Also useful:
Skin cream; cocoa butter, or lip-salve
Lomotil; Cipro (for stomach troubles)

Water: There is plenty of water, but do not drink it without either boiling it for at least ten minutes, treating it with disinfectant (e.g. iodine), or using a water-purifying pump.

Coca Leaves: An acquired taste, but good to have along on a high altitude trek *(see General Information, p. 14)*.

Doing It: Kilometer 88 to Machu Picchu

A *Trail Fee* is payable at Km. 88. Cost at this writing is US$17 or equivalent in soles. (This will change, so check in Cusco.) Paying in US$ gets you a slightly better rate. This fee includes the first day's entrance to Machu Picchu. Note, that if you arrive late at Machu Picchu and do not visit the ruins until next day, you can ask the ticket checkers not to stamp it, and use it next day. Even if you have used the ticket once, you can use it on subsequent days by paying half of the first day's fee.

Backpackers arriving at Machu Picchu will be steered by guards down a side trail that skirts the ruins, so that they can check in at the ticket gate. If you are late and do not plan to visit the ruins that day, make sure they do not stamp your Inca Trail ticket, so that you can use it to visit Machu Picchu for the first time next day.

The Inca Trail must be one of the loveliest walks in the world. Sadly, some hikers are disfiguring it with piles of tin cans, food wrappers, and worse. You have come all this way to escape the garbage of modern living, so why leave that very garbage behind you?

Please!—the trail is now so heavily used that it will no longer do to bury garbage. You must pack it out with you. Shit and toilet paper must likewise be concealed away from the main trail. Toilet paper can be burned. Some of the campsites now have latrines.

You will never forget the Inca Trail. Please take care of it.

Note. There are now some very interesting alternative hiking routes within the sanctuary. It is possible to extend the Inca Trail hike a bit by starting at Km. 82, thereby experiencing a very pleasant acclimatization hike at lower altitude before starting the steep climb beyond Patallaqta. This route and others are described on p. 182.

At various points in the following description you find distances marked in parentheses. Each one refers to the distance from the last similar reference. Added together they give the total distance for the walk: around 48 km. They are approximate, not exact.

The following are the approximate walking times (including resting, eating, and admiring the scenery) for typical hikers carrying all their own gear in reasonable weather:

Km. 88* to Wayllabamba*	3 hrs.
Wayllabamba to the Forks*	2 hrs.
The Forks to Llulluchapampa*	2 hrs.
Llulluchapampa to 1st Pass	2 hrs.
1st Pass to Pacamayo River*	1 hr.
Pacamayo to Runkuracay*	1 hr.
Runkuracay to 2nd Pass	1hr.
2nd Pass to Sayacmarca*	1 hr.
Sayacmarca to 3rd Pass*	1 1/2 hrs.
3rd Pass to Phuyupatamarca	15 mins.
Phuyupatamarca to Wiñay Wayna*	1 1/2 hrs.
Wiñay Wayna to Machu Picchu	2 1/2 hrs.

(*There are campsites at or near all these locations. Machu Picchu has campsites by the river on either side of the railroad station.)

Campsites are well spaced. There should never be any difficulty reaching a camp by nightfall if you take note of these directions.

The train is your only conveyance to Kilometer 88. This train is safer for travelers than it used to be, but nevertheless be alert and watch your gear carefully, especially at the Cusco station.

At Kilometer 88 the regular train stops (if you've splurged and taken the tourist *autovagon*, tell the crew you want to get off here). Be ready with your gear; the train does not stop long. You are at *Coriwayrachina* (Gold-sifter—a name coined by Bingham). Here you find a new suspension bridge standing on Inca foundations, and a man in a plastic helmet waiting to collect money from you.

A sidetrip: To your right after crossing the river, for about one kilometer downstream, lie the ruins of *Q'ente*, and *Wayna Q'ente*,

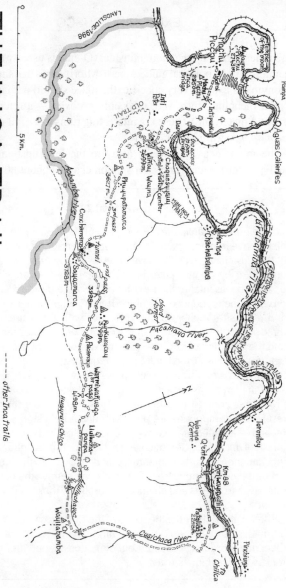

THE INCA TRAIL
AND NEW ROUTES TO MACHU PICCHU

© P. FROST - 1999

5 km.

LANDSLIDE 1998

Machu Picchu

- Temple of the moon
- Huayna Picchu 2743m.
- Hotel
- Machu Picchu 2450m.
- Inca Bridge
- Intipunku
- Inti Pata

OLD TRAIL

- Mandor Pampa
- Aguas Calientes

Dam

- Wiñay Wayna 2699m.
- Choquesuysuy hotel - visitor center

MINI INCA TRAIL

- Km.104
- Chachabamba

- Phuyupatamarca 3627m. V. 3rd pass
- Conchamarca
- Tunnel
- Sayacmarca 3128m.
- 2nd pass 3998m.

cloud forest

Pacamayo river

- Runkuracay 3799m.
- Pacamayo (1st pass) 4198m.
- Warmiwañusqa
- Llulluchapampa

Huayruro Chico

Huayllabamba

Llullchayoc

Cusichaca river

→ N

URUBAMBA RIVER

APPROXIMATE ROUTE OF NEW TRAILS

INCA TRAILS

- Torontoy
- Wayna Qente
- Km.88 Qoriwayrachina
- Patallacta 2565m.
- Pinchuya
- to Chilca

------ other Inca trails
▲ campsite
∴ ruins

which lies higher up the mountainside. (Q'ente is usually translated as "hummingbird," but local guide Alberto Miori claims that since Quechua toponymy is usually very specific, the place should perhaps be called Q'enti, meaning "furrowed, or deeply grooved"—a reference to the surrounding terrain.) These are interesting ruins to visit if one has time *(see map, preceding page)*.

The main Inca Trail winds away to the left (upstream) above a eucalyptus grove, crossing an irrigation channel about 800m from the

---

Patallaqta

The ruins of *Patallaqta* (Terrace Town) stand on the mountainside high above immense banks of agricultural terraces, on the west bank of the Cusichaca river. This well preserved and major Inca ruin was not part of the string of elite ceremonial centers that you will see later on—yet it was vital to their existence, because it produced the food on which they depended. Combined with Q'ente, further downstream, and other sites higher up the Cusichaca valley, this area produced three or four times more food than it consumed. Unlike Machu Picchu and the other Inca Trail sites, this one was settled by earlier cultures before the Incas arrived, with human occupation beginning at least 2,000 years ago, through to the present day.

Patallaqta was not a high-prestige settlement. A visit to the ruins provides a contrast to some of the sites you will see later on. The residential compounds are built with uncut field stone, in a strictly repetitive architectural style, characteristic of the type of site where transient *mit'a* labor contingents were housed. But the solid stonework, the attention to urban planning, and above all the quality and beautifully contoured style of the terracing betrays the hand of first-rate royal architects and engineers, most likely those of Pachacuteq's *panaca*.

Below the ruins, near the banks of the Cusichaca river here stands a small site called *Pulpituyoq* (Pulpit-having—a hybrid Spanish-Quechua word). This curved building, constructed around a huge rock, was Patallaqta's *waca*.

---

bridge, traversing the hillside and following the contours as they turn southeast up the valley of the river *Cusichaca* (Bridge of Joy), with the Inca site of *Patallaqta* above you to the right. There is an official campsite here.

Following the trail you descend to the river and cross just below a small ravine, adorned with an Inca buttress.   *(2km.)*

After crossing a small pass to the left of the ravine, your route follows an undulating course up the left bank of the Cusichaca. At first the valley is broad; after about 2 km. it narrows. At the end of this bottleneck you see a tributary stream, a valley, and traces of an old landslide on the right bank. Here there is a log bridge over the Cusichaca. Descend and cross it. Continue uphill along the main valley—on the right bank now—until you reach the village of *Wayllabamba* (Grassy Plain) at 3000m elevation. It's possible to camp in the Wayllabamba schoolyard.   *(7 km.)*

Are you carrying too much? Are you ready to croak? Well, the trail gets steeper ahead. But don't despair yet. The men of Wayllabamba work as porters for trekking companies, and sometimes there are spare hands (and strong backs) available. When you hire them, share food with them if you can spare it.

The trail now leaves the Cusichaca river, turning northwest up the side valley of the Llullucha (the name for a kind of herb). The climb becomes steep and unrelenting. You are ascending toward the first pass.

About 1 1/2 km. upstream (following the left bank) you come to The Forks (a.k.a. Three White Stones), where there is a small campsite— here two streams converge. The righthand stream is the Llullucha. Both valleys are steep-sided and densely forested. Follow the trail up the lefthand fork for roughly 500m beyond the confluence, then leave this trail to the right and descend to a log bridge across the stream, where there is a small meadow and campsite. Cross and ascend to a bluff, following a well-defined trail.

Beyond the bluff the trail winds steeply upwards above the left bank of the Llullucha, through a thick wood. This is humid *polylepis* woodland, one of numerous micro-environments within the sanctuary. It is a fragile habitat which supports various endemic bird species, and is highly endangered by human encroachment throughout the Peruvian Andes.

Eventually the trail drops to meet the stream's banks, at one place following the streambed itself. Stick to the left bank.

As you emerge from the woods you come to a section of stone trail which is essentially, as Peruvians say, "bamba"—a piece of fake "Inca" trail, newly-built by authorities who sometimes treat the Sanctuary as a sort of IncaWorld. Here you reach a small sloping area of crops, pasture, and dwarf forest, a transitional zone between the *polylepis* forest and the treeless grasslands of the *puna*. This spot is known as Llulluchapampa (official campsite) and stands at around 3600m. Although it's a moderate day from Km. 88, most hikers camp here at the end of the first day, because it's a long way to the next campsite. There are several good camping spots, so if the first ones you reach are occupied, keep going—there are others higher up. With luck you might see a white-tailed deer, or even the rare Andean taruca (a small barrel-chested deer with spiky little antlers).   *(7 km.)*

The trail is indistinct here, but the land is open and you cannot get lost. Bear toward the left side of the valley and you will soon see the pathway winding up the steep slopes to your left. This is the last, hard climb to the first pass, the *Abra de Warmiwañusqa* (Dead Woman's Pass; we have no record as to the origin of this name). Notice traces of ancient steps at the head of the pass, the first unmistakeable signs that you are following a pre-Columbian highway. This is the highest point of the trail at around 4200m.   *(3 km.)*

If visibility is good you can see two high passes ahead of you. The one on the right is your destination. You can pick out the two small lakes near the pass, and the circular ruin of Runkuracay below them.

Descend from Warmiwañusqa. A new stone trail winds down the steep slope to the *Pacamayo* (Hidden River). It is not Inca, but in this case, construction was justified because of the problem of loose rock and erosion on this section. As you near the valley floor you see the waterfalls of the river Pacamayo tumbling down the mountain to your

170

left. The valley floor of the Pacamayo is an official campsite. *(3km.)*

Seek a good place to cross the river near the valley floor, before you reach the woods that fill the valley ahead to the right. After crossing the Pacamayo locate the trail that begins to climb steeply ahead. Do not go down the main Pacamayo valley to your right: that way lies jungle, frustration and despair.

Here at last you begin to find real Inca stone steps built into the mountain as your route zig-zags up its slopes to Runkuracay. *(2 km.)*

The trail climbs on from Runkuracay toward the second pass, named after the ruins. Once again it follows the lefthand flank of the mountain, climbing between the twin lakes of Yanacocha (Black Lake); you see the lower one first, on your left, and the other behind you on the right as

Runkuracay

Hiram Bingham got the name *Runkuracay* from his local native porters. Victor Angles has suggested that, since the word *runku* doesn't exist in (Cusco) Quechua , Bingham must have misheard them, and the name should be Runturacay, meaning "egg [shaped] building." Toponymophile Alberto Miori points out that the building is round, not egg-shaped, and that *runku* does indeed exist in the Ayacucho/Apurimac Quechua dialect (close neighbors of this region). Thereby, the name translates as "basket [in shape and/or function] building." And there's also Runp'u, meaning "ball, or anthing circular/spherical in shape..." Gets complicated, this Andean toponymy.

The circular shape of the main structure at Runkuracay is unusual for a large Inca construction. The two concentric walls of the enclosure form two long, curved chambers and four small ones, all giving onto a central courtyard. The outer walls are massive and solid, and have no windows, but the eastern quarter of the courtyard is open, giving a magnificent view over the Pacamayo valley. The site might have served as a lookout point (most of the sites in this region command the landscape visually for kilometers in every direction), and also as a tambo—a place where travelers lodged, animals were corralled and cargoes were relayed.

you near the second pass, the Abra de Runkuracay (4000m). In clear weather the view ahead from here is fabulous—a breathtaking sweep of snow peaks, dominated by the 6,000 m. Pumasillo massif, the Puma's Claw. There is some egregious "Inca Theme Park" construction at the pass—a circular stone platform...built about 1995. *(2 km.)*

If you feel half dead with fatigue by now, take heart; most of the trail is downhill, or at least gentle, from here on.

Descend. As you do so the trail becomes more and more obviously an Inca highway. Below lies a long, shallow lake, green with algae. After about half an hour you can see ahead of you, clinging to a spur, the ruins of *Sayacmarca*. A trail to the left climbs abruptly, via a flight of steps hanging above a cliff, to reach these ruins, while the main highway toward Machu Picchu descends almost as abruptly to your right. *(5 km.)*

This next part of the trail skirts the edge of the cloud forest, which rises to 3400 m. at this point, nurtured by warm, humid air rising from the Urubamba valley. The route is a riot of exotic plant life—mosses, lichens, ferns, orchids, bromeliads—and some of the most colorful bird species of the Inca Trail are seen here.

Descend from Sayacmarca by the same route you entered. After 100 meters or so the trail cuts down to the left. There is a small campsite here, as you approach a wooden bridge over a small stream. Ahead of you lies a long but gentle haul to the third pass, and some of the most beautiful sections of the trail—perfectly preserved, two meters wide in places where the land is flat. About 15 minutes from Sayacmarca the trail crosses a shallow bowl known as *Ch'akicocha* (Dry Lake). This is a spacious official campsite—but be prepared for rather damp ground under your tent. Later you come to a tunnel, which takes advantage of a natural cleft in a rock face too steep and solid to pass around. So the Incas widened and cut steps into the cleft. The tunnel is 20 meters long.

The third and final pass at close to 4,000m., is really just the point at which the trail recrosses the long ridge that it previously crossed at the second pass, and is so gentle you may hardly notice it. Here you emerge onto a stupendous view of the Urubamba valley. The ruins of

Sayacmarca

Sayacmarca was discovered by Hiram Bingham in 1915. He called it Cedrobamba, meaning "Plain of Cedars." But since it is not a plain, nor are there any cedars, Paul Fejos, who visited the area in 1940, gave it a new Quechua name meaning "Dominant [or Inaccessible] Town." The complex is built at the end of an abrupt promontory commanding a sweeping view of the Aobamba valley, with the snowcapped Pumasillo in the distance.

The layout of the settlement is mazelike and tightly organized, almost cramped. There must have been some special motive or mindset behind the choosing of this site, because there is a small plateau nearby to the northwest known as *Ch'akicocha* (Dry Lake), which, from our perspective, would seem a much better location for a town. It has a more accessible water supply, and far more space for building. But it does not overlook its surroundings in the same way as the site that was chosen. This was surely the overriding factor for the Incas - Sayacmarca was not, in military terms, a defensible site: its water supply was easy to cut off, and it could be bombarded with missiles from the nearby mountain slope. What it does have, in common with all other sites along the Inca trail, is a commanding view of the landscape.

A line of observation platforms ran between here and Machu Picchu, and it seems likely that the Incas used a signalling system to send information - warning of the approach of important people, for example - up and down this line. Sayacmarca may also have served as a center from which to control travel and cargo along the two main highways visible from this point (the second of these being the trail that led down the valley directly south of Sayacmarca, to the Aobamba valley.

These are the utilitarian reasons for the location of Sayacmarca. But the deeper motives were metaphysical, and are harder to explain. The truth is that there was no real economic or strategic rationale for building Machu Picchu or the Inca Trail and its sites. The land is so rugged and steep it is hardly worth farming, and there were no significant mineral deposits. The quality and type of construction cannot be accounted for by a military threat, and in fact the settlements were so remote that they made no economic sense at all. If they had, they would never have been abandoned.

Machu Picchu and the Inca trail make no sense to our rational minds, but our hearts can readily understand. The Incas worshipped the natural world - particularly the snowcapped mountains which are visible from all the major sites - and tried to communicate with its spirits. They were willing to make an enormous investment in the contemplation of natural beauty. The man who had all this built was a warrior and imperial conqueror; this was his other face, the hidden aspect of Pachacuteq.

In the Ruins: The water supply (now defunct) ran down a cleft in the mountains behind, filling a large natural cistern. An aqueduct, probably consisting of a hollowed U-section log, then brought it onto a tall stone buttress (1) at the head of the ruins. The channel continues along the precipitous south wall of the complex (2) and descends through a series of three ritual baths (3). A fourth bath has been discovered outside the ruins, beside the trail shortly before the access stairway.

The unusual tongue-shaped building that dominates the site (4) has a curious feature: all of the trapezoidal openings on the west side have four pierced ring-stones set into the outside of the wall, one at each corner. Since the prevailing winds were from the west these might have been used to secure screens that would cover these openings when the wind was blowing hard.

At the lower end of the complex a broad triangular plaza (5) opens onto a wonderful vista of the Aobamba valley. To your right, northwest, you can see the Inca Trail crossing the flats of Ch'akicocha, and winding around the mountain flanks toward the third pass. The trail is surprisingly distinct, due to the white granite blocks used in its construction. Recognizing that too much beauty is intolerable, the authorities have considerately built a conspicuous stone-and-concrete latrine in the middle of this view, a few meters from the Inca Trail.

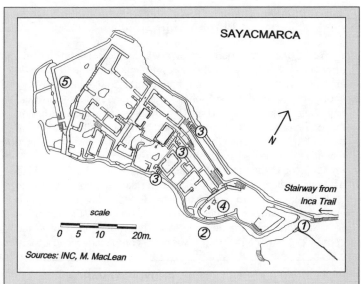

SAYACMARCA

Stairway from
Inca Trail

scale

0   5   10   20m.

Sources: INC, M. MacLean

Directly below Sayacmarca, stand the small ruins of Conchamarca, a cluster of three houses, standing on a finely constructed stand of stone terraces, which were only discovered in the early nineteen-eighties, and were not cleared until much more recently. They are currently in use as housing for INC guards.

Phuyupatamarca (Cloud-level Town) lie below you to the left. Looking south from here on a clear day you will see, starting from the left, the tip of snowcapped Palcay (ca. 5,600 m.) then the massive bulk of Salcantay (6,270 m.); 35 km. to the west stands Pumasillo (6,000 m.) and then a string of lesser snow peaks away to the west; then if you turn all the way around, there is Wakay Willka (a.k.a. Verónica) (5,750 m.) 15 km. away to the northeast.

At the pass lie several superb but very small campsites, with the best views of any on the Inca Trail.   *(6 km.)*

Phuyupatamarca

Phuyupatamarca (Cloud level town) was another of Hiram Bingam's discoveries. His name fits, because at night clouds tend to settle around this ridge. There are many agricultural terraces here, possibly enough to have made the site self-sufficient. Once again we find ritual baths here—a fine principal bath (1) at the outskirts of the ruins beside the road leading into the complex, and a chain of five almost identical baths (2) descending in a line along the pathway below. These have recently been cleared and restored to working order.

At the top of the site stands a large platform of bedrock (3) which has been leveled off by hand—an amazing feat when we consider the tools the Incas had to work with. The base of a fine double-jamb entranceway can be seen here, and this was evidently the beginning of a structure that was destined to be the most important in the complex. But we can see that it was never completed, because there

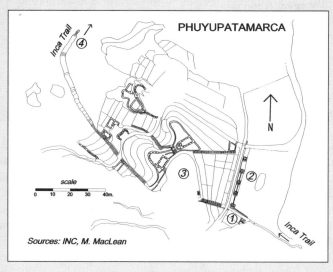

is no sign of the heaps of cut stones that we would inevitably find had there been finished walls which later collapsed.

Above the ruins stands a ledge littered with rocks that may have served as a quarry. There you can see a block of stone about three meters long, with three deep grooves cut into it, suggesting that someone was in the process of carving this stone into four separate blocks by the pounding technique described in Chapter Two (*p. 96*). The cliff edge was once crowned with a long wall at this point—the bedding-cuts in the rock can be seen clearly.

Each of the small groups of buildings in the ruins features a semi-circular or semi-ovoid structure, resembling a low, single-storey tower. Some of them have sinuous, irregular shapes that seem molded to follow the outlines of the rock on which they are built, and all of them look outwards over the immense Urubamba gorge. These miniature towers are a unique feature of Phuyupatamarca.

Where the trail exits from the ruins on the west side you come to two flights of steps pointing downward into the cloud forest. The first of these (#4 on Phuyupatamarca map) is a mind-boggling granite staircase that was probably once the principal route to Wiñay Wayna, the last major site along the Inca Trail before Machu Picchu. This trail and staircase is a recent discovery, dating from the early 1980s. The staircase is two meters wide in places— a sign of its importance as a thoroughfare. One steep section is cut into solid bedrock. Near the top you find a cave, and a kilometer or so beyond that another, both with walls and niches built inside them. The second of these probably served as a small rest stop and shelter. A lookout platform stands close by. From this point, in clear weather, you look down upon the ruins of Wiñay Wayna and the scabrous red rooftops of the adjacent modern visitor center—all some two air kilometers away.

Half a kilometer farther down the trail from the cave stands a pair of small structures perched on a rock outcrop at the left side of the trail, their entranceways facing each other.

The trail passes through another steep tunnel, cuts across the mountainside and eventually joins a new pathway that descends near a line of electricity towers. The original Inca trail probably led directly to Wiñay Wayna, but the lower part has disappeared over the centuries. The new trail is long, winding, dusty and very steep, with a vertical drop of approximately 300 m.

The scarred hillside and the mottled rooftops painted allergy-red below you, are part of a modern visitor center and hotel. (Twenty-fifth-century tourists, gazing upon its baleful ruins, will say: "How could they build this here? This, surely, was the work of devils!") This is where the trail emerges. The hotel has sixteen beds, basic lodging, drinks and meals. Reservations are theoretically possible (tel. 211147). There is a small, not-so-lovely official campsite as well. This complex is an ugly shambles, festooned with overhead cables and littered with trash— an abiding rebuke to the appalling insensitivity of those who dreamed up the whole eyesore. *(6 km.)*

Leaving Wiñay Wayna, you are on the last leg of the trail. This spectacular section traverses fairly steadily across open mountainside at

---

Inti Pata

The fan-shaped spread of agricultural terracing on the mountainside above Wiñay Wayna is known as Inti Pata (Sun-terrace). There are some buildings here, but the site was mainly for agriculture. It was discovered and named in 1915 by Hiram Bingham, who also cleared it of vegetation. It was allowed to become overgrown again, and was cleared again, and given the restoration treatment in the 1990s. Conservation experts cite this recent clearing of Inti Pata (clear-cutting, actually, which left not a tree standing), as an example of insensitive ecological management and lack of integrated planning. They say it destroyed some of the best orchid habitat, and probably eliminated several species from the Sanctuary.

Inti Pata can be visited, taking the access trail which begins at the Wiñay Wayna visitor center.

Wiñay Wayna

The ruins of Wiñay Wayna lie about five minutes walk off the trail around the hillside to the right (south) from the visitor center. The site is named after an orchid genus (here, *Epidendrum crassilabium* and *E. secundum*) with red, violet or yellow flowers, that was once abundant in this area, and is still to be seen. The plant blooms year-round, hence the Quechua name, which means "Forever Young."

The ruins here were discovered in 1941 by Paul Fejos, during the last days of the Viking Fund expedition. He had time only for rudimentary survey and clearing work. The Peruvian archaeologist Julio C. Tello conducted further investigations in 1942. The ruins are built on the steepest of mountain slopes, flanked by ancient farming terraces. Due east from here, the land plunges into the Urubamba gorge and then soars upward to the shining glaciers of Wakay Willka (Verónica).

In the Ruins: As you take the path from the visitor center to the ruins

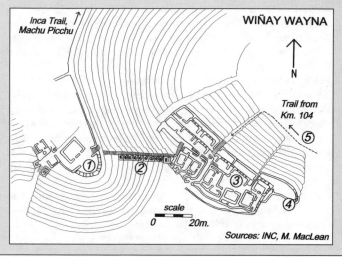

you pass from the ridiculous to the sublime, encountering one of those sudden, sensational first views that the Incas seemed to delight in creating. A magnificent sweep of curved terracing leads the eye down to a cluster of steep-roofed buildings perched at the end of a steep spur, while in the background a high waterfall sprays down the mountainside through dense cloud forest vegetation.

The trail leads into the complex along a broad terrace with a long, curved wall to one's right, which ends at a huge doorway. This leads into a large rounded structure (1) that commands the site in much the same way as the similar structure at Sayacmarca does, and the unfinished enclosure at Phuyupatamarca would have. Below the building a straight flight of stairs takes you down past a unique set of ten ritual baths (2). Historical data confirm that ritual bathing or cleansing was an important feature of Inca religious observance. The element of water itself was also worshipped. Ritual baths are a feature of every major Inca site, but they are particularly numerous on the Inca Trail sites. This is another factor among many which support the view that the Machu Picchu/Inca Trail network held a special spiritual significance for the Incas.

Another factor affecting the choice of location for this site, is that it looks directly across the Urubamba towards the glaciers of Wakay Willka (Verónica), thus linking Wiñay Wayna to that mountain as a place of worship.

If you follow the steps downhill past these waterworks you reach the dwelling area. Here there is a small square (3) overlooked by two open-fronted buildings, which might have been a communal area where the social and economic transactions of the community took place. At the lower extreme of the dwelling area you emerge onto a tiny, startling platform (4) (careful!) poised over two hundred meters of nothing - a vertical farewell to earth. To your right a small waterfall sprays down the cliff face.

The short "mini-Inca Trail" from Chachabamba at Km. 104 crosses the opposite side of this ravine, passes the waterfall, then enters the terraces of Wiñay Wayna at (5).

first, and then, rising and falling, enters an enchanted forest, scattered with giant ferns; careful observers will note many new plant species and a different type of cloud forest habitat here, with larger trees. When you come to a steep, imposing flight of stairs, you have almost arrived. Soon you reach the top of a ridge, where the path passes through a ruined gateway flanked by remains of buildings: this is *Intipunku* (Sun Gate). (*Birdwatchers*: right by these ruins on the east side of the ridge is a great viewing spot).

You have reached the city limits. Walk to the far side of the ruin and you see the climax of your journey, one of the world's breathtaking views. The tall peak of Wayna Picchu lies directly ahead. Before it, spread impressively over the ridge below you, lies the lost city of the Incas, Machu Picchu.   *(7 km.)*

New Trails around Machu Picchu

Several new routes have been opened within the Machu Picchu Historical Sanctuary in the late 1990s. All of the hiking within this region is spectacular, and these routes only fall short if compared to the Inca Trail itself. But the Inca Trail is often horribly crowded, and these are the trails less traveled. This is also the way to go for moderate hikers who recoil from the several days and 4,000 m. passes of the Inca Trail. See map on p. 167.

Km. 82 to Km. 88 A dirt road now reaches down the north bank of the Urubamba to the edge of the Machu Picchu sanctuary, through Ollantaytambo and Chillca to Km. 82 on the railroad line. At Km. 82 there is a new footbridge across the Urubamba river, so that you can walk on either side of the river. The south (non-railroad) side is shorter if you intend to take the main Inca Trail, because on the north side you have to walk somewhat downstream to reach the bridge at Coriwayrachina, and then double back to Patallaqta. However, north of the river there are some interesting ruins: Salapunku, a sort of miniature Sacsaywaman with zig-zag terraced walls and fine gateways; Pinchanuyoq, a small *waca*; and the Inca bridge built onto a huge carved outcrop at Km. 88, which is another *waca*. This route follows the railroad tracks, although the footpath travels mainly above it.

Km. 88 to Km. 104 & Machu Picchu or Aguas Calientes Inca trails follow the Urubamba valley down towards Machu Picchu. There are various places to camp along the trails, and again you have two choices: north or south of the river. There are footbridges at Km. 82, 88 and 104 of the railroad. Allow two days with an overnight camp to reach Machu Picchu or Aguas Calientes on these routes.

South bank: the agricultural terraces of Q'enti stretch along the first part of the hike after Km. 88. A sidetrip from here takes you up to the small Inca site of Wayna Q'enti. The trail undulates along the south bank of the river, through some delightful forest, which gradually becomes more tropical until you reach the bridge at Km.104. If you prefer to continue to Aguas Calientes, cross the bridge at Km. 104 and follow the railroad to Km. 110.

North bank: this trail follows close to the railroad. However, traffic is infrequent and hardly interrupts the peacefulness of the experience. The *waca* above the bridge at Km. 88 is worth a little time, before you continue down the valley to Torontoy, where there are also interesting ruins. Here there is an Inca construction stone which puts the famous 12-angled stone of Cusco to shame, by having 44 corner angles in one plane. Cross the bridge at Km. 104 for Machu Picchu, or stay on the north bank for Aguas Calientes.

Km. 104. - the Mini Inca Trail, a one-day or very leisurely two-day (with overnight at Wiñay Wayna) hike to Machu Picchu. Distance is about 6 km. to the visitor center at Wiñay Wayna, thus about 14 km. total to Machu Picchu. Take the train from Cusco or Ollantaytambo, and alight at the bridge at Km. 104. Shortly after the bridge, you will pass some recently-built concrete blockhouses (possibly designed to harmonize with the visitor center at Wiñay Wayna), where you will be charged a trail fee (currently US$2.00, plus US$10.00 entrance to Machu Picchu) Shortly after this point the trail passes through the interesting but heavily rebuilt ruins of Chachabamba, and then begins to climb around the mountainside into the ravine below Wiñay Wayna. After a spectacular waterfall, you climb through the ruins of Wiñay Wayna and join the main Inca Trail, continuing to Machu Picchu.

It's also possible to take a variant route from Km. 104, continuing on downstream along the banks of the river to the ruins of Choquessuysuy at Km. 107, and thence taking a very steep Inca path which climbs up the west side of the same ravine to join the other trail at Wiñay Wayna. This route is highly recommended for the forest and orchid habitat, though the final climb is hard.

Further progress along the south bank is not possible, because the route is blocked by the hydro-electric plant.

Trail to Putucusi. East of Machu Picchu on the north bank of the river stands the small rounded peak of Putucusi (soon to be adorned with its very own aesthetic outrage, the new cable car). A very steep trail leads to the top of it, starting near the railroad, just downstream from Aguas Calientes. Ask for directions to the trailhead in Aguas Calientes. About three hours round-trip.

Trail to Mandor ravine & waterfall. If you are staying at Aguas Calientes, it is possible to walk downstream along the railroad tracks, beyond the old railroad station at Puente Ruinas. About 3 km. beyond Puente Ruinas station Mandor ravine enters the Urubamba gorge from the north bank of the river. About twenty minutes climbing up this ravine brings you to Mandor waterfall, an exceptionally lovely spot. *(Birdwatchers:* early in the morning or at dusk, this walk features a lot of birdlife, including, if you are lucky, the spectacular Cock-of-the-rock *(Rupicola Peruviana saturata).*

Chapter Five

MACHU PICCHU

The Fabled City

For centuries the Lost City has been the most durable and evocative of myths about ancient Peru. El Dorado. Paititi. Vilcabamba. The names have lured treasure hunters, adventurers and explorers ever since the Conquest. In early colonial times the jungle swallowed up hundreds of gold-hungry Spaniards and thousands of their press-ganged Indian porters. All in vain. They found nothing, except the Amazon. But the irony was that there *were* lost cities buried in the forested eastern slope of the Andes. The 20th century has seen the discovery of more than one: Gran Pajatén in northern Peru; Espiritu Pampa in Vilcabamba; and, most famous and awe-inspiring of all, Machu Picchu.

Hiram Bingham, known today as the scientific discoverer of Machu Picchu, was actually seeking the site of Vilcabamba the Old, the remote last stronghold of Manco Inca and his sons. Today we have virtually watertight evidence that he did actually find that site, without realizing it, when he visited Espiritu Pampa near the Apurimac River, some 100 km. west of Machu Picchu *(see Vilcabamba; Chapter Eight)*. But Bingham only saw part of the ruins at Espiritu Pampa, and eventually came to dismiss them as insignificant. He solved the conceptual problem of having found the totally unexpected and unreported site of Machu Picchu while searching for Vilcabamba, by declaring that Machu Picchu *was* Vilcabamba.

Bingham was a historian, a Yale graduate, and later a U.S. Senator. He first came to South America in 1908 to participate in the first Pan-

American scientific congress in Santiago, Chile. Early the following year he traveled through the Andes, and saw his first remote Inca ruin, when he was invited by the prefect of Abancay to join an expedition to the spectacular site of Choquequirau, above the Apurimac canyon. He was fascinated by Peru, and returned in 1911 as leader of the Yale Peruvian expedition, whose goals included surveying the 73rd meridian; climbing Coropuna, a mountain near Arequipa then thought to be a candidate for "highest peak in the Americas"; and searching for the lost Inca capital of Vilcabamba. He had read some of the sources on the history of the last Inca refuge, and had become curious about its location.

While in Cusco at the outset of this expedition, Bingham learned from Albert Giesecke, the American-born rector of the Cusco university, that there were unexplored ruins on the ridge above Mandor Pampa. Alberto Duque, who lived downstream from Mandor Pampa, gave him similar information.

Bingham decided to take the relatively new mule trail down the Urubamba, en route to the area thought to contain Vitcos and Vilcabamba the Old, two of the most important, but as yet unidentified, settlements mentioned in the chronicles of the Vilcabamba Inca resistance. On July 23rd, 1911, he camped at Mandor Pampa, the flat strip of valley floor that curves around the north and west flank of the Wayna Picchu and Machu Picchu ruins. The next day a local farmer and innkeeper who knew the ridgetop ruins, one Melchor Arteaga, guided Bingham through the perilous river crossing and grueling climb, for a reward of one silver dollar.

Some local campesinos were farming in the ruins, and had helpfully cleared the central part of the site (which was therefore not completely overgrown, as Bingham later claimed), so that the fortunate Yankee was able to see much of what was there. But Bingham was not unduly excited at first by Machu Picchu; he spent five hours at the ruins, took some pictures, made a rough sketch map, and jotted a few laconic notes in his diary. That was all. He left his camp at Mandor the next day, and did not return to Machu Picchu until the following year.

Before leaving the camp, he wrote in his journal: "Agustín Lizárraga is discoverer of Machu Picchu." Lizárraga was a farmer who lived at San Miguel bridge, just downstream from Mandor Pampa; Bingham had seen his name chalked on a rock at the ruins.

One reason Bingham did not think Machu Picchu worth delaying his journey may have been that it did not correspond to the information he had been given in Lima by the Peruvian scholar Carlos A. Romero, as to the probable location of Vilcabamba. Later Bingham would ignore those inconvenient topographical details, and proclaim that Machu Picchu was the lost Inca capital of Vilcabamba the Old.

The value of his find slowly dawned on him. On July 26th he wrote, in a letter to his wife: "[Machu Picchu] is far more wonderful and interesting than Choquequirau. The stone is as fine as any in Cusco! It is unknown, and will make a fine story." He sent three members of his expedition back there in September of 1911 to clear and map the ruins, while he pressed on with his goal of making the first ascent of Coropuna. But in his preliminary report on the findings of the Yale Peruvian expedition the following year, he devoted only seven lines to Machu Picchu, and more than two pages to some prehistoric human bones he had discovered in a glacial deposit near Cusco, which he thought were of epoch-making significance.

Even when Bingham returned to Peru a year later, with the Yale Expedition of 1912, the study of Machu Picchu still was not specifically mentioned as an objective. He was more interested in Peruvian geography; and in his prehistoric bones. But the latter soon turned out to be relatively recent, so he at last decided to throw most of his expedition's energies into months of clearing and excavating at Machu Picchu. He spent two weeks in July getting his crew started, and then, typically, set off on new explorations. He returned for a spell in mid-August, departed again to cope with political problems in Lima, and returned again in November to wrap up the expedition. Bingham was an excellent photographer, and in these three visits he assembled a vast collection of seven hundred photographs. The best of these were published in the National Geographic magazine in 1913, and soon afterwards he was famous.

Hiram Bingham was extraordinarily lucky, and hilariously blind to his luck. He longed for fame, and today, 90 years later, with all that we have learned since then, one laughs to read of his manic pursuit of spurious bones and first ascents (he bagged the wrong peak), right after he had become the first western scientist to see Machu Picchu.

As with most scientific discoveries, numerous people were involved. Giesecke and Duque, Bingham's informants in Cusco, had not visited Machu Picchu themselves; Lizárraga had, but perhaps he was not well enough connected or educated to make anything of it. Melchor Arteaga knew the ruins, and there were campesinos actually living there. But none of these people had recognized the site's historic significance. In the end, it *was* Hiram Bingham who, rather hesitantly, announced Machu Picchu to the world.

Butterfly motif from ceramic plate, found at Machu Picchu

After his first visit to Machu Picchu, Bingham went on to locate the ruins of Vitcos and those of Vilcabamba the Old, at Espiritu Pampa *(see Vilcabamba; Chapter Eight)* These were the sites he had originally been seeking, the remote last strongholds of Manco Inca and his sons. Ironically, at first he identified both ruins correctly. But somewhat later, now dazzled by the response to his spectacular find on the Urubamba gorge, he retracted, declaring that Machu Picchu *was* the location of Vilcabamba the Old.

Nevertheless, Bingham's mistake was understandable. He only saw part of the ruins at Espiritu Pampa, which were thoroughly buried in dense vegetation—and who would imagine that there were not one, but two major lost cities in the forest north of Cusco? Today no one believes Machu Picchu was Vilcabamba the Old. Firstly, there is too much high-quality stonework that must have taken many years and employed a great labor force in its construction at Machu Picchu, whereas Manco's capital was a post-Conquest city, built hurriedly with limited resources. Secondly, Machu Picchu is purely an Inca city; there are no traces of the Hispanic influence one would expect to find at Vilcabamba. Furthermore, the Spaniards actually discovered Manco's capital and burned it, before its location was lost to memory, yet there are no clear signs of destruction at Machu Picchu; even the setting fails to conform to historic Spanish accounts of the terrain around Vilcabamba. The name itself (Vilcabamba means Sacred Plain) flatly contradicts the hypothesis, given the precipitous terrain around Machu Picchu. Finally, and most convincingly, the true site of Vilcabamba the Old at Espiritu Pampa seems to have been confirmed by the Savoy expeditions of 1964 *(see Vilcabamba; Chapter Eight)*.

So Bingham discovered an enigma even deeper than he imagined. Machu Picchu was not Vilcabamba the Old—then what was it? Bingham's explorations in 1912 and 1915, discovered a string of other ruins and a major Inca highway (now known to us as the Inca Trail) to the south of Machu Picchu. Later still, in 1941, the Viking Fund expedition led by Paul Fejos discovered the important ruins of Wiñay Wayna *(see Inca Trail; Chapter Four)* above the Urubamba gorge, about 4 1/2 km. due south of Machu Picchu.

The Lost Province

A popular and alluring myth portrays Machu Picchu as some kind of Andean Shangri-la perched alone on its remote crag, and it is easy to believe this if one sees only Machu Picchu itself, without walking the Inca Trail. But many more discoveries, large and small, have been made in the region since 1941. Taken as a whole they support and expand an emerging view of Machu Picchu as the ceremonial and possibly administrative center of a large and quite populous region—not a lost city, but an entire lost province.

The U.S. archaeologist and ethnohistorian J.H. Rowe recently presented a newly-discovered 1568 document that refers to a place called "Picho" (Picchu) north of Cusco. According to the document, the natives were farming coca in the Urubamba valley at "Picho" after the Spanish Conquest, a site that was formerly a "royal estate" belonging to the Inca Pachacuteq. So Machu Picchu was built and populated by the *panaca* (royal lineage) of Pachacuteq. Very little is known about the nature and function of the estates belonging to individual Inca emperors, so this detail on its own does not tell us very much about the site itself.

If indeed Machu Picchu was built for Pachacuteq, and we accept the standard dates of the reign of the Incas, we can speak of the construction dates of Machu Picchu with reasonable confidence. Most academics accept that the Inca expansion began around the year 1438, after Pachacuteq's defeat of the invading Chanca tribe. (Some scholars are sceptical of the 1438 date of the Chanca war and the beginning of the Inca expansion, putting it further back in time. And indeed, it is hard to see Machu Picchu and accept that the whole site—along with the surrounding sites, and all the other vast works of the Incas—could have been built in so short a time).

Various chronicles tell us that for strategic reasons (to contain the retreating Chancas) this region was the first to be settled in the headlong rush toward empire. The building style of Machu Picchu is "late imperial Inca," which supports this thesis, and, unlike many other Inca sites, this one bears no sign of pre-Inca occupation. Nor are there signs of post-Conquest occupation. So Machu Picchu may have been built, occupied and abandoned in the space of less than one hundred years. The rest is speculation. And who can resist speculating when faced with something as affecting, and yet impenetrable, as the mystery of these silent stones?

What kind of settlement was Machu Picchu? Hemming states that Machu Picchu has only 200 habitation structures, leading him to estimate a permanent population of about 1000 people. In previous editions I wrote (considering the great areas of agricultural terracing in and around the settlement) that "the agricultural output of the area would greatly have exceeded the needs of the population".

Not so, it appears—in fact, quite the opposite. Cusco archaeologists Alfredo Valencia and Arminda Gibaja surveyed the area, including the main satellite sites, and calculated production at about 28 metric tons of maize per year, assuming only maize was cultivated. This does not add up to a great abundance of food. The terraces at Machu Picchu were dry farmed, not irrigated. The region is rainy for much of the year, but the dry season would have prevented the harvesting of two maize crops per year. If each inhabitant needed 1/4 Kg. of maize per day, the 28 ton figure gives us food for only just over 300 people. Even if production were twice that, they still fed only 600 people.

The terraces may have been used partly to grow corn dedicated to the making of special chicha, for use in ceremonies. There are also hints in the 1568 document that the population here were growing crops to be burned in ritual sacrifices. It is clear, at least, that Machu Picchu must have been supplied with food from elsewhere—probably the site of Patallaqta near Km. 88 on the Santa Ana railroad *(see p. 168)*.

Some archaeologists have proposed that a principal function of the Machu Picchu region was to create a reliable supply of coca leaves for the priests and royalty of Cusco. Today Machu Picchu itself is too high to grow coca, but old documents show that the Incas had developed many crop varieties—since lost—that would flourish at altitudes far above where they grow today. The Incas built many agricultural centers which seem to have been designed and used for plant adaptation, and this Inca settlement may have been partly designed as a center for the adaptation of coca to higher altitudes. Soil samples currently being studied for pollen content may tell us if coca was being grown here. Whether it was or not, Machu Picchu was probably a conduit to Cusco for coca grown lower down the Urubamba valley.

The school of thought fostered by Bingham held that the city existed primarily for strategic and defensive purposes. He pointed to the outer wall (by the main ruins entrance) and inner walls, the latter flanked by a deep trench (#3 on ruins map), as evidence of fortifications. There was also the strategic draw-bridge to the west of the ruins, and the lookout platforms atop Wayna Picchu and the peak of Machu Picchu.

However, Mecca is also surrounded by walls and has closely guarded gateways, yet it is not a fortress. Machu Picchu contains an unusually high proportion and quality of religious architecture, and modern opinion leans more to the view that Machu Picchu was essentially a site of spiritual and ceremonial significance, perhaps with important agricultural functions. Its strategic purposes, if any, were secondary.

One very popular and durable myth has it that Machu Picchu was the secret refuge of the Virgins of the Sun—whose existence was known only to a select few, and concealed from the Spaniards. A more plausible variant of this theory proposed that the Chosen Women were sequestered at Machu Picchu after the Conquest had begun, when it became clear that the Spaniards respected nothing and nobody of native origin. This story leans on the finding of Bingham's osteologist, Dr. George Eaton, that 75% of the human remains discovered were female. Sadly for both romance and plausibility, however, scientists at Yale, using modern technology, restudied these remains in the 1980s, and concluded that many of Eaton's identifications were wrong; the male/female proportion was roughly equal. Machu Picchu was not a 75% female domain.

One enduring mystery is why the Spanish never heard about and visited Machu Picchu. Along with its outlying sites, it remains the most perfect surviving example of Inca architecture and planning, because it was never looted and destroyed. The same 1568 document that attributes Machu Picchu to Pachacuteq also tells us that the valley floor below Machu Picchu was being farmed at that time, and perhaps visited occasionally by Spaniards, but 34 years after the Conquest the farmers may have been only dimly aware of the overgrown site on the ridgetop 700m. above them.

The Cusqueño historian Dr. Victor Angles has argued that it would have been impossible for the Incas to conceal Machu Picchu from the Spanish. He claims that nothing so important as the location of an entire active and populated region could have been kept secret. Little was hidden from Pizarro's troops in the early days of the Conquest. The Cusco Incas, losers in the civil war against Quito, greeted them as liberators because they had captured and killed the northern usurper, Atawallpa. Yet the Spaniards did not know of Machu Picchu's existence. Why? Angles speculates that it was because the surviving Incas did not know of it either—and that the total amnesia concerning its location occurred because Machu Picchu was a rebel province, one that was dealt with so ruthlessly by the Incas that its population was annihilated and its existence erased from official memory.

It is certainly likely that Machu Picchu was abandoned before the Spanish invasion, but it is possible to imagine less dramatic causes. The Incas suffered a terrible civil war lasting several years just before the Spanish arrived. This war was triggered by a pestilence—probably European smallpox—which ravaged the Inca empire, killing the reigning emperor Wayna Capac, along with his designated heir. The plague may have reached Machu Picchu, or perhaps this costly ceremonial settlement simply became an unacceptable drain on Cusco's dwindling resources during the civil war, and thus was abandoned. Any treasure would have been removed at that time, which would explain why no precious objects were found by Bingham's team. Once abandoned, Machu Picchu was forgotten.

Another theory concerning the abandonment of Machu Picchu is that it ran out of water. There are signs of an unfinished project to augment the water supply. However, core samples of the Quelccaya ice cap south-east of Cusco, show that the weather in southern Peru was actually getting wetter during the early 16th century, so this theory does not quite...ahem...hold water.

Finally, a Spanish document of 1562 states that the rebel Incas of Vilcabamba had "burned and pillaged all the Indian houses" of this area, probably to establish a secure zone between themselves and the Spanish in Cusco, and to prevent the Spaniards discovering and using the access routes from Machu Picchu to Vilcabamba. So Machu Picchu still could have been abandoned after the Conquest, during the period of Inca resistance.

New Discoveries: (Information provided by Instituto Nacional de Cultura, Cusco.) The most extensive finds have been made just across the river to the northeast, on a sloping plateau about 100m above the valley floor known as Mandor Pampa. Its outstanding feature is an enormous wall about 3.5m high and 2.5m wide, and more than a kilometer long, which runs straight up the mountainside, toward a distinctive pointy peak known as Yanantin. This wall was apparently built to protect the adjacent agricultural terraces from erosion, and may also have served to demarcate two areas with separate functions. At this writing the wall has become overgrown with vegetation, but its line can still be discerned in the forest beyond the river from Machu Picchu. Other finds on the pampa include quarries, circular buildings, a large number of stone mortars (emphasizing the utilitarian nature of this area), and a large observation platform to the west.

Closer to Machu Picchu itself, the sector known as the "Temple of the Moon" (on the north slope of Wayna Picchu) has been cleared to reveal another subterranean temple, a superb wall with an imposing gateway, and an observatory directed toward the aforementioned Yanantin peak.

Farther upriver two important burial sites known as Killipata and Ch'askapata have been discovered, and the ruins of Choquessuysuy, just upstream from the hydroelectric project, now appear to be larger than had been previously believed. Of these sites only the Temple of the Moon and Choquessuysuy have been opened to the public so far.

In 1997, a forest fire on the west slope below Machu Picchu revealed an unknown Inca trail down to the river, which is not currently open to the public.

In the years following Bingham's discovery the ruins were cleared of vegetation, excavations were made, and visitors became more frequent. Later a railroad was blasted out of the sheer granite cliffs of the imposing canyon. In 1948 a sinuous 12-km. road from the river banks to the ruins was named for and inaugurated by Hiram Bingham himself (who came to visit his famous discovery for the first time since 1915). Today there are a hotel, a daily train shuttle, a minibus service, official guides, and official guards.

Nowadays Machu Picchu is often quite crowded. March, April and November tend to be the quietest months. Avoid visiting between July 28th & August 10th, when Peruvian national holidays are in full swing.

"Cusco week," leading up to Inti Raymi (June 24th), is also busy; it's best to enjoy the festivities in Cusco, and visit Machu Picchu afterwards).

Conservation Note: one of the charms of Machu Picchu is its great variety of wild flowers, including many varieties of orchid. But they are fewer every year because of irresponsible collecting by visitors. *Please don't pick them!* And don't buy them from people offering them for sale at the train stations.

The Train Journey

The normal time for the journey from Cusco is about 3 hours in the tourist train, 4 hours in the Pullman, about 5 hours on the local train. *(For schedules etc., see Transportation, p. 20)* Note: A shuttle has recently been developed, and during busy periods some trains now run from the town of Ollantaytambo, with a bus connection via Chinchero and Urubamba from Cusco.

The experience of visiting Machu Picchu is not limited to the ruins themselves; the journey by train from Cusco is without a doubt one of the most spectacular in the world. The first leg out of Cusco is notable for a switchback ascent up a hillside too steep to permit normal railway curves. Past the top of this section you see a piece of abandoned Inca highway to your left. The train crosses rolling uplands, twisting and turning as it crosses a pass and descends past the town of *Poroy* . Here

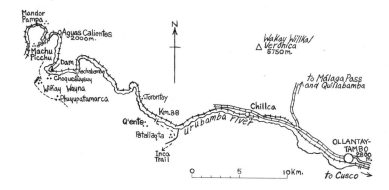

you see a graveyard of ancient railway engines and rolling stock to the right of the track, and to the left, a brand new White Elephant tourist railroad station that has never been used (and never will be). Supposedly, the idea was to run shuttle buses between there and Cusco, to avoid the time-consuming Cusco switchbacks (but what's *time* to a government-owned railroad?). Next comes the fertilizer and explosives factory of *Cachimayo* to the right of the tracks, followed by *Izcuchaca*, a cross-road and market town on the highway from Cusco to Lima via Abancay. Now you are crossing the *Pampa de Anta*, a high plateau where Inca armies are said to have defeated the Chanca tribe at the beginning of their expansions, and where later the rebel Gonzalo Pizarro was defeated, captured and beheaded in 1548. Far off across this plain to the west (the left side of the train) the huge Inca terraces of *Zurite* can be seen hugging the base of the next range of mountains. *Huarocondo*, the following town, stands close to the head of the valley of the Huarocondo river, down which the railway descends to meet the Urubamba valley. Look out for the striking endemic Andean torrent ducks all along the river to Machu Picchu, often seen perched in pairs on boulders in the stream.

There is another switchback at the lower end of the Huarocondo valley, then the train reaches the railroad halt of *Pachar*. Here the ruins of Inca storehouses can be seen on cliffs above you to the left. At Pachar the railroad turns westward as it meets the Sacred Valley of the Incas and the Urubamba river. The train passes by ruined Inca forts and huge areas of terracing, then stops at *Ollantaytambo*. After it pulls out of the station you see across the terraces to the right the impressive remains of the Inca temple and the long ramp that served for dragging huge stones up to the site. Soon the railway enters the beginnings of a gorge which grows ever narrower and deeper as you pass *Chillca*. As the train continues its descent of the valley you may catch occasional glimpses of snow-

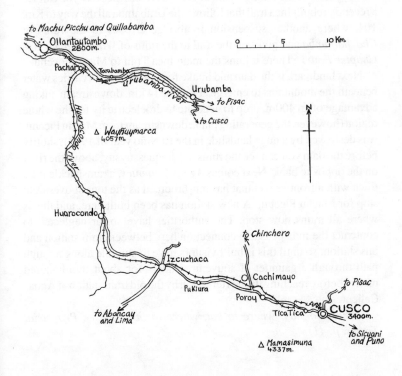

capped*Wakay Willka /Verónica* (5750m/18865 ft.) to the right.

As you approach *Kilometer 88* the extensive ruins of *Patallaqta* can be seen on the mountains across the river on the left. Soon a modern suspension footbridge across the Urubamba, built on Inca foundations, comes into view below the train tracks. This is Km. 88, where you must get off the train if you are planning to walk the Inca Trail. After a short tunnel you see rows of solid Inca terracing across the river, the ruins of *Q'ente*. The vegetation grows more prolific—you are leaving the highlands and entering the mountainous cloud forest, known locally as the "eyebrow of the jungle" *(ceja de selva)*. Across the river you can see a recently rebuilt Inca trail that follows the Urubamba all the way to Km. 104, where another suspension footbridge crosses to the ruins of *Chachabamba* and picks up the trail to the ruins of *Wiñay Wayna (see Chapter Four)*. There it joins the main Inca Trail to Machu Picchu.

Next landmark is the dam and intake for a tunnel which carries water beneath the mountains to emerge at a point 14 km. downstream, taking advantage of an 400m. drop to generate hydroelectric ity for the whole region (however, the generating plant, downstream from Machu Picchu, was destroyed by a huge landslide in the El Niño year of 1998); shortly before the dam you can see the ruins of Choquessuysuy, above the river on the opposite bank. Next comes *Aguas Calientes*, a ramshackle little town with a frontier feel that has mushroomed as the tourist overnight stop for Machu Picchu. A new station has been built here, and this is where all trains now stop. The authorities have so far neglected to construct the indispensable connection here between train station and bus station, so until this is built visitors have to stumble along a rough path through a gauntlet of souvenir vendors for about two hundred meters before reaching the bus terminal, by the old train station at Aguas Calientes.

(Where to stay, where to eat, where to boogie—see Provincial Towns, p. 41)

In the Ruins

Hiram Bingham studied and excavated at Machu Picchu, later classifying the ruins into sectors, naming some of the buildings, and so on. His categories are often quoted as gospel by local guides and guidebooks. But Bingham himself noted that words like "temple" and "palace" are used tentatively, and merely record the impressions conveyed by a careful examination of the buildings.

If his conclusions often appear wide of the mark to modern archaeologists, nevertheless we still need some way of designating the different sectors, and since nobody has come up with a better system than Bingham's, here we go:

You enter the ruins through Bingham's *"House of the Terrace Caretakers"* (1) This entrance did not exist in Inca times, and has been artfully inserted to make tourist access easier. This entrance opens onto the *Agricultural Sector* (2). This great area of terracing undoubtedly was for agricultural purposes. Currently archaeologists are studying soil samples in hopes of determining via pollen traces what was grown here. Most likely it was corn, much of it for making the chicha that was consumed abundantly at Inca ceremonies. Some of the corn itself was probably sacrificed during these ceremonies, too.

It is amazing that these terraces were found standing firm and upright on this vertiginous ridge, 400 years after they were abandoned to the forest. Excavations have revealed that the Inca engineers carefully prepared the subsoil of terraces and plazas for drainage, by recycling the vast quantities of stone chippings left by their stone masons into thick, permeable foundations, before filling in the topsoil that would be used for planting crops. They also built innumerable subterranean buttressing walls in crucial places to prevent subsidence. It was all this invisible engineering that made the terraces so resilient.

The terraces end in a *Dry Moat* (3), beyond which lies the city itself. If you turn left here and ascend the steps which parallel the moat, you come to the the top of the agricultural terraces, high above the city. This is a considerable climb from the main part of the ruins, taking about 20-

MACHU PICCHU

to Wayna Picchu and
Temple of the Moon

N

1. "House of the Terrace Caretakers"
2. Agricultural Sector
3. Dry Moat
4. "Watchman's Hut"
5. "Funerary Rock"
6. Fountains
7. Main Fountain
8. Temple of the Sun
9. "Palace of the Princess"
10. "Fountain Caretaker's House"
11. Royal Sector
12. Quarries
13. Temple of Three Windows
14. Principal Temple
15. "Sacristy"
16. Intiwatana
17. Sacred Rock
18. "Common District"
19. "Mortars"
20. Temple of the Condor
21. Intimachay

▲ "Echo Stones"

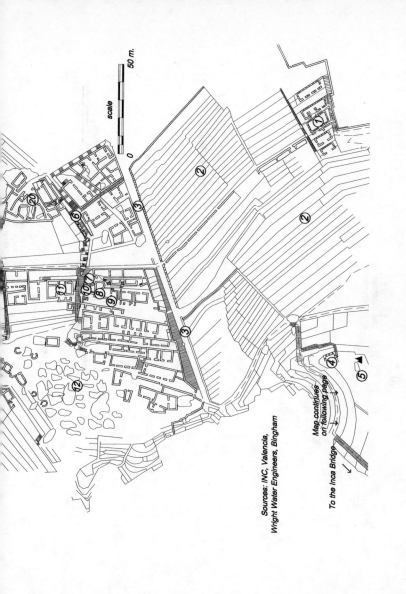

scale

50 m.

0

Sources: INC, Valencia,
Wright Water Engineers, Bingham

Map continues
on following page

To the Inca Bridge

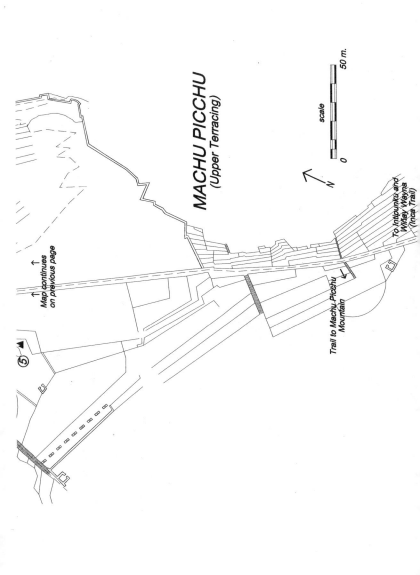

MACHU PICCHU
(Upper Terracing)

N

scale

0   50 m.

Map continues
on previous page

⑤

Trail to Machu Picchu
Mountain

To Intipunku and
Wiñay Wayna
(Inca Trail)

30 mins., but this is the spot for the classic picture-postcard panorama of Machu Picchu. Here stands a lone open-fronted structure, often called the *Watchman's Hut* (4), which faces back onto a gently-sloping area known as the cemetery. Bingham found many bones and mummies in this area. This is a great place for an overall view of the ruins. A few meters from the hut lies a curiously-shaped carved rock , known as the *Funerary Rock* (5). Bingham speculated that this rock was used as a place of lying-in-state for the dead, or as a kind of mortician's slab, on which bodies were eviscerated and dried by the sun for mummification.

If you continue straight ahead into the ruined city instead of climbing the stairs by the moat, you come to the *Fountains* (6), which are actually small waterfalls in a chain of sixteen little "baths," varying in the quality of their construction, with the finest at the top. Scholars believe that these were for ceremonial purposes relating to the worship of water, or perhaps ritual ablutions. The *Main Fountain* (7) is so called because it is the largest, with the finest stonework and the most important location; it is just above you to the left as you arrive from the agricultural terraces.

The fountains are fed by a channel 750 meters long, which brings water across the terraces from a spring. According to an ongoing investigation started by U.S. hydrologist Kenneth Wright and Cusco archaeologist Alfredo Valencia in 1994, this, too, is a small miracle of durability. Carefully engineered, sealed with clay, and graded so that excess water would spill off where it would not cause erosion, it still runs perfectly today. The Wright study has so far discovered no less than 127 drainage outlets in the Urban Sector, all contributing to the stability of Machu Picchu's structures. "The elevation and location of the drainage outlets proves that the Inca engineers followed a master plan... Drainage was neither left to chance nor worked out later, as is so often the case with modern city planning," states Mr. Wright.

Next to the main fountain stands the *Temple of the Sun* (8). This round, tapering tower features the most perfect stonework of Machu Picchu. It contains sacred niches for holding idols and offerings, and the centerpiece is a great rock, part of the actual outcrop onto which the temple was built. Archaeo-astronomical studies carried out in the 1980s by David Dearborn and Raymond White have shown how this temple was used as an astronomical observatory. The rock in the center of the tower has a straight edge cut into it. This is precisely aligned through the adjacent window to the rising point of the sun on the morning of the June solstice. The pegs on the outside of the window may have been used to support a shadow-casting device, which would have made observation much simpler. The purpose of another almost identical window in this building, which faces roughly S.E., has not been determined.

There is an entrance-like opening on the north-east wall of the tower, which presumably was not really a doorway because it has no steps leading down to the next level. It has holes drilled about the jamb, much like a rather similar opening at the Qoricancha in Cusco *(see Chapter One)*. Speculative interpretations portray these holes encrusted with precious stones or with snakes crawling through them, but in truth nobody has the slightest idea what their purpose was. The adjacent building (9) has two storeys and, though small, is of fine quality, and was obviously the house of someone important, perhaps a priest who attended the Sun temple. Bingham named it the *Palace of the Princess*.

The base of this rock forms a grotto which Bingham casually named the Royal Tomb, without actually finding human remains there. It contains exceptionally high quality stonework, and part of the bedrock across the threshold is cut in the ubiquitous step pattern that appears in textiles, pottery motifs and architecture over millenia of Andean civilization. It certainly had a ceremonial function, and indeed it could have been a tomb for some important personage. Today some call it the Temple of Pachamama (Mother Earth).

Next to the Sun Temple, just above the main fountain, is a three-walled house (10), which has been restored and its roof thatched as an example of how these structures looked in Inca times—although Inca thatch was much more perfectly laid. (In his monograph *The Lost Half of Inca Architecture*, Vincent Lee proposes that the ceilings of Inca structures were highly decorated, with a rattan mat woven in elaborate geometric designs stretched between the roof poles and the thatch). It is usually called the *Fountain Caretaker's House*—but it's unlikely to have been a house at all, since it is open to the elements on one side. The thick stone pegs high up in the wall are thought to have served as hangers for heavy objects.

There is an interesting (and probably unverifiable) proposition relating to this cluster of four structures—the Main Fountain, the Sun Temple, the "Royal Tomb," and the Open-fronted Building. Some see these as having represented four temples to the four elements of Water, Fire, Earth and Air, respectively.

The structures directly across the staircase, north of the Sun Temple, have been classified as the *Royal Sector* (11), because of the relative roominess of the buildings, and also for the huge rock lintels (weighing up to three tons) which generally characterized the homes of the Inca potentates. This must have been where the Inca Pachacuteq resided when he came visiting his sacred precinct (unless some fabulous marquee was set up for him on the spacious esplanade). It's a modest dwelling for a mighty emperor, but small quarters are typical of Inca sites.

Notice that the very first fountain of the chain mentioned above is a small but beautifully carved structure, directly across from the entrance to this complex, so that Pachacuteq's compound would have had first use of the water; further testimony to a carefully designed master plan behind the building of Machu Picchu.

At the top of the staircase leading up from the fountains you come to a great jumble of rocks (12) that served as a *quarry* for the Inca masons. There is a fascinating discovery in this sector—a partially-split rock that seems to show precisely how the builders cut stone from the quarry. The rock bears a line of wedge-shaped cuts where tools were hammered in to form a crack. The problem with this rock, though, is that it was reportedly cut by a 20th-century archaeologist, Dr. Manuel Chavez Ballón!

Follow the ridge north-west away from the quarry, with your back to the staircase, and you come to one of the most interesting areas of the city. Here is the *Temple of Three Windows* (13). Its east wall is built on a single huge rock; the trapezoidal windows are partly cut into it. Bingham based a whole theory on this temple, speculating that the three windows symbolized the three caves from which the mythical Ayar brothers stepped forth into the world, and that Machu Picchu therefore represented the origin place of the Incas. However, close inspection reveals that the temple once had five windows, two of them having later been blocked off.

On the open side of this three-walled building stands a stone pillar

which once supported the roof. On the ground by this pillar is a rock bearing the sacred step motif so common to many other Inca and pre-Inca temples.

The huge corner-stone at the north end of the building is unfinished, and shows clearly how the masons were pounding away the face of the wall after it had been erected, to leave the smooth surface we are accustomed to seeing. There is even a shallow groove in the end face of the stone which showed the workers how far they were supposed to cut.

Next to this site is the *Principal Temple* (14), another three-walled building with immense foundation stones and artfully-cut masonry. In the ground at the western end of this building stands a kite-shaped stone pointing south, which is said to represent the Southern Cross. The Principal Temple is so named because of its size and quality, and also because it is the only temple with a kind of sub-temple attached to it, (around the west side, to the rear of the Principal Temple). Bingham called this the *Sacristy* (15), because it seems a suitable place for the priests to have prepared themselves before sacred rites. A stone which forms part of the left-hand door-jamb has no fewer than 32 angles in its separate faces.

At the western edge of this square, overlooking a drop onto steep terraces, stands a small rounded balustrade whose base is of beautifully carved and fitted stones, while the upper portion is rough and crude. The wall remains exactly as Bingham found it—and this is only one among many pieces of evidence that there was a later phase of hastier construction at Machu Picchu.

Ascending the mound beyond this temple leads you to what was probably the most important of all the many shrines at Machu Picchu, the *Intiwatana* (16), the "Hitching Post of the Sun," so-called because the Incas are said to have ritually "tied" the sun to such stones during those critical solstice sunrises to prevent it from wandering any further away down the horizon. The term was popularized by the American scholar Ephraim Squier in the 19th century. Every major Inca center had such a stone, but—other than the inadequate "sun-hitching" explanation -nobody has ever proposed a plausible theory of how they were used. Modern archaeologists sometimes refer to these stones as "gnomons" which in its simplest definition means only a vertical column. It seems very likely that the stones served for making astronomical observations and calculating the passing seasons.

Johan Reinhard has shown that the Intiwatana was at the centerpoint of alignments of both important solar events and sacred peaks. The tip of Wayna Picchu lies due north, while the peak of Salcantay (not visible from this point) is due south. From here at the equinox the sun rises over the peak of Wakay Willka (Verónica) and sinks behind the highest summit of nearby Cerro San Miguel, across the river to the west, where Reinhard, Fernando Astete and Leoncio Vera discovered an Inca platform with a small standing stone. At the December solstice it sets behind the distant snow peak of Pumasillo, the highest peak in the snowcapped range to the south-west, which is visible from here on clear days. Reinhard also suggests that the Intiwatana was itself a stylized representation of Wayna Picchu, creating a similar play of shadows across its face with the passing of the day, and the seasons.

There was at least one other "Intiwatana" in the vicinity, located near the old hydro-electric power station, traces of which are visible on the valley floor down to the west. This second gnomon was probably situated to make a specific astronomical alignment with the main one. The Machu Picchu stone itself is a sculpture of surpassing beauty. It is the only one in all Peru which escaped the diligent attention of the Spanish "extirpators of idolatry" and survived in its original condition.

It is worth noting here that this aspect of "sacred geography" constitutes the very essence of Machu Picchu. The Incas worshipped nature, and the earth itself, and at Machu Picchu so many of the sacred elements came together; not for nothing did Reinhard describe Machu Picchu as the "Sacred Center". The city is built in a saddle at the northern end of an immense ridge about 40 km. long, reaching down from the snows of Salcantay, which to this day is the most venerated and powerful Apu west of Cusco (the Inca Trail follows this ridge, starting at the second pass), while the soaring mass of Wayna Picchu stands like an exclamation point, as a dramatic ending to the ridge. These details alone would have been enough to establish Machu Picchu's sacred importance, but there was more, because at the end of the ridge nothing less than the Willcamayu, the Incas' most sacred river, made a huge snaking loop, almost surrounding the city. And the encircling crescent of mountains north of the river, was another long ridge, reaching westward from the sacred snows of another important Apu, Wakay Willca (Verónica), which lies to the east. Even today, the most jaded visitor cannot fail to sense the extraordinary beauty and power of the setting.

Sadly, the integrity of this landscape will soon be lost forever. The government has authorized a private consortium to build a cable car which will swing across the Urubamba gorge on a huge span of steel cables, anchored halfway up the face of Putucusi, the low, rounded mountain that stands across the river to the east. Good business, no doubt—but business was never the point of Machu Picchu.

The group of buildings east of the level grassy esplanade in the center of the ruins comprises another, more utilitarian sector of the city. At the north end of this sector, farthest from the entrance to the ruins, you find two three-sided buildings opening onto a small plaza, which is backed by a huge stone (17), generally called the *Sacred Rock*.

An intriguing aspect of this plaza is that the outline of the great flat rock erected at the northeast edge is shaped to form a visual tracing of the mountain skyline behind it. Then, if you step behind the *masma* (three-sided hut) on the southeast edge and look northwest, you find another rock that echoes the skyline of the small outcrop named Uña Wayna Picchu in the same way.

Inca culture was oral, and many spaces must have been designed for performing the poetry and song through which information was transmitted. It is easy to imagine this plaza as such a place, with the audience seated in the square or the huts, and the bards standing on the stone ledge that skirts the sacred and acoustically useful rock like a narrow stage.

Walking back toward the main entrance along the east flank of the ridge you pass through a large sector of cruder constructions that has been labeled the *Common District* (18). At the end of this sector you come to a building with two curious *disc-shapes* cut into the stone of the floor (19). Each is about two feet in diameter, flat, with a low rim carved around the edge. Bingham called these mortars for grinding corn, but this is a dubious proposition. The normal mortar used by the Quechua people today is much deeper and more rounded within; also it is portable, not fixed in one spot. However, to date nobody has suggested a more plausible explanation for these enigmatic carvings.

Just across the next staircase you come to a deep hollow surrounded by walls and niches known as the *Temple of the Condor* (20). Bingham called this the "Prison Group," because there are vaults below ground, and man-sized niches with holes that might have been used for binding wrists. But the concept of "prison" probably did not exist in Inca society; punishments tended to involve loss of privileges, or physical suffering, or death. Some early Spaniards reported pits full of snakes or pumas into which offenders were dropped to see if they would survive, but this hardly constitutes a prison. More likely, the complex was a temple. A rock at the bottom of this hollow bears a stylized carving of a condor, with the shape of the head and the ruff at the neck clearly discernible. If you face this carving and look up you see a splayed rock formation which some interpret as the wings of the condor.

There is an underground cavern here through which one can climb. It contains a large niche big enough for a human to squat in, which may have held a mummy in accordance with the Inca custom of worshipping their ancestors.

There is a small cave known as *Intimachay* (21) above and to the east of the Condor Temple. It has been identified by archaeo-astronomers Dearborn & White as a solar observatory for marking the December solstice. The cave is faced with coursed masonry and features a window carved partially from a boulder that forms part of the front wall. This window is precisely aligned with the winter solstice sunrise, so that morning light falls on the back wall of the cave for ten days before and after this date.

Puma-head pot handle, found at Machu Picchu

Walks Close to the Ruins

Intipunku: Above the ruins to the southeast you can see a notch in the ridge, with a small ruin at the center. This is Intipunku, the Sun Gate. The trail you see traversing the mountainside from this point is the last section of the Inca Trail, arriving from Wiñay Wayna and other sites further south. It is well preserved, and makes for a fairly easy climb, taking typical walkers about an hour and a half there and back—but allow time for enjoying the view of Machu Picchu from Intipunku, which is magnificent.

Wiñay Wayna hike: Physically active people who are staying overnight at or near Machu Picchu can consider taking the Inca Trail beyond Intipunku, as far as Wiñay Wayna and back. This walk takes about five hours altogether, including some time to look at the ruins.

(*Note:* at Intipunku you will be charged a fee, currently US$2.00, for doing this hike.) The journey itself is rewarding, since the trail passes through exotic tropical cloud forest. The beautiful site of Wiñay Wayna *(see Chapter Four, p. 179)* is also very much worth the effort of reaching it. The route follows the trail to Intipunku described above, and continues on along the well-marked Inca Trail to Wiñay Wayna. It is a fairly strenuous hike, and you probably have a train to catch, so start early.

The Inca drawbridge: A trail winds back from the heights of the ruins, by the cemetery, leading along the west flank of the mountain behind Machu Picchu. This trail grows narrower, until it is cut into the side of a sheer precipice, and you find yourself taking each step with great care. Follow it until you come to a spot so abrupt that the ancients had to build a huge stone buttress to create a ledge for the path to cross. They left a strategic gap in the middle of the buttress, bridged by logs which they could withdraw to prevent unwanted visitors from entering. Beyond this point the trail quickly peters out, becoming unstable and extremely dangerous. The path has been fenced off shortly before the bridge, ever since a hiker tried to cross it and fell to his death. To the bridge and back is an exciting one-hour walk demanding a cool head for heights. The trail is closed after 1 p.m.

Machu Picchu Mountain: An Inca pathway winds eastward up through the woods on the north flank of the mountain, until it meets the ridgetop. Here it turns westward, still climbing along the ridge until it reaches the summit, where the Incas built a series of platforms. The beginning of this trail is a set of sunken stairs that climbs through the terraces to the right of the roadway to Intipunku, shortly after it passes below (12) on the map. The trail winds diagonally to the left, up the north flank of Machu Picchu mountain. When it reaches the ridgetop it turns sharply to the right, following the line of the ridge until it ends at an Inca platform on the summit. This is a tough climb. Allow at least three hours round trip.

Wayna Picchu and the Temple of the Moon: Hardy visitors like to climb the towering granite peak that overlooks Machu Picchu to the north. The path is very steep; it's the original Inca path, stepped in places. Approach it with caution—but don't be put off by the peak's fearsome appearance. It's not as exposed as it appears from a distance.

Everyone planning to climb Wayna Picchu must sign in at the control point along the trail leaving the principal ruins. No one is allowed to begin the climb after 1:00pm.

As you near the top of Wayna Picchu you pass through ancient terraces, so inaccessible and so narrow that their value for agricultural purposes would have been negligible. Hence, it's thought that these were probably ornamental gardens, bright patches of color on the mountain to be admired from the city below. About an hour to an hour and a half gets the average person to the peak for a stupendous view of the ruins, the road, the valley, the mountains—everything. It is possible to continue down from the peak to the Temple of the Moon (*see circuit below*).

The *Temple of the Moon* is located inside a cavern halfway down the north face of Wayna Picchu. It contains some of the most impressive stonework of the entire Machu Picchu complex. There is a large and magnificent gateway just beyond the temple, with a long, narrow building tucked into the rocks behind it. Another, more roughly worked subterranean temple lies about 50m downhill from there. This gateway and cave complex was an important ceremonial center, and a major threshold to Machu Picchu via a trail leading up from the river, which still exists, but is not open to the public at this writing.

According to Fernando Astete, resident INC archaeologist at Machu Picchu, an early manager of the ruins hotel gave this place its fanciful name, which then stuck. It almost certainly has nothing to do with the Inca uses of the site, since this is not a good place for observing the moon. Human remains were found here. These caves may have been a place of venerating the Inca mummies.

The main Inca pathway which leads to the temple forks off the main trail to the left, about one third of the way up to the peak of Wayna Picchu. It takes about two hours round-trip to reach the temple. Note that parts of the trail are quite exposed, with a long sheer drop-off to one side. Not really dangerous, but scary.

Wayna Picchu/Temple of the Moon circuit. From the peak of Wayna Picchu an Inca stairway leads down the north face of the mountain, arriving at the Temple of the Moon. It is incredibly steep, and broken in places. About five minutes down from the peak there is a place where the stairs have collapsed, and ropes and a ladder have been installed to make it easier for daredevils to descend. Even so, this is a heartstopping experience for the average person.

If you succeed in reaching the Temple of the Moon this way, you can return via the easier route which climbs around the north flank of the mountain to rejoin the main trail up Wayna Picchu.

Future project: One day it should be possible to walk a trail down past the Temple of the Moon to the river and across it to see the new discoveries on Cerro San Miguel and at Mandor Pampa. (This has been a Future Project for many years, however).

Chapter Six

CHINCHERO & MORAY

The High Plateau North of Cusco

The Incas had every climate and ecological zone from torrid rainforest to bleak, desolate *puna* within a day or two's march of their capital; the modern visitor can reach these locations in even less time. Just northwest of Cusco lies a highland area, colder and windier than the sheltered valley of the city. It is flatter, too, forming a rolling plateau between the Cusco valley and the middle Urubamba valley to the northwest, which is known as the Pampa de Anta. This is an agricultural belt of mainly potato, wheat and barley production; yellow and seemingly barren in the dry season when most visitors see it, in the rainy months it becomes a multicolored mosaic of red earth squares interspersed with fields in every shade of green and yellow.

The first stretch of the railway to Machu Picchu crosses this *altiplano*, and a major road parallels it, climbing out of Cusco then descending onto this plateau, heading west. It divides shortly after Poroy, the right fork heading towards Chinchero and Urubamba, the left toward Limatambo, Abancay, and the coast.

CHINCHERO

Chinchero was the Pampa de Anta's chief center of population in Inca times. It may have been a considerable city; some historians think it could once have been the capital of a small state, before the fusion and expansion of the Inca culture. Later it is thought to have become the royal estate of Topa Inca, son of Pachacuteq. Under Spanish rule the

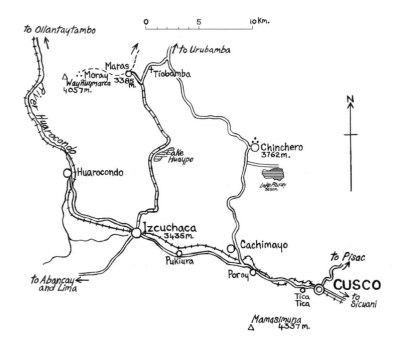

town dwindled into a village, and remained a backwater off the main Cusco-Izcuchaca highway until very recently, when the paved road was completed.

Chinchero is mainly visited for its Sunday market, which is the best known in the area after Pisac's. Nowadays the handcrafts market is located in the plaza in front of the church, and the produce market is at the foot of the hill. *(For transportation from Cusco see p. 19)*. These days the handcrafts market carries similar items to that of Pisac, though there are fewer vendors. However, the setting here is spacious, it is easier to wander off into open, uncrowded areas, and shopping here feels more relaxed. For those interested in Andean textiles, some good weavings can sometimes be found here.

The town itself is spread over a commanding rise at the head of a valley which leads down and away northeast to the Urubamba river. On a clear day the views from Chinchero are tremendous: to the west and northwest stretches a vista of rolling altiplano, ringed in the distance by the dramatic snowcaps of the Cordilleras Vilcabamba and Urubamba.

The main square of the town is famous for its massive Inca wall, set with ten of the largest trapezoidal niches known among Inca structures. This was probably the base-wall of a palace—perhaps that of Topa Inca—that once overlooked the square, situated where the church now stands. The church has a colonial fresco around the portico. Inside it was once beautiful, entirely painted, walls and ceiling, with multicolored flowers and patterns. Centuries of neglect almost destroyed these works of art, but much restoration has been done in recent years. Note the image of a saint dressed as a peasant, carrying a ploughshare and ears of wheat, by the altar on the right.

As you stand in the square facing the church, you see to your left, beyond the village, the head of the valley that descends several kilometers to meet the Urubamba at Urquillos, just east of Wayllabamba. The slopes close to the town here are heavily sculpted with ancient terracing. This is an Inca site far larger than it would seem just by looking at it from the village square.

If you walk northward down the terraces from the near the church, then follow the terraces downvalley a little way, keeping to the righthand slopes, you come to a large rock outcrop which has been carved and shaped to an amazing degree. Climb over it and you will find staircases, seats, water channels, an intricately worked drainpipe cut vertically into the rock, and (careful!) a 30-meter plunge into a kind of grotto beneath the outcrop. Farther down the valley you can see another of these rocks, with a long staircase winding up the side of it; a deep niche—perhaps this once housed a mummy—facing the valley; and what seems to be a little conference-room or get-together place with seats carved in a circle at the top of the outcrop.

Walks: Chinchero lies close to the edge of the plateau, where it drops away into the Sacred Valley. To make a full day of your visit to Chinchero, combine it with a walk to the Urubamba river. After crossing the river you can reach the paved highway, where you can pick up a ride to one of the valley towns, and from there to Cusco. The walks are fairly easy—mostly downhill—but leave Chinchero by noon at the latest—preferably earlier—to be sure of reaching the valley before dark.

Chinchero to Wayllabamba. This route follows the old Inca highway down the small valley from Chinchero, to meet the Urubamba near Huayllabamba (Grassy Plain—not to be confused with a village of the same name on the Inca Trail). It takes about four hours to reach the modern roadway between Pisac and Urubamba.

Cross the valley heading north, with your back to the terraces of Chinchero, and pick up the trail you see leading upward to your right on the opposite side of the valley. Once you pick up this main trail, just follow it. There are no major turn-offs to confuse you. The path is wide and safe. It keeps to the lefthand heights of the valley, which becomes something of a gorge as you descend. There is a staggering drop to the valley floor on your right. About 45 minutes out of Chinchero you come upon the well-preserved ruins of an Inca tambo, or post-house. The trail gradually leads you down into a lush, bountiful valley, filled with orchards and green meadows.

You reach the Urubamba valley at the village of Urquillos. Here the trail turns downstream (left). By now you are on a motor road—follow it to the village of Wayllabamba, then cross the bridge to meet the main Valley highway. To return to Cusco, take any ride you can get in the direction of Pisac (to your right). Once you reach Calca it is easy to get a ride to Cusco (but be there before about 8 p.m.).

Salineras: On the way from Maras to Pichinjoto in the Urubamba valley is a remarkable site known as the Salineras. This is a huge accumulation of terraces, watered by a saline underground stream, that collect salt by evaporation (a small entrance fee is charged to visitors). The Salineras have been worked since pre-Hispanic times—there are

Foods of Cusco

There are three basic places to support your food habit in Cusco: restaurants, street vendors and the mercado, the public market where campesinos sell their produce. There are, of course, corner stores and supermarkets that sell conventional foodstuffs, but unless you are homesick you will find the other options more fun.

Most visitors will only sample the foods in Cusco's many inexpensive restaurants. There is much to choose from: beef (carne or lomo); chicken (pollo or gallina); pork (cerdo or chancho); fish (pescado), such as local freshwater whitefish (pejerrey) or trout (trucha), sea-bass (corvina), flounder (lenguado), prawns (camarones) and shrimp (langostinos). All are cooked in myriad ways. The rich sauces are usually beef- or chicken-stock based, with vegetables cooked in. Dishes are generally served with either white rice (arroz) or potatoes (papas), with a bit of lettuce or tomato on the side. (But beware: raw lettuce harbors microbes as does no other vegetable; even hardened travelers avoid it.)

Suggestions for some good restaurant dishes: ají de gallina (spicy chicken); rocoto relleno (stuffed chili, often very spicy); adobo (pork in a spicy broth, served only in the mornings); lomo saltado (chopped beef with rice and vegetables); and chupe de camarones (prawn soup).

Soups in particular are often very good. I recommend locro (corn-based, with chunks of meat and vegetables); chairo (similar, but with potato and ch'unu, the Andean freeze-dried potato, instead of corn); caldillo de huevo (egg soup); and sopa a la criolla (chopped beef with noodles and mild chilis).

Street vendors offer a variety of meals and snacks, some of which can be sampled without fear—the ones which are not served on the vendor's dishes and are thoroughly cooked before your eyes. Try anticuchos (beefhearts on bamboo skewers, with a potato) or tamales, usually reliably well-cooked, they come *dulce* (sweet) or *salado* (salted). Fresh-baked empanadas (flaky pastries stuffed with cheese, chicken or beef) are good, as are the many varieties of bread and sweet pastries.

The main market by the San Pedro station is a must to visit (don't carry any valuables). Unless you will be hiking or plan an extended stay in Cusco you probably won't buy much food here. But there are a few things for sale worth trying anytime, such as the fruits: pepino (a yellow, purple-streaked fruit that tastes something like a melon; chirimoya (a green, knobby, soft-skinned fruit with white pulp and black seeds—sweet and delicious); granadilla and its cousin maracuyá, the passion fruits, with egg-like shells containing a white bag of tasty seeds, which are both gelatinous and crunchy; and several varieties of banana—the small ones about the size of frankfurters, and the fat ones with reddish skin and pink pulp inside are the best. Then there are the usual tropical favorites: papaya, mango, and avocado, all at a low price and high quality that—if you choose carefully—will knock your socks off.

¡Buen provecho!

- Carol Stewart

small Inca ruins close by. The dazzling, salt-encrusted terraces make an extraordinary sight, especially for photographers. Local families own and work them by hand, digging out the salt and loading it onto donkeys.

A dirt road takes you there via the well-marked Maras turn-off, to the left from the Chinchero-Urubamba highway, but there's no public transport there. However, there are taxis which will take you to Salineras from the Maras turn-off on the Urubamba highway *(see Transport, p. 20)*. If walking on your own, the best way to go is to start from Maras, and walk straight down the valley, which lies a few kilometers uphill from the Salineras. Once at the salt pans it is easy to follow the trail down the left side of the valley to the Urubamba river. Turn right as you near the river, and you soon meet a footbridge. Cross it and follow the trail another 500m or so to the main Urubamba-Ollantaytambo highway.

MORAY

If you are keen to leave the beaten track and see something different, go to Moray. Moray is beyond different—it is truly unique. This site is not the ruin of a city or a fortress, it is an earthwork. The ancient peoples of the region took four huge natural depressions in the landscape and sculpted them into levels of agricultural terraces that served, hundreds of years ago, as an experimental agricultural station for the development of different crop strains. This was possible due to the discovery of a fascinating phenomenon: the climates of many different ecological zones were present at a single site.

Much of the terracing survives intact, leaving regular concentric layers flowing harmoniously into the land. There are no great ruined

Moray
three main depressions

structures here to impress visitors. Moray is more for the contemplative traveler with an affinity for such phenomena as the Nazca Lines, the stone rings of Avebury and the menhirs of Brittany.

How to Get There: It is normally possible to reach Moray by car (but prepare for trouble after heavy rain). There is a good paved road as far as Maras—the nearest town—and then a rural track that leads westward across the open country of the plateau. This track passes to the right (north) of the footpath—ask for directions in Maras to pick it up. The difficulty here may be some rather shaky log bridges over the three streams that lie between Maras and Moray. If you are taking a taxi, best bet would be to hunt for a driver who has been there; some drivers might balk at the bridges.

You can reach Maras by bus from Cusco, and then taxi from the main highway *(see Transportation, p. 20).*

Where to Stay: Nowhere. You must camp. Maras has no hotels, and Moray itself is in the country, far from even rudimentary comforts. Two ways to see Moray in one day, without an overnight stop, are to have your own motor tranpsort, or to go by mountain bike—an excellent way to see both the ruins and the surrounding plateau *(see Mountain Biking, p. 33).*

If you decide to camp, bring all your food, fuel for your stove—everything you need, because there is nothing available at Moray itself, and you have about a 1 1/2 hour walk to Maras, where you will find only very basic supplies.

The terraces of Moray themselves make a pleasant campsite, but there is no water. Nearest source is the farmhouse above the ruins, where they will be glad to let you use the tap—but ask first. Nowadays there is an INC post here, with a guard charging an entrance fee.

The Route to Maras: This town lies near the paved highway from Cusco to Urubamba. The turn-off is well-signposted, and lies about 10 minutes by car beyond Chinchero.

The Walk: Maras is a colonial town, quite large but smaller than it was years ago when it thrived on mining the salt deposits in the cliffs to the north. The salt deposits are still being worked *(see Salineras, above)*, but nowadays most of Cusco's salt comes from the coast.

The walk from Maras to Moray is about 7 km., and takes about an hour and a half. The trail to Moray leads westward, away from the town in roughly the same direction you followed from the highway, perpendicular to the main street of Maras. Best ask for directions here, as the path is hard to find at first.

Once found the trail is easy, with only one real opportunity for getting lost. You cross three minor ravines en route. The first is only 20 to 25 feet deep. The second is large, perhaps a hundred feet deep. As you climb out of this second quebrada what appears to be the main trail continues diagonally up its slopes. This is the wrong trail. (It goes off northwest toward Pachar in the Urubamba valley.) The Moray trail leaves this path and climbs to the left almost straight up the slopes. Next landmark is a farmhouse to the right of the path, followed immediately by two small ponds, one on either side of you (these might be dry sometimes, of course). Soon you can see in the distance a large INC signboard, bearing the name of the ruins. The path does fork a second time, but you are now in view of the signboard, so aim for that. Cross the third ravine, about 50 feet deep, to arrive on the rim of the main bowl of Moray.

In the Ruins: The plateau around Maras lies on a shaky bed of salt and soluble minerals. The soil is highly calcitic, rich in calcium sulphate and carbonate. In places the land has collapsed into a honeycomb of subterranean erosion and potholes. Moray is one such place, a cluster of great sinkholes like craters in the landscape. They have never flooded and become lakes, because the rock below is riddled with tunnels that drain water away northward to the Urubamba valley.

Long ago the ancient Peruvians made a curious discovery here. The deep natural bowls caught sunlight and shade in such a way as to create drastic variations in temperature within a very small area. In the thirty or so meters of altitude between the bottom and top levels of Moray's main depression one scientist, John Earls, has recorded a full 15 degrees

Celsius difference in temperature. That is about equal to the difference between the mean annual temperatures of London and Bombay.

Nature had created at Moray the conditions modern man creates artificially in a row of greenhouses. And the development of Andean civilization followed, step by step, the development of varying high-altitude crop strains—particularly strains of maize, the crop that enabled Andean peoples to settle in large communities.

Conceivably it was Moray itself that played the key role in the original transformation of maize into a high-altitude crop. If so the site is a monument of immense importance, for scholars agree that without Andean maize there could have been no Andean civilization on any scale—none of the earlier highland civilizations like Tiwanaku, and no Incas. Other crops like potato and quinoa could not, they say, have sustained such large population centers.

With Moray the ancients were able to develop in one place crops adapted to the challenging range of local climates found in the tropical Andes. According to Earls, they probably measured temperature differences by placing water in cups to freeze at night on the terraces and checking the rate of thaw in the morning sunshine. Quechua has a subtle vocabulary for ice, snow, freezing, etc., so we know that the Incas understood these characteristics of water.

We can be more certain about the purpose of this site than with other pre-Columbian sites in Peru. The terraces are clearly agricultural. The remains of the irrigation system are well preserved. And yet for ordinary agriculture this location would have been disastrously inappropriate, since no one crop variety, or even two or three, could thrive on the terraces. The local people still refer to the ruins as the "Greenhouses of the Incas," and the influence of the ruins is manifest to this day in the extraordinarily complex crop rotation and plantings practiced by the campesinos of the district. In fact, the nearby villages have a rich mythical tradition about Moray. A very old man told anthropologist Gary Urton that the terrace walls were once covered in plates of gold and silver to trap and reflect celestial light. Another told him that the Inca

Wayna Capac is alive and dwells underground beneath the largest bowl.

How old is Moray? It definitely seems pre-Inca in origin. Probably it spanned more than one culture, starting millenia ago, since pottery fragments from the Chanapata culture—dated around the time of Christ—have been found there. It seems unlikely that the terraces were built so long ago, but there is strong evidence for a link with the Wari culture, a pre-Inca "middle horizon" civilization dating from about 1000 A.D. or earlier. The Waris were no master stonemasons, but they had a distinct ceramic style, which has been found on the bottom six levels of the main depression.

The higher levels are clearly different, and probably Inca. In accordance with their usual pattern, the Incas took Moray over, refined it, and enlarged it. They added a horseshoe-shaped extension to the main depression, leveling off a large area for planting, and another area in a second adjacent depression to the west.

The largest depression, known as *Quechuyoc* (Warm-being), has fifteen levels of terracing. The other depressions—smaller and less well preserved—are called *Simiyoc* (Grass-having; or possibly Tongue-having); *Ñustahispanan* (Where the Princess Pee'd)—a curiosity common in Inca legend: a spring rises at this spot, and Inca myths often attribute this to a royal lady having urinated there; and *Intiwatana*, the familiar name indicating that an Inca "calendar stone" may once have stood on this spot.

For a view of all four *muyus* (as they are called in Quechua), make a half-hour climb to the middle of the three peaks of *Wañuymarca* (House of the Dead), the mountain which looms over the ruins to the south.

Chapter Seven

THE VALLEY ROAD SOUTHEAST

The Road to Collasuyu

Many travelers take the southeast road or railway toward Lake Titicaca and Arequipa en route to Bolivia or southern Peru. Yet few visitors know of the many fascinating places close to Cusco along this valley. This chapter describes some of the most interesting spots.

Figures in kilometers indicate distances from the city of Cusco. Directions (left, right) are given for people traveling south; if you are traveling north you should, of course, reverse them.

Explorers should find many interesting places along some of the lesser side roads off the main valley. But it is just about essential to have your own transport to do this, unless time is unimportant. These roads carry little traffic.

The best way to see the main valley if you do not have your own transport would be to select two or three places to visit. Then catch a bus early from Cusco *(see Transport, p. 18)* and get off at the first place you intend to see, moving on later with the next available transport. The main road is quite busy in both directions and buses are available well into the evening. Nowadays the valley highway is paved all the way to the Bolivian border at Yunguyo, and traveling has become much easier in recent years. If you should happen to get stranded, there are hotels of sorts in Quiquijana (72 km.), Combapata (110 km.) and Sicuani (138 km.).

One useful item to carry if you plan to visit churches would be a powerful flashlight, since some are dark inside and this is the only way to see the paintings clearly. A pair of binoculars is also useful for picking out the details of paintings high up on walls or ceilings.

Another problem here is that churches are often locked. The church of Andawaylillas is usually open, and the one at Urcos has a key-carrying caretaker on the premises, but it may take time and dogged persistence to find the caretaker in other places. Try enlisting the aid of the police or local authorities, and do remember to give a tip to the *guardián* who opens up a church for you.

San Sebastián (5 km.) is known for its fine church, which stands on the site of a chapel built to commemorate the victory of the Pizarro brothers over Diego de Almagro. The original collapsed in the earthquake of 1650. The present church has two towers—identical, despite the fact that 135 years separated the building of the two. The baroque portico gets a worthy mention from connoisseurs of porticos.

Saylla (12 km.) is the spot if you like *chicharrón de chancho* (fried pork)—a whole village of restaurants devoted to pigging out. And just beyond it, off the highway to left, is *Huasao*, known as the sorcerer's village, where the local specialties are magic, ritual, and the casting of spells.

Tipón (turn-off: 23 km.) is an Inca site of considerable interest to ruin junkies (a small entrance fee is charged). The turn-off (left) is about 2 km. before Oropesa, marked by the standard INC signboard for archaeological monuments. The site lies 4 km. off the highway, much of it fairly steep climbing (allow about 1 1/2 hours on foot) and can be reached by car up a reasonably good dirt road.

The ruin consists of a long series of high, beautifully-constructed agricultural terraces—some of the finest in existence—running up the head of a narrow valley. The irrigation system was unusual in that it featured deep, vertical channels in the terrace walls. The system was fed by a natural spring from the mountainside which still flows today. Tipón may have been a site for developing special crop strains, like Moray *(see*

Chapter Six) as it seems too elaborate for routine agriculture. There are remains of some habitations, but it does not seem to have been a large population center.

An aqueduct 1400m long flows down the mountain spur to the west of the terraces. It passes underground beneath the ruins group known as Intiwatana. At the heights above the top end of this aqueduct, a couple of hours climbing from the main terraces, stand the remains of an ancient walled enclosure, perhaps a fort.

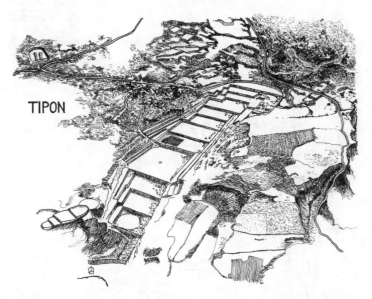

TIPON

Shortly after the Tipón turn-off lies another to *Oropesa* (25 km.), which boasts 47 bakeries, and a colonial church with fine murals.

Beyond the lefthand turn-off for Paucartambo*(see below)* and the Sacred Valley, the road begins to climb to a small pass. To your right is the Laguna de Lucre, a beautiful reed-lined lake. At Urpicancha, a beautiful spot about 1 km. off the main road on the south shore of the

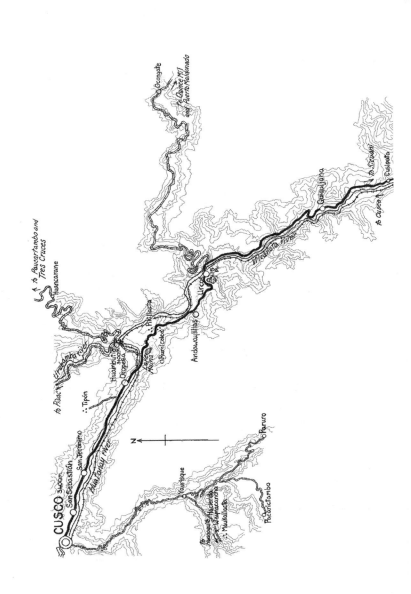

THE VALLEY ROAD
SOUTH-EAST

rail
paved highway
dirt road

© P. FROST – 1999

0   10   20   30 Km.

lake, there is a small hotel, recently refurbished, which serves lunches. Nearby are some seldom-visited Inca ruins known as the "Morada de Wascar"—Wascar's Dwelling—because this is thought to have been the birthplace and country palace of the Inca Wascar, who fought and lost in the civil war against his half-brother, Atawallpa.

Pikillaqta—Flea Town—(30 km.) stands above the road to the left as you climb past the lake. This is a huge sprawling site, of interest primarily because it is the only major ruin of a pre-Inca settlement in the Cusco region. The site was built by the Wari culture, which arose near Ayacucho, northwest of Cusco, and flourished c. 600-950 A.D. Pikillaqta (entrance by T.T.) stands at the narrow southern approach to the Huatanay valley, and seems strategic in location. It appears powerful and menacing, with its many hectares of tall, two- and three-story buildings surrounded by a enclosing wall, much of which still stands. It is a huge site, about the size of pre-Conquest Cusco. And it lies across a rolling slope in a precisely squared-off grid as if it had been designed elsewhere and set down here with utter disregard for the landscape, in striking contrast to the harmonious integration of nature and architecture at the Inca sites.

The appearance of control over the valley was symbolic, however, because this was not a military garrison. Neither was it a city, in the ordinary sense of the word. According to U.S. archaeologist Gordon McEwan, who has excavated the site, Pikillaqta was a curious sort of ceremonial center; local vassal lords were brought here for alliance-building feasts and rituals. At one of the three basic types of structure at Pikillaqta—described by McEwan as "lineage halls"—venerated ancestors were kept in niches, presiding over the festivities. Two nearly simultaneous looting expeditions in 1927 unearthed two very similar sets of 40 tiny turquoise figurines in one of these halls. One set is now one of the major treasures belonging to the Cusco Inka Museum, and the other ended up, minus one figurine, in a private collection in Madrid.

Pikillaqta is a puzzling site. Very few people actually lived there. People *came* here, and then left. All of its buildings were covered in a white gypsum stucco, quarried in the surrounding hills, which must have made it unbearably dazzling in the Andean sunshine. Floors were also of gypsum, 5 cm. thick. Many of its rooms were windowless and utterly dark, so that they were once thought to be for storage; but archaeology reveals that these enigmatic spaces were apparently designed for some other purpose. The only entrance to the entire complex was a narrow street lined with very high walls, also stuccoed, so one could see nothing of the surroundings. The effect of arriving there as a vassal of the Wari must have been profoundly intimidating.

Beneath the modern town at nearby *Huaro*, the remains of a major Wari center have been discovered. This settlement was probably the residential site for the people who built and maintained Pikillaqta.

Some unknown violent catastrophe befell the Wari empire, while it

Turquoise figurines, found at Pikillacta

was still expanding. As a result the Wari deliberately and systematically abandoned Pikillaqta sometime between 850-950 A.D. The Wari filled in partially-built temples with clay, and dug up some of the offerings they had buried. Then, after they left, someone came along and torched the place. Perhaps this was the vengeance of the local vassals.

Just up the main highway from Pikillaqta (about 500m) stands *Rumicolca* (Stone Storehouse), the southern gateway to the Cusco valley. The ruin can be seen to the right of the road. From ground level it looks like a huge Inca work, with its sheer walls of fine-cut stone. However, the tiered stonework on either side of the gate is much cruder. The structure was originally a Wari aqueduct—part of the Pikillaqta complex. The remains of the water channel can clearly be seen along the top. The Incas altered it—probably demolished some sections—and turned it into a great double gateway to the Cusco Valley.

Just down the hill from Rumicolca lie some stone quarries which were the source of much of the characteristic grey andesite which was used in the construction of Inca Cusco. The flat area by the Vilcanota river just beyond here, is called *Piñipampa*, and is the major center of production for the terracotta roofing tiles of Cusco.

Andawaylillas (37 km.), a small community just off the main highway to the right, is the most attractive village for miles around. The main square is delightful, with its canopy of trees and the colonial houses surrounding it, some with murals painted on their façades. The village hall is graced with a proud Inca doorway in Imperial stonework—a sign that the structure which once stood here housed a noble of very high rank. The major attraction of the village is the church of San Pedro, which someone in a fit of hyperbole once called the "Sistine Chapel of the Americas." It certainly is a splendid church, with a stunning multicolor and gold-leaf ceiling, beautiful murals and some especially fine colonial paintings. There is no church in the city of Cusco to compare with it.

The church dates from the early 17th century and was built by the Jesuits. The purpose of covering the inside of this church and others with murals was to evangelize the illiterate natives, often using imagery that harmonized with the indigenous belief system. The Moorish influence evident in the frescoes on the ceiling, for example, evidently appealed to Quechua aesthetic sensibilities, being geometrical and abstract, like many Andean textile motifs.

Local guides claim that the painting above the arch is by the 17th-century Spanish master, Murillo. A mural over the main doorway, no doubt designed to instruct the natives, depicts a sumptuously attractive (and crowded) path to hell versus a drearily virtuous path to heaven. The painting in the nave reflects the Cusco school, characterized by a surfeit of gilt ornamentation on top of the paint, whereas the chancel was painted by adherents of Italian Renaissance masters. The entrance to the baptistry to the left of the main door is crowned with a mural whose inscription is written in five languages—latin, spanish, Quechua, Aymara and the now-extinct pukina, language of the Uru and Chipaya peoples of the altiplano.

The sponsor of most of the church's artistic content was a priest called Juan Pérez de Bocanegro, whose image, kneeling before Saint Peter, appears on the pulpit. Many of the paintings were done around 1626-28 by one Luis de Riaño, whose signature sometimes appears. The parish has produced an informative pamphlet (in spanish) with detailed information on the works of art in the church, on sale at the entrance.

Decent restaurants are hard to find along this road, but the *Restaurante Las Tunas*, just before Huaro, 39 kms from Cusco, is a cheerful outdoor lunch spot with good, simple food.

The church at *Huaro* (44 km.) is another fine colonial church, decorated with beautiful murals and well worth visiting. These works are much later than Andawaylillas, signed by the artist and head of the project, Tadeo Escalante, and dated 1802. A terrifying painting of Hell occupies the righthand wall, and the ceiling is entirely covered with floral and animal motifs, among which native Peruvian species feature prominently. There are also scenes of the tree of life, and of pleasure, death and dying.

Recent excavations at Huaro have revealed the site of an important settlement of the Wari empire, virtually all of it buried beneath the modern town. An intricate and difficult study led by Cusco archaeologist Julinho Zapata is today revealing the extent of this site.

The chapel of the Virgin at *Canincunca*, just beyond Huaro, and about 1 km. before Urcos (47 km.), is even more heavily decorated with murals than the other churches in this area. It stands to the right of the highway at the small pass from which you can see Urcos and the lake into which—legend says—a solid gold chain belonging to the Inca

Wascar was dumped to save it from Pizarro's ravening wolves. The chapel is dedicated to the Virgen de Candelaria. Knock on the side door and ask the caretaker to unlock it for you.

At *Checacupe* (99 km.) there is a church partly built on Inca or transitional walls, and worth seeing for those interested in colonial art. The building is often locked. Try to get the policeman across the road to find the caretaker for you.

A road leads off the main highway northeast from Checacupe to *Pitumarca*. Little traffic, but it's only about a two-hour walk. The village is very traditional. A lot of fine weaving comes from this area, which is a major center of alpaca production. Weaving enthusiasts from all over come to visit the store of former mayor Timoteo Ccarita, who is a leading expert and collector. About a half-hour walk from the village there are some pre-Inca ruins known as Machu Pitumarca. To return to the highway, it's said that the people of this village are so trusting they will sometimes rent you a bike on the understanding you will leave it at the police station in Checacupe.

Raqchi (119 km.) is the last major place of interest on the route within an easy day's journey of Cusco. This ruin site covers a big area, lying to the left of the main highway, about 4 km. before the town of San Pedro. Look out for a series of very tall adobe columns capped with rooflets of Spanish-style tiles, beyond a small village.

You can reach the main square of the village by car. The church here looks like the prototype for all those fairy-tale ceramic churches from Ayacucho that are so popular with tourists. The villagers of Raqchi make excellent rustic pottery during the dry season, when the fields are idle.

The ruin at Raqchi is called the "Temple of Viracocha." Legend has it that the temple was raised to propitiate the Inca creator god after the area's devastation by a volcanic eruption. The stone of the district is indeed predominantly volcanic. The building itself is unique in Inca architecture for its sheer size (outer walls 90m long, 15m high), and also

Herds and Herders of the Andes

Animal herding in pre-Columbian America was developed only in Peru. Llamas *(Lama glama)* and alpacas *(Lama pacos)* were the domesticated species, both descended from the guanaco *(Lama guanicoe)*, which exists in the wild to this day, along with its more distant cousin the vicuña *(Vicugna vicugna)*. The evolutionary prototype of both the camel and the South American cameloids appeared in North America 40 million years ago. One branch of the evolutionary tree went north, crossing the Bering strait and becoming the two Asian camel species, while another went south across the isthmus of Panama and evolved into the cameloid family of South America. In the interim, the proto-camel became extinct in its place of origin.

Hunter-gatherers of the *puna* (the grasslands of the high Andes) began the domestication of llamas and alpacas seven thousand years ago, a process which culminated in the appearance of herding societies, five thousand years ago. Since then herding has been a complex adaptive process, especially at the high altitudes where it has been most highly developed, and where today's herders live.

Llamas and alpacas acquired their greatest economic and strategic importance under the Incas. They supplied wool for textiles and meat for consumption, but above all llamas were used for transport. Their load-carrying capacity made the Inca expansion possible. Llamas carried the supplies of the imperial Inca armies to places as far away as southern Colombia, the sierra of Ecuador, and northern Chile and Argentina.

They played an important part in Andean religion, too. The priesthood kept herds, from which they took animals for sacrifice. In the Aucaypata, the central square of Inca Cusco, numerous llamas were sacrificed every day.

The Sapa Inca joined in the festivals of the herders, to dance and sing with them. One of the royal symbols of the Sapa Inca was the *napa*, a pure white llama covered with a red cloth, which walked

ALPACA

EARS: Straight, pointed, shorter than llama's

FACE: small; short nose; woolly

FACE: long nose; no wool; haughty look

TAIL: usually carried low

LEGS: wool below knee — not much wool

LLAMA

EARS: long and curved

TAIL: often carried high, like a flag

ahead of him during processions. In Inca culture the iconography of llamas and alpacas is diverse, abundant, and esthetically sophisticated.

The 16th-century Spanish invasion brought with it cattle and sheep, which displaced llamas and alpacas to marginal areas, especially the great highland punas above 4000 m., truly the "refuge regions" where modern herders graze them.

There are about 100,000 herding families today, tending to three million alpacas and half a million llamas. Their remoteness has not prevented them, since the last century, from participation in the world fibers market, given that alpaca wool is used in high fashion clothing. Nevertheless, they conserve ways of life and traditions which have hardly changed since Inca times, although they adopt the modern innovations which interest and suit them.

La Raya is the Experimental Center for South American Cameloids of Cusco's National University. It is the world's principal center for the study of llamas and alpacas. It lies on the route to Puno, 160 kms. from Cusco. (It is possible to visit the La Raya facility, by first obtaining written permission from the *Vice-Rector Administrativo,* Dr. Jorge Villafuerte, on the University campus in Cusco; tel. 238192). Traditional herding regions accessible to a day excursion from Cusco lie on the roads from Ollantaytambo to Quillabamba at the Abra de Málaga (4000m), and at the Abra de Amparaes (4200m) on the Calca-Lares road.

-Jorge Flores Ochoa

Today llamas and alpacas are becoming popular in other parts of the world, particularly the U.S. where they serve as pets and pack animals. They are valued for their low impact on the environment compared to horses and mules, because their soft hoof-pads do not chew up trails, and their grazing habits are exemplary. Sheep ranchers have also discovered that a few llamas kept in the herd will drive away the coyotes which kill their lambs. - P.F.

for its configuration. It consists of a central wall with bases of Imperial Inca stonework and a top section of adobe, with a line of rounded columns on either side of this wall, which once supported the roof. Columns like these are otherwise unknown in Inca structures. Only the bases of these columns remain, though one has been reconstructed. The ruin has been roofed with tiles to protect the adobe from erosion.

Adjacent to the temple are rows of identical houses grouped neatly around identical squares: six squares, 36 buildings. Then, toward the road, stand perhaps the most remarkable sturctures of the ruins: the remains of 200 stone storehouses. These are cylindrical in shape, grouped in dead-straight rows of ten, and each measures some six meters in diameter by two-and-a-half in height. All of this represents a colossal volume of storage space, and is the most impressive remaining testimony in the region to the degree of social organization attained by the Incas.

The residence of the nobles or high priests seems to have been located near the hillside, to the left as you enter the ruins from the village. Over there you will find the stone base of what was probably once a palace; and also a very fine set of baths, which has been partly excavated and restored. The remains of a complex system of water ducts can be clearly seen.

Paucartambo lies in a valley above the eastern jungles, 115 km. from Cusco. *(To get there see Transport, p. 20.)* The road there is a twisty mountain affair that carries little traffic. There are now daily buses from Cusco, however. If you have your own car, take the left turn into the Sacred Valley about 3 km. beyond Oropesa, and cross the bridge over the Vilcanota at Huambutío.

The town itself is small and out of the way. Expect to rough it if you stay the night.

Paucartambo is a picturesque but quiet place, best known for its yearly Christian-on-Pagan festival of the Virgin of Carmen (15th-17th July), a very colorful local fiesta with the best traditional dances, and the most varied and exotic masks and costumes to be seen anywhere in the Cusco region. The dances and characters include malaria victims, gringos (warty, evil-looking ones), bear-men, condor-men, black slaves and warlike jungle Indians.

About 50 km. beyond Paucartambo lies *Tres Cruces*, at the eastern rim of the Andes, perched over the last breathtaking drop into the Amazon basin. The Incas held this place sacred for the uncanny optical effects that appear there during sunrise at certain times of year, notably the winter solstice (June). Here you are at 3600 m., looking down over the flat, endless lowlands of the Manu Biosphere Reserve; the horizon lies an immense distance away, and on clear mornings observers report multiple suns, haloes, rainbows, a brilliant rosy glow covering land and sky. This phenomenon is at its most intense and frequent during May, June and July.

Explorer's Note: South of Cusco, near the road that goes to Huanoquite, lie the Inca ruins of Maukallaqta and Puma Orqo.

Maukallaqta was an extensive and important ceremonial and administrative center, now largely destroyed. Puma Orqo is a carved-rock outcrop, a waca, about 20 minutes walk from Maukallaqta. Some archaeologists believe that this pair of sites forms the true location of Tampu Tocco, celebrated in one of the Inca origin myths. (There is a cave locally known as Tampu Tocco near Pacarictambo, to the south, but it shows no traces of Inca occupation.) To visit Maukallaqta take the highway south to Yaurisque and follow the right fork towards Huanoquite. After about 8 km. stop at the Hacienda Waynacancha and ask directions. The ruin lies south of the highway, about 45 minutes walk from here.

VILCABAMBA
a rough guide to trails, settlements and ruins

© P. FROST-1999

0   10   20   30 Km.

to San Miguel

Espíritu Pampa
Vilcabamba the Old
Concevidayoc

Vista d. Concevidayoc river
Alegre

Pampaconas

Vilcabamba the New

Salinas Pass

Collpaccasa Pass 3690 m.

Punkuyoc

Yupanca 2600 m.
Lucma
Puquiura
Vitcos (Rosaspata)
Huancacalle ~2930 m.
Ñusta hispana

Quillabamba 950 m.

Choquechaca Bridge

bridge out (1998)

Chaullay

Santa Teresa

Vilcabamba river

Urubamba river

Km. 88

Inca Trail

Wayllabamba

Huayna Picchu

Huiñay Huayna

to Ollantaytambo and Cuzco

Salcantay 6264 m.

to Mollepata

Soray 5838 m.

Vilcabamba

Collpapampa

Yanama Pass

Yanama

Choquequirau

to Cachora

Cordillera

Pumasillo 6000 m.

Choquetacarpo 5742 m.

Choquetacarpo Pass

Santa 5667 m.

Osambre

Apurímac river

to Ayacucho

N

to Ayacucho

Chapter Eight

VILCABAMBA

Refuge of the Rebel Incas

The fate of the last Incas is a mystery that has intrigued historians and explorers for many years. After the Conquest some members of the royal line chose a comfortable but impotent existence in Cusco under Spanish tutelage; some collaborated openly with the new order. At one point there were two Incas. The Spaniards had their own candidate, Paullu Inca, fighting at their side against the natives under Manco Inca throughout the second rebellion.

But Paullu was blatantly a Spanish puppet. Diego de Almagro had declared him Inca in 1537, stripping the reigning Inca, Manco, of his title in absentia. Manco himself was recently installed in his jungle redoubt of Vilcabamba, where he was preparing to mount the guerrilla war that he would pursue doggedly against the Spanish until his death seven years later.

The rebel Inca Manco had abandoned the fortress of Ollantaytambo in July 1537, seeing that the Spanish forces arrayed against him in the Cusco region were now overwhelming. He retreated by way of the Panticalla pass, with the Spanish under Rodrigo Orgoñez close on his heels. Evidently the Inca had prepared his retreat; he made straight for the bridge over the Urubamba at Choquechaca, by the modern settlement of Chaullay—the gateway to the remote wilderness of Vilcabamba.

The Incas already had a foothold in this area: the fortress city of Vitcos, a few kilometers from the river. Manco took refuge there but the Spanish were onto him before he could regroup or prepare defenses.

They captured the Choquechaca bridge, crossed it, and swiftly took Vitcos. Only the conquistadors' greed saved Manco on this occasion. They discovered loot and women at Vitcos, and paused to sack the place, allowing Manco to escape.

The Spanish later had cause to regret this. Vilcabamba under Manco became a legend: a source of fear and unease to Spanish settlers and an inspiration to millions of Inca loyalists in Spanish-occupied Peru; the springboard from which Manco launched the second rebellion and countless lesser raids against Spanish life and property.

Gonzalo Pizarro led a force into Vilcabamba in 1539 in an attempt to crush for all time the rebellious Inca state. Pizarro overran all the main settlements, including Manco's new capital of Vilcabamba. But Manco, in the best guerrilla style, vanished into the jungles to fight another day.

Gonzalo Pizarro's expedition was costly, unproductive and inconclusive. The Spanish found the area of Vilcabamba almost uninhabitable and certainly not worth fighting for. First they tried diplomacy to get Manco out, and when this failed they murdered his captured wife, burned to death a number of Inca commanders, and finally withdrew, abandoning the problem of Vilcabamba in the hope that it would simply go away. They were, in any case, becoming embroiled in their own civil wars.

But Manco organized the inhospitable territory into a solid native state that continued to harass the Spanish until his death in 1544. In the end Manco made the mistake of trusting seven renegade Spaniards—disaffected members of the Almagrist faction, wanted by the authorities—and offering them sanctuary. They repaid Manco by murdering him in an attempt to regain favor with the crown.

Manco's appointed heir, Sayri Tupac, emerged from Vilcabamba in 1557 after prolonged negotiations with the Spanish Viceroy. He traded the hardships of a jungle kingdom for a grant of estates and nominal recognition of his title by the Spanish. But the diehards remained in Vilcabamba, and when Sayri Tupac died in 1561 raids against Spanish territory resumed under the direction of a tough new Inca, Sayri's half-brother Titu Cusi. Titu Cusi was a skillful diplomat as well as a resolute leader. He played off the Spanish, constantly assuring them that he was ready to surrender on this or that condition, never actually doing so. Thereby he kept alive Spanish hopes of a negotiated settlement and stalled the invasion the Spanish always contemplated.

Titu Cusi allowed Christian missionaries into Vilcabamba, to appease the Spanish. He dictated a long memoir to one of them, Fray Marcos Garcia, which is a major contemporary source of information about Vilcabamba and the Conquest in general. He died in 1571. A Spanish priest, Padre Ortiz, was accused by the Inca priests of poisoning the Inca, and the unfortunate friar was tortured and beaten to death. His martyrdom, and the killing of a crown envoy to the new Inca soon afterward, provoked the long-delayed invasion of Vilcabamba in 1572. This time the expedition was large, thoroughly prepared, and implacably determined to kill or capture the Inca. They still believed they were after Titu Cusi, whose death had been kept secret, but the Inca was now Tupac Amaru, yet another son of Manco, half-brother of Titu Cusi and Sayri Tupac.

The invasion, under Hurtado de Arbieto, captured all the major fortifications of Vilcabamba and reached the capital city, which they found a smoking ruin, abandoned and burned by the retreating Incas. Tupac Amaru fled by canoe down the Cosireni river, deeper into the jungle, but this time the Spaniards tailed the Inca doggedly, resolved to put an end, once and for all, to the Inca resistance. They finally came upon him in appropriately pitiful circumstances: huddled over a fire in the heart of the forest; betrayed by some of his captains; almost alone; destitute; defenseless; his followers scattered—the last remnant of an empire that once stretched halfway from the Equator to the Pole now overrun by the terrifying alien warriors.

The royal line of the Incas comes decisively to an end with Tupac Amaru. Viceroy Francisco de Toledo made sure of that. The Inca was taken in chains to Cusco, converted to Christianity with the utmost dispatch, and beheaded in the main square three days later. Members of his family—even collaborators with the Spanish—were exiled, scattered and dispossessed. Not even a Spanish puppet Inca remained. The Incas were finished.

The conquistadors occupied the territory of Vilcabamba and exploited it for what it was worth—which was not much—over the next few decades. They founded the new settlement of San Francisco de la Victoria de Vilcabamba and began to work a couple of silver mines in the area. The remnants of Vilcabamba's native population were conscripted to labor in them. But the mines proved disappointing. Sugar and coca plantations were established, too—but all in all the Spaniards found the humid jungles uninviting, the discomforts many, and the rewards meager. The final dethroning of the Incas meant there were no longer strategic reasons for occupying the region.

By the mid-seventeenth century Vilcabamba was little more than a memory. And its capital city was not even that; its location was entirely forgotten. None of the chroniclers who recorded the invasion, the memoirs of Titu Cusi, and the martyrdom of Padre Ortiz had thought to record its exact situation. And now the forest had covered the roads leading to it.

And so when during the 19th century men of science began to take an interest in such questions, Vilcabamba was already a mysterious and shadowy place whose very existence was open to doubt. The chronicles themselves were buried in the then-impenetrable archives of Madrid. (Some of the most important sources relating to Vilcabamba have only come to light during the 20th century.)

At first Choquequirau *(see below)*, a ruin perched on a mountain spur high above the Apurimac River was thought to be the site of Vilcabamba the Old, as it had come to be known. Later this was amended to a belief that this had been merely an outpost of the Inca state. Hiram Bingham visited Choquequirau in 1909 and pronounced it an unlikely candidate.

Machu Picchu, the city Bingham discovered in 1911, was, in retrospect, an equally unlikely candidate *(see Chapter Five)*. Remarkably, in the same year of his discovery of Machu Picchu, Bingham actually did find the ruins now thought to be those of Vilcabamba, at a place known as Espiritu Pampa (Plain of Spirits). But perhaps because this site was more spread out and more deeply buried in forest than Machu Picchu, he uncovered only a small part of the complex, and dismissed the ruins as insignificant. Intoxicated with his magnificent discovery on the Urubamba river, he pronounced Machu Picchu to be the site of Vilcabamba the Old. Such was his reputation that, even though the evidence he presented was incredibly flimsy, this claim stood unchallenged for the next 50 years.

Then a revisionist explorer arrived in the person of Gene Savoy. This flamboyant American moved in with everything from dollars to more dollars—plus a lot of grit and determination—and took large expeditions into Vilcabamba in 1964 and 1965. In 1911 Bingham had established beyond doubt the location of Vitcos, Manco's fortified city near the Choquechaca bridge. The real argument revolved around the probable location of the capital itself. Machu Picchu, Choquequirau and Espiritu Pampa were all about the same distance from Vitcos. But nothing else about the former two ruins seemed to fit the descriptions supplied by contemporary accounts. Savoy believed that Espiritu Pampa was the real location of Vilcabamba, and when his party cleared some of the dense jungle away from the ruins the evidence in favor began to pile up.

Savoy's hypothesis has eloquent and authoritative support from John Hemming. In *The Conquest of the Incas* Hemming makes a convincing case for Espiritu Pampa as Vilcabamba the Old, noting that these ruins are much larger than Bingham realized (they cover about 500 acres), and that new sources have emerged to which Bingham did not have access. Hemming demonstrates that everything about Espiritu Pampa—and conversely, nothing about Machu Picchu—conforms to contemporary accounts of the city and its setting: altitude, topography, rivers, climate, flora and fauna, and the locations of several important landmarks on the route to Vitcos. Finally, perhaps most conclusively, Savoy found Spanish-style roofing tiles at the site. Bingham noticed these, too. But roofing tiles were never seen in Peru until after the Conquest (the Incas only used thatch) and certainly were not found at Machu Picchu. Vilcabamba was a post-Conquest Inca city, probably the only one to have existed in Peru. And we now know that the city at Espiritu Pampa was at least partly built after the Conquest, whereas there is no evidence for this conclusion at any other known ruin site.

As Hemming puts it: "Unless someone can discover another ruin that so exactly fulfills the geographical and topographical details known about Vilcabamba, and that also contains imitation Spanish roofing-tiles, the lost city of Vilcabamba has finally been located at Espiritu Pampa."

In the 1980s Vilcabamba suffered a waves of notoriety and controversy. In 1976 a Lima historian had claimed to have "discovered" Bingham's ruins at Espiritu Pampa, and suddenly the place was off limits. In time the restrictions lapsed, only to reappear in more radical form when the feared "Shining Path" terrorists appeared in the area, around 1983. For a while the Vilcabamba "annex" (being so remote and sparsely populated, it doesn't qualify as a province in the Peruvian political structure) was overrun with soldiers and police.

Happily, this troubled period is over, and it is no longer necessary to obtain a permit to enter the area.

Getting There: to visit the Vitcos/Espiritu Pampa axis of Vilcabamba, the final road destination is the town of Huancacalle. Early in 1998 a gigantic landslide came down the Aobamba side valley, just below Machu Picchu, and then surged down the Urubamba valley towards Quillabamba, wiping out five bridges and many kilometers of the railroad. Thus, the famous Choquechaca bridge at Chaullay, which had become a road bridge with Inca stone foundations, was totally obliterated. Until it is rebuilt, travelers entering Vilcabamba from the Urubamba valley must either a) cross the river at Chaullay, using the temporary *oroya*—a cable-and-sling device which is scary, but not as bad as it sounds, or b) travel downstream on the north bank of the river to

248

Quillabamba, whence there are daily minibuses and trucks back upstream to Chaullay and Huancacalle on the south bank road.

The damage to the Quillabamba railroad from Km. 120 downstream was so severe that the train will probably never run here again. Thus Quillabamba can now be reached from Cusco by road only, a spectacular journey of approx. ten hours, over the 4,300m. Abra de Málaga. *(see Transportation, p. 19)*

To get to Espiritu Pampa only: truck from Quillabamba to San Miguel, a.k.a. Chuanquiri. A gruelling truck ride, 8-12 hours of bad road. Plenty of trucks on Fridays, returning Saturdays; other days less certain.

From San Miguel it's an easy day's walk to Espiritu Pampa, up the valley of the Rio Concevidayoq. If you need mules there are more animals and drovers in town on Saturday than any other day.

Where to Stay: in *Quillabamba*: the Hostal Lira, Hostal Quillabamba and Hostal Cusco are all reasonable and close to the center. At *Huancacalle*, there is a small new hotel sponsored by explorer Vincent Lee and friends and run by the Cobos family—the Hostal Sixpac Manco. Clean, inexpensive, friendly.

Hiking to Vitcos and Espiritu Pampa

You need to spend two or more nights in the Huancacalle area to visit Vitcos, and about ten days for a trip to Vilcabamba the Old—Espiritu Pampa. Take your supplies in with you, and basic camping gear as for the Inca Trail *(see Chapter Four)*. Check with the *South American Explorers Club* in Lima or Cusco, or the Instituto Geográfico Nacional *(see General Information p. 15)* for detailed maps of the region (the IGN map for this area is named "Machupicchu").

The area known as Vilcabamba forms a roughly square block of territory bounded in the south and west by the Apurimac River, in the east by the Urubamba. The southeast corner is walled in by the massive glacial ramparts of the Cordillera Vilcabamba. And the northern sector is ringed by the dense jungle lowlands beyond the Cosireni river. The ruins of Vitcos—known nowadays as Rosaspata—stand on a bluff on the east bank of the Vilcabamba river, roughly equidistant (about 45 mins. on foot) from Huancacalle and Puquiura. The excellent plans in Vincent Lee's *Sixpac Manco (see Bibliography)* may be used to tour this site and others, including Espiritu Pampa.

The Spanish captured the citadel of Vitcos three times during the occupation of Manco Inca and his descendants. In the ruins you can see a large square where, it's said, Manco Inca was playing quoits with his Spanish guests when they set on him and stabbed him to death. The remains of a complex of buildings survives on the knoll above this square. Some very fine agricultural terracing survives on the eastern flank of the mountain. In a valley below the southern slope of the mountain you will find the Yurac Rumi—the White Stone—which was once the holiest shrine of Vilcabamba. (Nowadays this site is known as "Ñustahispanan.") It is a huge rock about eight meters high by twenty meters wide, carved with mysterious knobs and recesses over much of its surface. Once it overlooked a pool (now silted up) in whose mirror surface the Inca priests used to call up images of demons—according to the Augustinian priests who later desecrated the shrine. The rock itself is not white but dark, almost black, because of the lichen that now covers it.

You will definitely need guides and perhaps mules to get to Espíritu Pampa. Setting this up can take patience and luck. A group with more money to spend and a need for more mules to hire stands a better chance of finding someone quickly. In this transaction trade goods speak louder than money. If you can offer a good knife or machete, flashlight, fishing rod, quality camping gear or any other item of locally unobtainable hardware as part of the deal you may find yourself in demand. The Cobos family are the best-known guides in the area. Inquire at the Sixpac Manco Hostal in Huancacalle. At Yupanca, back down the highway towards Quillabamba, a man with the resonantly Incan name of Paullu Quispe Cusi has been recommended. If you can provide food and shelter (a plastic tarp) for the guides you will travel faster, since you won't have to depend on local settlements as stopping places.

The walk to Espiritu Pampa (Plain of Spirits) takes about three days from the roadhead. The ruins themselves are extensive and very interesting, but may be heavily overgrown. Every so often an expedition will do some clearing, but the jungle grows back fast. You will see more if you have a local guide who knows his way around them. Juvenal Cobos and José Salas Cobos of Huancacalle are probably the most knowledgeable.

The shortest way to return to Cusco from Espiritu Pampa is to continue downriver one easy day's walk to San Miguel (Chuanquiri). From there trucks to Quillabamba are available, though you may have to wait a day or so. This is a long ride over a terrible road. If you should choose to return the way you came you can vary the route a little by crossing the Abra de Salinas and taking the trail which emerges at Yupanca.

Punkuyoq This is another very interesting ruin in the Vilcabamba region, about one day's long, climbing walk north of Yupanca. It is a small ruin, but very well preserved, and the location is spectacular. If the weather is fine, all the peaks of the Cordillera Vilcabamba are visible from here. The aforementioned José Salas Cobos is the man to take you there.

Choquequirau (Cradle of gold ore— probably not the original Inca name).

This magnificently situated ruin became almost a legend during the 19th century. It was thought to have been the elusive last refuge of the Incas. It was mentioned by the Peruvian chronicler Cosme Bueno in 1768, and rediscovered by the French Comte de Sartiges in 1834. Thereafter it received occasional visits from treasure hunters and explorers. The French consul in Peru, Leonce Angrand, visited and did the first known drawings of the site in 1847. Hiram Bingham went there in 1909—his first taste of a lost city. Even today Choquequirau is rarely visited because of its remoteness, but it has become easier to reach since COPESCO constructed a footbridge over the Apurimac river below the ruins (formerly one crossed on an *oroya*, a steel cable and sling).

After Bingham no serious documentation was done until the 1990s, when COPESCO architect Roberto Samanez mapped the main sectors of the site. The importance of Choquequirau has been widely underrated, partly because of its remoteness, but perhaps essentially because the stonework seems poor compared to that of the well known high-status sites. U.S. explorer Gary Ziegler, who has studied Choquequirau extensively, was the first to point out that this is because the type of stone available here is a frangible metamorphic rock which cannot be worked into the subtle interlocking shapes that are possible with granite and andesite. But when one looks at the style and quality of construction, and the layout of the settlement at Choquequirau, to say nothing of its size, one's perceptions shift.

Choquequirau *was* an important Inca site. Its utterly spectacular location, on a ridge spur almost 1,800m. above the roaring Apurimac river, reminds one of Machu Picchu itself. The buildings around its central plaza represent extremely fine ceremonial and high-status residential architecture. There is a chain of ritual baths, an enormous, curving bank of fine terraces, numerous intriguing outlier groups of buildings—a large group of buildings whose existence was hitherto unsuspected was discovered buried in forest on a ridge spur below the main site during the 1990s—and a vast area of irrigated terracing on a nearby mountain slope, evidently designed to feed the local population.

In short, a huge investment of time and energy; another large, mysterious, remote ceremonial center that nobody in their right mind would build, but the Incas did.

Choquequirau is all the more enigmatic because it is not mentioned in any of the recorded incidents and invasions of the 40-year period of the Vilcabamba resistance. Bingham and others dismissed it as a candidate for the last refuge of the Incas, which today has been almost incontrovertibly located at Espiritu Pampa. It is the remotest of the major sites, and may have been some secret refuge; Ziegler suggests it may have been the place where the last Inca, Tupac Amaru, was raised among Inca priestesses. Double jamb doorways and niches, which point to high status in Inca architecture, are abundant at this site. Vincent Lee, who has also studied and mapped here, proposes that it may originally have been built as a "royal estate" for Topa Inca, the son of Pachacuteq.

In the ruins. Arriving at Choquequirau on foot, you come to the *Curved Terraces* (1), an imposing set of four massively constructed walls, 350m. long and each about six meters high. At the foot of these lies a roadway, the *Avenue of the Cedars* (2), so-called because it is lined on the left with tall Andean cedars, a fairly rare tree nowadays, but common at this site. One wonders if the Incas planted them here. This roadway exhibits typically exquisite Inca architectural sensitivity to landscape, as it leads you and your eye towards the *Sacred Platform* (3), a levelled-off hilltop overlooking the site. It commands the entire horizon—which features the snow peaks of Panta, to the west, Quiswar, across the Apurimac to the south, and nearby Cerro Yanama—and was probably used for celestial observation. At the end of the terraces you climb to the *Main Plaza* (4), which has imposing structures on three sides: the *Main Fountain* (5); an enigmatic and oddly shaped building (6) which seems to have been a *shrine*, perhaps a place where ancestral mummies were kept; the *Great Hall* (7) whose doorways look out towards the Apurimac, has been heavily reconstructed. The hall was probably used for banquets, because right behind it are some rough structures (8) identified from potsherds and mortar stones as *kitchens*. A *Lesser Hall*, or *Hall of Niches* (9), on the east side of the plaza appears to have held high-status or ceremonial significance, because its niches are triple-recessed and edged with puzzling ring stones. The first enclosure of a high-status residential group of *two-story buildings* (10), also fronts onto the Plaza. Some of the inside walls of these buildings display traces of a clay stucco that once covered them entirely.

Follow the *water channel* (11) up the hill, passing the *Giant Stairway* (12), a curious narrow set of terraces, to the *Upper Plaza* (13), where there is another *fountain* (14), and an odd little building containing a large niche (15). Returning to the Main Plaza, a worthwhile walk takes you over the Sacred Platform and down the knife-edge ridge to a small, delightful courtyard (16), two structures which may have been very exclusive residences, having the finest view up and down the Apurimac of any building in the entire site.

At this writing, the Ridge Group (17) documented by Vincent Lee in 1996 has not been cleared, but may turn out to contain more interesting surprises. The trail leading beyond the Upper Plaza climbs over a notch in the nearby ridge and descends to a huge area of terracing known as Pincha Unuyoq (Water bursting forth) containing some curious structures in the Inca fountain tradition. COPESCO archaeologist Percy Paz suggests that these terraces were used for growing coca.

(Sources: Inca Choqek'iraw, Vincent Lee, self-published-Wilson, Wyoming, 1997 e-m: sixpacmanco@compuserve.com; The Empire Strikes Back, Choquequirao, the Inca's Last Secret—Gary Ziegler, self-published—Westcliffe, Colorado 1998 e-m: adventur@rmii.com).

Getting there. Basically, there are two ways:

Cachora. The "short" visit is a hike in and out the same way, via the village of Cachora, which lies on the south side of the Apurimac river, on a side road below the main highway to Abancay from Cusco.

Take any transport from Cusco heading for Abancay. (If you have your own transport, it's worth stopping to visit the Inca ruins of Tarawasi, at Limatambo, and the famous stone of Sayhuite, along the way). Alight at the turn-off to Cachora, which is shortly after Sayhuite, and before the Abra de Abancay, about 5 hours from Cusco by bus. The village of Cachora lies about a half-hour walk from the main highway. You will find lodging, guides and mules at the village. Allow four days to get to Choquequirau and back, and at least one day (two is better) to explore there. You will descend more than 2000m into the astounding Apurimac Canyon, and climb almost as much on the far side. This is a difficult hike. From Cachora to the river takes one full day, and the climb to the ruins takes another (leave this camp very early to escape the heat of the canyon).

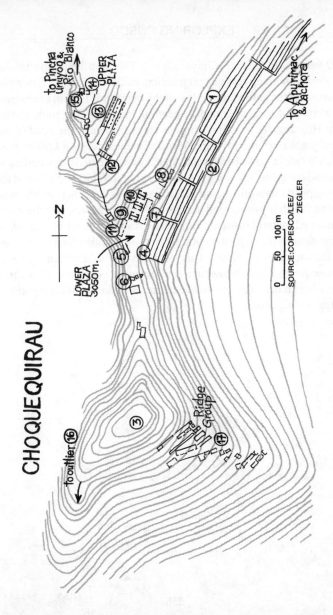

Huancacalle-Yanama-Choquequirau. This is a long, spectacular and strenuous hike, requiring preparation, guides, horses etc. Since you are crossing the entire huge Vilcabamba range, it is hard to exaggerate the amount of ascending and descending involved. The route climbs from Huancacalle to a first camp in the meadows at the head of the Vilcabamba river, then over the Abra de Choquetacarpo, a 4,600m. pass which divides the Urubamba and Apurimac watersheds, descending to a second campsite below the spectacular granite spires at the foot of the snowcapped Pumasillo massif. Third camp is at the village of Yanama, and the fourth is just beyond the pass at Minas Victoria, past the many abandoned shafts of disused silver mines. Another long descent leads to a fifth camp at the edge of the Rio Blanco, and another long ascent past the Inca terraces of Pincha Unuyoq leads across a forested pass to Choquequirau. Camp here is at a site somewhat below the ruins. From here, after taking a day or two to explore, continue on to the Apurimac bridge, and Cachora.

GLOSSARY OF QUECHUA AND SPANISH TERMS

aclla	chosen woman, a special caste in Inca society
altiplano	high plain or plateau
andesite	type of grey basalt, used extensively by the Incas in the building of Cusco
Antisuyu	eastern (jungle) quarter of the Inca empire
Apu	sacred peak, worshipped by the Incas and many modern Quechua people
ayllu	Quechua kinship group or community
Aymara	people and language of the southern Titicaca region
ayni	Andean reciprocal system of sharing labor and goods
campesino	rural worker; peasant farmer
cancha	courtyard enclosure, corral
ceque	radial ritual line on the landscape surrounding Cusco and other Inca settlements
chacra	cultivated plot of land
charango	small, mandolin-like stringed instrument
chaski	Inca messenger
chicha	corn beer, brewed in the Andes from ancient times to the present
Chinchaysuyu	northern quarter of Inca empire
choque	gold in its natural state
chronicles	Spanish documents and commentaries,

mainly written in the 16th & 17th centuries, which are used by ethnohistorians to interpret the Inca civilization

Collasuyu	southern quarter of Inca empire
Contisuyu	western quarter of Inca empire
Coya	the Inca queen, wife and sister of the emperor
creole	Peruvian-born person of Spanish descent
huayno	an Andean music style, usually with vocals
ichu	highland bunch grass, staple of llamas and alpacas
inti	sun
intiwatana	literally, "for tying up the sun"; a stone pillar characteristic of Inca ceremonial sites, whose most famous surviving example is at Machu Picchu
kallanka	type of Inca building, a large hall with many entrances, used for assemblies and transient lodging
mestizo	person of mixed Caucasian/Amerindian descent
mit'a	Inca system of drafted labor
orejón	Spanish name for an Inca noble, after the huge earplugs they wore; literally, "big ears"
oroya	cable and sling arrangement, for getting people and light cargo across rivers where no bridge exists
pampa	flat place (rule of thumb: any flat place big enough for a village soccer pitch)
panaca	royal Inca lineage group
pucara	fortified area

GLOSSARY

puna	the treeless grasslands of the high Andes
quinoa	Andean high altitude grain
qori	gold that has been worked by human hands
quena	Andean flute
quipu	Inca recording device made of knotted cords
runa	Quechua word meaning people, humans
Sapa Inca	the Inca emperor
soroche	hypoxia, altitude sickness
tambo	a lodgehouse and transit point on the Inca highway system
Tawantinsuyu	the Inca empire, which translates as Four Quarters joined together
usnu	tiered platform where the Inca élite stood during ceremonies and parades
Viracocha	the Inca creator god; also a term of address used by Quechua speakers today to mean something like "sir" or "gentleman"
waca	a sacred landscape feature, often a carved rock, or sacred object, such as an idol
zampoña	Andean pan pipes

ABBREVIATIONS
USED IN THIS BOOK

a.k.a.	also known as
COPESCO	The co-ordinating agency for UNESCO-funded tourism infrastructure projects in the Cusco region.
e-m	e-mail
ENAFER	Empresa Nacional de Ferrocarriles (the government-owned railroad company).
IGN	Instituto Geográfico Nacional (National Geographic Institute, responsible for mapping the country)
INC	Instituto Nacional de Cultura (National Cultural Institute, responsible for archeological sites)
INRENA	Instituto Nacional de Recursos Naturales (National Institute for Natural Resources, responsible for parks and reserved zones).
m.a.s.l.	meters above sea level
MITINCI	Ministry of Industry and Tourism
T.T.	Boleto Turístico Unico, the $10 ticket for visitors which gives access to many sites and museums in and around Cusco.
SAEC	South American Explorer's Club
UNSAAC	Universidad Nacional San Antonio Abad de Cusco. Cusco's main university, located on Avenida la Cultura a short taxi ride from the city center.
web	Internet web site

BIBLIOGRAPHY

Guidebooks

Peru Handbook - Alan Murphy — Footprint Handbooks, Bath 1997. Excellent new guidebook from the publishers of the South American Handbook.

Peru, a Travel Survival Kit - Rob Rachowiecki, 3rd edition, 1996. Lonely Planet Publications, Hawthorn, Australia. Thorough job, regularly updated, by a veteran travel guide, author, backpacker and mountaineer.

The Rough Guide to Peru - Dilwyn Jenkins, London & New York, 1997. Thoughtful guidebook, very good on social and cultural life, by an anthropologist and seasoned Peru traveler.

The Insight Guide to Peru - Tony Perrottet et al. - APA Publications, Singapore. A tour of Peru via the essays of various insiders, with scores of sumptuous full-color photos.

Backpacking in Peru & Bolivia - Hilary Bradt. U.K., 1995. 6th edition of a classic trail guide.

A Traveler's Guide to El Dorado and the Inca Empire - Lynn Meisch, New York, 1987. A guide to the Andean republics (excluding Chile), packed with cultural background and superb information on how to travel in this region. A new edition is in preparation at this writing. Try amazon.com for copies of the old edition.

Nature

Wildflowers of the Cordillera Blanca - Helen & Kees Kolff - the Mountain Institute, 1997. (bilingual Sp./Eng.) Most of these plants also grow in the Cusco region, although some of the northern Quechua names are different. A sorely-needed addition to the Andean bookshelf. Illustrated with color photos.

Birds of the High Andes - Jon Fjeldsa & Niels Krabbe - U. Copenhagen Zoological Museum, Svendborg, Denmark, 1990. At nearly 900 pages, not portable - but some ruthless folks rip out the section of color plates and carry them along as a field identification guide.

Coming soon:

A Field Guide to the Flora and Fauna of the Sacred Valley, Inca Trail and Machu Picchu- Edited by Michel Lemoine. Bilingual Spanish/English publication with over 200 color plates. (Publication projected for July, 1999).

Birds of the Machu Picchu Historical Sanctuary - a field guide by Peru birding expert Barry Walker, and others (publication late '99 or early 2000). **Orchids of the Machu Picchu Historical Sanctuary -** a field guide compiled by various experts (publication mid-'99).

Exploration

Lost City of the Incas - Hiram Bingham. New York, 1972. Classic account of Bingham's explorations. Outdated theories, but a great read.

Sixpac Manco: Travels among the Incas - Vincent R. Lee. Self-published, Wilson, Wyoming, 1985; e-m: sixpacmanco@ compuserve.com. Amusing and informative record of the author's extensive explorations in the Vilcabamba region. A must for travelers to that area. Excellent maps and diagrams. Available in Cusco bookstores. *By the same author:* **The Building of Sacsayhuaman, 1987,** monograph presenting a new theory on Inca stoneworking. **The Lost Half of Inca Architecture,** 1988. About the nature and quality of Inca roof design. **Inca Choqek'iraw,** 1997. A summary of the author's surveys, explorations and theories of this remote Inca site. **The Sisyphus Project,** 1998. In which the author reveals Ultimate Truth (probably) about how the Incas moved huge stones.

Antisuyo - Gene Savoy - NY, 1970. Fascinating book, long out of print, by a man with an incredible nose for lost cities.

BIBLIOGRAPHY

Non-fiction

The Conquest of the Incas - John Hemming, London, 1970.
A major contribution to modern knowledge and theories about the
Incas, and an extraordinary story brilliantly told.

Monuments of the Incas - John Hemming & Edward Ranney. New
York, 1982. Luminous black-&-white photos, with narrative by the
respected historian, about the best-known Inca sites.

The Inka Empire and its Andean origins - Adriana von Hagen &
Craig Morris - Abbeville Press Publishers, NY 1993. Lavish and
thorough hardcover job on the origins of Andean civilization, through to
its demise.

The Cities of the Ancient Andes - Adriana von Hagen & Craig
Morris — Thames & Hudson, London 1998. Life in the major urban
settlements from early times through the Incas.

Living Incas - enchanting photography by Jeremy Horner, with text
by various distinguished authors - Villegas Editores, Bogotá 1996.

The Incas and their ancestors - Michael Moseley - Thames &
Hudson, London 1993. A very useful paperback tour of Peruvian
prehistory, with a few minor errors and eccentric spellings.

Machu Picchu Historical Sanctuary - Jim Bartle & Peter Frost,
Lima 1995. A guide to Machu Picchu and the surrounding protected
area, with scores of color photographs.

Speculation

The Secret of the Incas - Myth, Astronomy, and the War Against
Time - William Sullivan - Crown, NY 1996. Fearless and intriguing
mytho-historical acrobatics upon a well researched but ultimately
rather slender framework of data.

Biography

Portrait of an Explorer - Alfred M. Bingham. Iowa State U., Ames,
1989. A well researched, warts-and-all portrait by a son of the
famous explorer.

Scholarly works

The Stone and the Thread: Andean Roots of Abstract Art — Cesar Paternosto — U. Texas Press, Austin 1996. An intriguing and unusual perspective on Inca stonework and textiles, by an art historian and artist.

At the Crossroads of the Earth and the Sky - Gary Urton - U. Texas Press, Austin 1981 - a seminal and influential work on the Andean cosmovision.

Astronomy and Empire in the Ancient Andes: The Cultural Origins of Inca Skywatching — Brian S. Bauer & David Dearborn. U. Texas Press, Austin 1995. Recent investigations by two distinguished Andean scholars.

The Development of the Inca State — Brian S. Bauer, U. Texas Press, Austin 1992. In which the author reveals how the Inca state developed gradually over a period of more than three hundred years before beginning its explosive expansion.

Inca Architecture and Construction at Ollantaytambo — Jean-Pierre Protzen, Oxford U. Press, NY, 1993. A thorough investigation of a complex and still puzzling site. Demolishes the more fanciful ideas about how stones were moved and fitted.

Archaeological Explorations in the Cordillera Vilcabamba - Paul Fejos, New York, 1944. Hard to find but fascinating record of the first systematic survey of the Inca Trail.

Inca Architecture - Graziano Gasparini & Louise Margolies. Bloomington, 1980. Still the most complete book on the subject.

INDEX

INDEX

271

INDEX